ALSO BY CHUCK KLOSTERMAN

Fargo Rock City: A Heavy Metal Odyssey in Rural Nörth Daköta

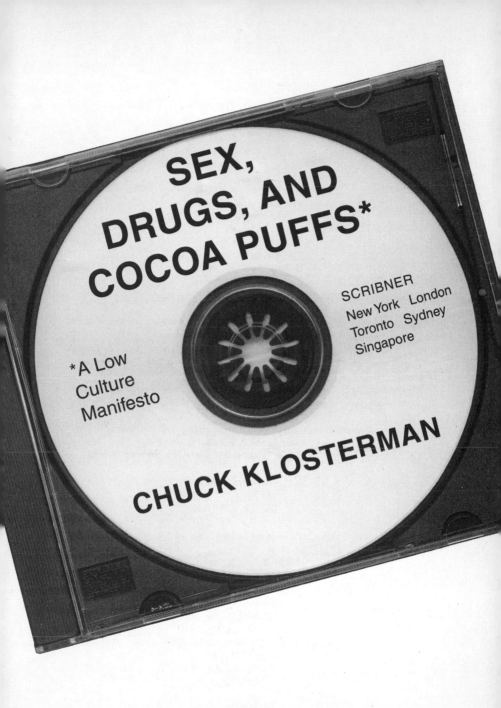

SEX, DRUGS, AND COCOA PUFFS*

*A Low Culture Manifesto

SCRIBNER
New York   London
Toronto   Sydney
Singapore

CHUCK KLOSTERMAN

SCRIBNER
1230 Avenue of the Americas
New York, NY 10020

"33" was previously published in a different form in GQ. "Appetite for Replication" was previously published in a different form in *The New York Times Magazine*.

SCRIBNER and design are trademarks of Macmillan Library Reference USA, Inc., used under license by Simon & Schuster, the publisher of this work.

For information about special discounts for bulk purchases, please contact Simon & Schuster Special Sales: 1-800-456-6798 or business@simonandschuster.com

DESIGNED BY ERICH HOBBING

Text set in Electra

Manufactured in the United States of America

1 3 5 7 9 10 8 6 4 2

Library of Congress Cataloging-in-Publication Data
Klosterman, Chuck.
Sex, drugs, and cocoa puffs : a low culture manifesto / Chuck Klosterman.
p. cm.
1. Popular culture—United States. 2. United States—Civilization—1970–. I. Title.
E169.12.K56 2003
306'.0973—dc21
2003045535

ISBN 0-7432-3600-9

There are two ways to look at life.

Actually, that's not accurate; I suppose there are thousands of ways to look at life. But I tend to dwell on two of them. The first view is that nothing stays the same and that nothing is inherently connected, and that the only driving force in anyone's life is entropy. The second is that everything pretty much stays the same (more or less) and that everything is *completely* connected, even if we don't realize it.

There are many mornings when I feel certain that the first perspective is irrefutably true: I wake up, I feel the inescapable oppression of the sunlight pouring through my bedroom window, and I am struck by the fact that I am alone. And that everyone is alone. And that everything I understood seven hours ago has already changed, and that I have to learn everything again.

I guess I am not a morning person.

However, that feeling always passes. In fact, it's usually completely gone before lunch. Every new minute of every new day seems to vaguely improve. And I suspect that's because the alternative view—that everything is ultimately like something else and that nothing and no one is autonomous—is probably the greater truth. The math does check out; the numbers do add up. The connections might not be hard-wired into the superstructure to the universe, but it feels like they are whenever I put money into a jukebox and everybody in the bar suddenly seems to be having the same conversation. And in that last moment before I fall asleep each night, I understand Everything. The world is one interlocked machine, throbbing and pulsing as a flawless organism.

This is why I will always hate falling asleep.

What you are about to read is an evening book. It was written in those fleeting evening moments just before I fall asleep, and it's built on this ethos: Nothing can be appreciated in a vacuum. That's what accelerated culture does; it doesn't speed things up as much as it jams everything into the same wall of sound. But that's not necessarily tragic. The goal of being alive is to figure out what it means to be alive, and there is a myriad of ways to deduce that answer; I just happen to prefer examining the question through the context of Pamela Anderson and *The Real World* and Frosted Flakes. It's certainly no less plausible than trying to understand Kant or Wittgenstein. And while half of my brain worries that writing about *Saved by the Bell* and *Memento* will immediately seem as outdated as a 1983 book about *Fantasy Island* and Gerry Cooney, my mind's better half knows that temporality is part of the truth. The subjects in this book are not the only ones that prove my point; they're just the ones I happened to pick before I fell asleep.

In and of itself, nothing really matters. What matters is that nothing is *ever* "in and of itself."

1   This Is Emo   0:01
(carnivore interlude)
2   Billy Sim   0:12
(reality interlude)
3   What Happens When People Stop Being Polite   0:26
(Pat Benatar interlude)
4   Every Dog Must Have His Every Day,
Every Drunk Must Have His Drink   0:42
(Monkees = *Monkees* interlude)
5   Appetite for Replication   0:56
(an interlude to be named later)
6   Ten Seconds to Love   0:71
(metaphorical fruit interlude)
7   George Will vs. Nick Hornby   0:86
(Ralph Nader interlude)
8   33   0:97
(Fonzie recalibration interlude)
9   Porn   1:09
("kitty cat as terrorist" interlude)
10   The Lady or the Tiger   1:19
(hypothetical interlude)
11   Being Zack Morris   1:27
(50–50 interlude)
12   Sulking with Lisa Loeb on the Ice Planet Hoth   1:41
(anti-homeless interlude)
13   The Awe-Inspiring Beauty of Tom Cruise's Shattered,
Troll-like Face   1:51
(punk interlude)
14   Toby over Moby   1:66
(Johnny Cash interlude)
15   This Is Zodiac Speaking   1:79
(Timothy McVeigh interlude)
16   All I Know Is What I Read in the Papers   1:95
(boom!)
17   I, Rock Chump   2:11
(waiting to die interlude)
18   How to Disappear Completely and Never Be Found   2:20

All tracks by Chuck Klosterman and Crazy Horse, except "The Lady and the Tiger"
(Lennon/McCartney) and "This Is Zodiac Speaking" (Klosterman /Desmond Child).
Additional vocals by Shannon Hoon and Neko Case on "Being Zack Morris."
Produced by Bob Ezrin at Little Mountain Sound Studio LTD., Vancouver.
No keyboards, synthesizers, or outboard gear were used in the typing of this manuscript.

Sol-ip-sism (sol'ip siz'em) , *n. Philos.* The theory that only the self exists or can be proved to exist.
—The Random House College Dictionary,
Revised Edition

"I remember saying things, but I have no idea what was said. It was generally a friendly conversation."
—*Associated Press reporter Jack Sullivan,*
attempting to recount a 3 A.M. *exchange*
we had at a dinner party and inadvertently
describing the past ten years of my life.

SEX, DRUGS,
AND COCOA PUFFS

1 This Is Emo 0:01

No woman will ever satisfy me. I know that now, and I would never try to deny it. But this is actually okay, because I will never satisfy a woman, either.

Should I be writing such thoughts? Perhaps not. Perhaps it's a bad idea. I can definitely foresee a scenario where that first paragraph could come back to haunt me, especially if I somehow became marginally famous. If I become marginally famous, I will undoubtedly be interviewed by someone in the media,[1] and the interviewer will inevitably ask, "Fifteen years ago, you wrote that no woman could ever satisfy you. Now that you've been married for almost five years, are those words still true?" And I will have to say, "Oh, God no. Those were the words of an entirely different person—a person whom I can't even relate to anymore. Honestly, I can't image an existence without _____. She satisfies me in ways that I never even considered. She saved my life, really."

Now, I will be lying. I won't really feel that way. But I'll certainly *say* those words, and I'll deliver them with the utmost sincerity, even though those sentiments will not be there. So then the interviewer will undoubtedly quote lines from *this* particular paragraph, thereby reminding me that I swore I would publicly deny my true feelings, and I'll chuckle and say, "Come on, Mr. Rose. That was a literary device. You know I never really believed that."

But here's the thing: I *do* believe that. It's the truth now, and it will be in the future. And while I'm not exactly happy about that truth, it doesn't make me sad, either. I know it's not my fault.

It's no one's fault, really. Or maybe it's everyone's fault. It

---

1. Hopefully Charlie Rose, if he's still alive.

should be everyone's fault, because it's everyone's problem. Well, okay . . . not *everyone*. Not boring people, and not the profoundly retarded. But whenever I meet dynamic, nonretarded Americans, I notice that they all seem to share a single unifying characteristic: the inability to experience the kind of mind-blowing, transcendent romantic relationship they perceive to be a normal part of living. And someone needs to take the fall for this. So instead of blaming no one for this (which is kind of cowardly) or blaming everyone (which is kind of meaningless), I'm going to blame John Cusack.

I once loved a girl who almost loved me, but not as much as she loved John Cusack. Under certain circumstances, this would have been fine; Cusack is relatively good-looking, he seems like a pretty cool guy (he likes the Clash and the Who, at least), and he undoubtedly has millions of bones in the bank. If Cusack and I were competing for the same woman, I could easily accept losing. However, I don't really feel like John and I were "competing" for the girl I'm referring to, inasmuch as her relationship to Cusack was confined to watching him as a two-dimensional projection, pretending to be characters who don't actually exist. Now, there was a time when I would have thought that detachment would have given me a huge advantage over Johnny C., inasmuch as *my* relationship with this woman included things like "talking on the phone" and "nuzzling under umbrellas" and "eating pancakes." However, I have come to realize that I perceived this competition completely backward; it was definitely an unfair battle, but not in my favor. It was unfair in Cusack's favor. I never had a chance.

It appears that countless women born between the years of 1965 and 1978 are in love with John Cusack. I cannot fathom how he isn't the number-one box-office star in America, because every straight girl I know would sell her soul to share a milkshake with that motherfucker. For upwardly mobile women in their twenties and thirties, John Cusack is the neo-Elvis. But here's what none of these upwardly mobile women seem to realize: They don't love John Cusack. They love Lloyd Dobler. When they see Mr. Cusack, they are still seeing the optimistic, charmingly loquacious teenager he played in *Say Anything,* a movie that came out more than a decade ago. That's the guy they think he is; when Cusack played Eddie Thomas in *America's Sweethearts* or the sensitive hit man in *Grosse Pointe Blank,* all his female fans knew he was only acting . . . but they assume when the camera stopped rolling, he went back to his genuine self . . . which was someone like Lloyd Dobler . . . which was, in fact, someone who *is* Lloyd Dobler, and someone who continues to have a storybook romance with Diane Court (or with Ione Skye, depending on how you look at it). And these upwardly mobile women are not alone. We all convince ourselves of things like this—not necessarily about *Say Anything,* but about any fictionalized portrayals of romance that happen to hit us in the right place, at the right time. This is why I will never be completely satisfied by a woman, and this is why the kind of woman I tend to find attractive will never be satisfied by me. We will both measure our relationship against the prospect of fake love.

Fake love is a very powerful thing. That girl who adored John Cusack once had the opportunity to spend a weekend with me in New York at the Waldorf-Astoria, but she elected to fly to Portland instead to see the first U.S. appearance by Coldplay, a British pop group whose success derives from their ability to write melodramatic alt-rock songs about fake love. It does not matter that Coldplay is absolutely the shittiest fucking band I've ever heard in my entire fucking life, or that they sound like a mediocre photocopy of Travis (who sound like a mediocre photocopy of Radiohead), or that their greatest fucking artistic achievement is a video where their blandly attractive frontman walks on a beach on a cloudy fucking afternoon. None of that matters. What matters is that Coldplay manufactures fake love as frenetically as the Ford fucking Motor Company manufactures Mustangs, and that's all this woman heard. "For you I bleed myself dry," sang their blockhead vocalist, brilliantly informing us that stars in the sky are, in fact, yellow. How am I going to compete with that shit? That

sleepy-eyed bozo isn't even making sense. He's just pouring fabricated emotions over four gloomy guitar chords, and it ends up
sounding like love. And what does that mean? It means she flies
to fucking Portland to hear two hours of amateurish U.K. hyper-
slop, and I sleep alone in a $270 hotel in Manhattan, and I hope
Coldplay gets fucking dropped by fucking EMI and ends up like
the Stone fucking Roses, who were actually a better fucking
band, all things considered.

Not that I'm bitter about this. Oh, I concede that I may be taking this particular example somewhat personally—but I do think
it's a perfect illustration of why almost everyone I know is either
overtly or covertly unhappy. Coldplay songs deliver an amorphous, irrefutable interpretation of how being in love is supposed
to feel, and people find themselves wanting that feeling for real.
They want men to adore them like Lloyd Dobler would, and they
want women to think like Aimee Mann, and they expect all
their arguments to sound like Sam Malone and Diane Chambers.
They think everything will work out perfectly in the end (just like
it did for Helen Fielding's Bridget Jones and Nick Hornby's Rob
Fleming), and they don't stop believing, because Journey's Steve
Perry insists we should never do that. In the nineteenth century,
teenagers merely aspired to have a marriage that would be better
than that of their parents; personally, I would never be satisfied
unless my marriage was as good as Cliff and Clair Huxtable's (or
at least as enigmatic as Jack and Meg White's).

Pundits are always blaming TV for making people stupid,
movies for desensitizing the world to violence, and rock music for
making kids take drugs and kill themselves. These things should
be the least of our worries. The main problem with mass media
is that it makes it impossible to fall in love with any acumen of
normalcy. There is no "normal," because everybody is being
twisted by the same sources simultaneously. You can't compare
your relationship with the playful couple who lives next door,
because they're probably modeling themselves after Chandler
Bing and Monica Geller. Real people are actively trying to live like

fake people, so real people are no less fake. Every comparison becomes impractical. This is why the impractical has become totally acceptable; impracticality almost seems cool. The best relationship I ever had was with a journalist who was as crazy as me, and some of our coworkers liked to compare us to Sid Vicious and Nancy Spungen. At the time, I used to think, "Yeah, that's completely valid: We fight all the time, our love is self-destructive, and—if she was mysteriously killed—I'm sure I'd be wrongly arrested for second-degree murder before dying from an overdose." We even watched *Sid & Nancy* in her parents' basement and giggled the whole time. "That's us," we said gleefully. And like I said—this was the *best* relationship I ever had. And I suspect it was the best one she ever had, too.

Of course, this media transference is not all bad. It has certainly worked to my advantage, just as it has for all modern men who look and talk and act like me. We all owe our lives to Woody Allen. If Woody Allen had never been born, I'm sure I would be doomed to a life of celibacy. Remember the aforementioned woman who loved Cusack and Coldplay? There is absolutely no way I could have dated this person if Woody Allen didn't exist. In tangible terms, she was light-years out of my league, along with most of the other women I've slept with. But Woody Allen changed everything. Woody Allen made it acceptable for beautiful women to sleep with nerdy, bespectacled goofballs; all we need to do is fabricate the illusion of intellectual humor, and we somehow have a chance. The irony is that many of the women most susceptible to this scam haven't even *seen* any of Woody's movies, nor would they want to touch the actual Woody Allen if they ever had the chance (especially since he's proven to be an *über*-pervy clarinet freak). If asked, most of these foxy ladies wouldn't classify Woody Allen as sexy, or handsome, or even likable. But this is how media devolution works: It creates an archetype that eventually dwarfs its origin. By now, the "Woody Allen Personality Type" has far greater cultural importance than the man himself.

Now, the argument could be made that all this is good for the sexual bloodstream of Americana, and that all these Women Who Want Woody are being unconsciously conditioned to be less shallow than their sociobiology dictates. Self-deprecating cleverness has become a virtue. At least on the surface, movies and television actively promote dating the nonbeautiful: If we have learned anything from the mass media, it's that the only people who can make us happy are those who don't strike us as being particularly desirable. Whether it's *Jerry Maguire* or *Sixteen Candles* or *Who's the Boss* or *Some Kind of Wonderful* or *Speed Racer*, we are constantly reminded that the unattainable icons of perfection we lust after can never fulfill us like the platonic allies who have been there all along.[2] If we all took media messages at their absolute face value, we'd all be sleeping with our best friends. And that does happen, sometimes.[3] But herein lies the trap: We've also been trained to think this will *always* work out over the long term, which dooms us to disappointment. Because when push comes to shove, we really *don't* want to have sex with our friends . . . unless they're sexy. And sometimes we *do* want to have sex with our blackhearted, soul-sucking enemies . . . assuming *they're* sexy. Because that's all it ever comes down to in real life, regardless of what happened to Michael J. Fox in *Teen Wolf*.

The mass media causes sexual misdirection: It prompts us to *need* something deeper than what we *want*. This is why Woody Allen has made nebbish guys cool; he makes people assume there is something profound about having a relationship based on witty conversation and intellectual discourse. There isn't. It's just another gimmick, and it's no different than wanting to be with someone because they're thin or rich or the former lead singer of Whiskeytown. And it actually might be worse, because an intel-

2. The notable exceptions being *Vertigo* (where the softhearted Barbara Bel Geddes gets jammed by sexpot Kim Novak) and *My So-Called Life* (where poor Brian Krakow never got any play, even though Jordan Catalano couldn't fucking read).
3. "Sometimes" meaning "during college."

lectual relationship isn't real *at all*. My witty banter and cerebral discourse is always completely contrived. Right now, I have three and a half dates worth of material, all of which I pretend to deliver spontaneously.[4] This is my strategy: If I can just coerce women into the last half of that fourth date, it's anyone's ball game. I've beaten the system; I've broken the code; I've slain the Minotaur. If we part ways on that fourth evening without some kind of conversational disaster, she probably digs me. Or at least she *thinks* she digs me, because who she digs is not really me. Sadly, our relationship will not last ninety-three minutes (like *Annie Hall*) or ninety-six minutes (like *Manhattan*). It will go on for days or weeks or months or years, and I've already used everything in my vault. Very soon, I will have nothing more to say, and we will be sitting across from each other at breakfast, completely devoid of banter; she will feel betrayed and foolish, and I will suddenly find myself actively trying to avoid spending time with a woman I didn't deserve to be with in the first place.

Perhaps this sounds depressing. That is not my intention. This is all normal. There's not a lot to say during breakfast. I mean, you just woke up, you know? Nothing has happened. If neither person had an especially weird dream and nobody burned the toast, breakfast is just the time for chewing Cocoa Puffs and/or wishing you were still asleep. But we've been convinced not to think like that. Silence is only supposed to happen as a manifestation of supreme actualization, where both parties are so at

4. Here's one example I tend to deploy on second dates, and it's rewarded with an endearing guffaw at least 90 percent of the time: I ask the woman what religion she is. Inevitably, she will say something like, "Oh, I'm sort of Catholic, but I'm pretty lapsed in my participation," or "Oh, I'm kind of Jewish, but I don't really practice anymore." Virtually everyone under the age of thirty will answer that question in this manner. I then respond by saying, "Yeah, it seems like everybody I meet describes themselves as 'sort of Catholic' or 'sort of Jewish' or 'sort of Methodist.' Do you think all religions have this problem? I mean, do you think there are twenty-five-year-old Amish people who say, 'Well, I'm *sort of* Amish. I currently work as a computer programmer, but I still believe pants with metal zippers are the work of Satan.'"

7

peace with their emotional connection that it cannot be expressed through the rudimentary tools of the lexicon; otherwise, silence is proof that the magic is gone and the relationship is over (hence the phrase "We just don't talk anymore"). For those of us who grew up in the media age, the only good silence is the kind described by the hair metal band Extreme. "More than words is all I ever needed you to show," explained Gary Cherone on the *Pornograffiti* album. "Then you wouldn't have to say that you love me, cause I'd already know." This is the difference between art and life: In art, not talking is never an extension of having nothing to say; not talking always means something. And now that art and life have become completely interchangeable, we're forced to live inside the acoustic power chords of Nuno Bettencourt, even if most of us don't necessarily know who the fuck Nuno Bettencourt is.

When Harry Met Sally hit theaters in 1989. I didn't see it until 1997, but it turns out I could have skipped it entirely. The movie itself isn't bad (which is pretty amazing, since it stars Meg Ryan *and* Billy Crystal), and there are funny parts and sweet parts and smart dialogue, and—all things considered—it's a well-executed example of a certain kind of entertainment.[5] Yet watching this film in 1997 was like watching the 1978 one-game playoff between the Yankees and the Red Sox on *ESPN Classic*: Though I've never sat through the pitch sequence that leads to Bucky Dent's three-run homer, I know exactly what happened. I feel like I remember it, even though I don't. And—more important—*I know what it all means*. Knowing about sports means knowing that Bucky Dent is the living, breathing, metaphorical incarnation of the Bo Sox's undying futility; I didn't have to see that game to understand the fabric of its existence. I didn't need to see *When Harry Met Sally*, either. Within three years of its initial release, classifying any intense friendship as "totally a *Harry-Met-Sally* situation" had a recognizable meaning to every-

5. "A certain kind" meaning "bad."

one, regardless of whether or not they'd actually seen the movie. And that meaning remains clear and remarkably consistent: It implies that two platonic acquaintances are refusing to admit that they're deeply in love with each other. *When Harry Met Sally* cemented the plausibility of that notion, and it gave a lot of desperate people hope. It made it realistic to suspect your best friend may be your soul mate, and it made wanting such a scenario comfortably conventional. The problem is that the *Harry-Met-Sally* situation is almost always tragically unbalanced. Most of the time, the two involved parties are not really "best friends." Inevitably, one of the people has been in love with the other from the first day they met, while the other person is either (a) wracked with guilt and pressure, or (b) completely oblivious to the espoused attraction. Every relationship is fundamentally a power struggle, and the individual in power is whoever likes the other person less. But *When Harry Met Sally* gives the powerless, unrequited lover a reason to live. When this person gets drunk and tells his friends that he's in love with a woman who only sees him as a buddy, they will say, "You're wrong. You're perfect for each other. This is just like *When Harry Met Sally*! I'm sure she loves you—she just doesn't realize it yet." Nora Ephron accidentally ruined a lot of lives.

I remember taking a course in college called "Communication and Society," and my professor was obsessed by the belief that fairy tales like "Hansel and Gretel" and "Little Red Riding Hood" were evil. She said they were part of a latent social code that hoped to suppress women and minorities. At the time, I was mildly outraged that my tuition money was supporting this kind of crap; years later, I have come to recall those pseudo-savvy lectures as what I *loved* about college. But I still think they were probably wasteful, and here's why: Even if those theories are true, they're barely significant. "The Three Little Pigs" is not the story that is fucking people up. Stories like *Say Anything* are fucking people up. We don't need to worry about people unconsciously "absorbing" archaic secret messages when they're six

9

CHUCK KLOSTERMAN

years old; we need to worry about all the entertaining messages people are consciously accepting when they're twenty-six. They're the ones that get us, because they're the ones we try to turn into life. I mean, Christ: I wish I could believe that bozo in Coldplay when he tells me that stars are yellow. I miss that girl. I wish I was Lloyd Dobler. I don't want anybody to step on a piece of broken glass. I want fake love. But that's all I want, and that's why I can't have it.

I designed the perfect girlfriend once. She was a friend of a friend, and—from the moment I never met her—I decided she was the seamless combination of intellect, wit, and altruistic sincerity (she was also supposedly an English major). My love for this girl was spawned before I ever laid eyes on her; her physical appearance was merely described to me by other people, and I quite suddenly convinced myself that this woman was my soul mate. I'm not sure why I did this; maybe it just seemed like an interesting decision to make in advance. I do this sort of thing quite often (sometimes I buy records and pick which song is my favorite before I actually play them, and I find that I am right almost half the time).

Since I had never spoken to this woman (her name was Annette) and had only an anecdotal understanding of what she looked like, my best avenue for cementing our future passion was to send her a letter, which is what I did. And since David Letterman was very popular at the time (and since I am not creative, and since I was nineteen), I sent her a comically agile Top 10 List, which I titled "The Top 10 Reasons Annette Should Fall In Love with Chuck Klosterman." My assumption was that we would share our first kiss forty-eight to seventy-two hours after she received this missive, particularly because of the cleverness of reason number 4, which was as follows:

4) I am almost a carnivore.

Unfortunately, Annette wasn't my soul mate. She also was not an English major, a fact that became abundantly clear when our mutual friend told me he talked to her on the telephone and asked her about my letter, to which she replied, "Why would I possibly want to date someone who eats other humans?" And the thing that broke my heart wasn't that she didn't know the definition of the word *carnivore*; I could live with that. What killed me was that she thought I had claimed to be "almost a cannibal," and that didn't work, either.

I am not a benevolent God.

I am watching myself writhe in a puddle of my own urine, and I offer no response. I have not slept or eaten for days. My cries go unrecognized and my loneliness is ignored. I am watching myself endure a torture worse than death, yet I decline every opportunity to end this self-imposed nightmare. Darkness . . . imprisoning me . . . all that I see, absolute horror. I cannot live, I cannot die, trapped in myself; my body is my holding cell.

I am the master, and I am the puppet. And I am not the type of person who still plays video games.

I realize there is a whole generation of adults born in the seventies who currently play Sega and Nintendo as much as they banged away on their Atari 5200 and their George Plimpton–endorsed Intellivision in 1982. I am not one of them. I agree with *Media Virus* author Douglas Rushkoff's theory that home video game consoles were the reason kids raised in the 1980s so naturally embraced the virtual mentality—we never thought it seemed strange to be able to manually manipulate what we saw on a video screen—but I'll never accept pixels killing other pixels as an art form (or a sport, or even a pastime). A homeless man once told me that dancing to rap music is the cultural equivalent of masturbating, and I'd sort of feel the same way about playing John Madden Football immediately after filing my income tax: It's fun, but—somehow—vaguely pathetic.

However, some things are just too enchanting (and just too weird) to ignore. Those were my thoughts when I first read about The Sims, arguably the most wholly postmodern piece of entertainment ever created. Much like the TV show *Survivor*, the Pokémon phenomenon, and Parliament Funkadelic, The Sims is a keenly constructed product that seems hopelessly absurd to anyone unfamiliar with it but completely clear to anyone who's experienced it even once. Developed by Electronic Arts, The Sims is a video game where you do all the things you would do in real life if you weren't playing a video game. You create a human character, and it exists. That's it. Your character does things like read the newspaper. He takes naps, plays pinball, and empties the garbage. Your character invites friends over to his house, and they have discussions about money and sailboats. You buy oak bookcases and you get pizza from Domino's. *This is the whole game*, and there is no way to win, except to keep yourself from becoming depressed. The Sims is an escapist vehicle for people who want to escape to where they already are, which is why I thought this game was made precisely for me.

WHO AM I? OR (PERHAPS MORE ACCURATELY) WHO ELSE COULD BE ME?

The Sims is the only video game I have ever purchased. My goal—and probably the initial goal of most people who buy The Sims—was to create a perfect replica of the life I already have. I would build a character who looked just like me, and I would name him "Chuck Klosterman." I would design his home exactly like my own, and I would have him do all the things I do every day. Perhaps I unconsciously assumed I would learn something about myself through this process, although I have no idea what that could possibly be. Maybe it was just the desire to watch myself live. Pundits like to claim that a game like The Sims taps into the human preoccupation with voyeurism, but it's really the complete opposite. I don't care about peeping into anyone else's keyhole; I only want to see into Chuck's.

I designed my digital self as accurately as possible: pasty skin, thick glasses, uncommitted haircut, ill-fated trousers. Outlining my character's personality traits was a little more complicated, because nobody (myself included) truly knows how they act. I've never met anyone I'd classify as self-aware: It's been my experience that most extroverted people think they're introverts, and many introverted people make a similarly wrongheaded juxtaposition about being extroverts. Maybe that's why extroverts won't shut up (because they always fear they're not talking enough) while introverts just sit on the couch and do nothing (because they assume everybody is waiting for them to be quiet). People just have no clue about their genuine nature. I have countless friends who describe themselves as "cynical," and they're all wrong. True cynics would never classify themselves as such, because it would mean that they know their view of the world is unjustly negative; despite their best efforts at being grumpy, a self-described cynic is secretly optimistic about normal human nature. Individuals who are truly cynical will always insist they're pragmatic. The same goes for anyone who claims to be "creative." If you define your personality as creative, it only means you understand what is *perceived* to be creative by the world at large, so you're really just following a rote creative template. That's the *opposite* of creativity. Everybody is wrong about everything, just about all the time.

But ANYWAY . . . I eventually created a Chuck in my own image and dropped him into 6 Sim Lane, a $15,000 home on the outskirts of an underdeveloped suburb of SimCity, a relic from an earlier incarnation of this particular game. SimCity was the first "simulated reality" game to capture people's imagination, although SimCity seemed (at least retrospectively) oddly innocuous: The object of that game was to design a vibrant community (transportation systems, hospitals, animal shelters, etc.). It was really just a game for amateur city planners, which is actually less boring than it sounds. SimCity led to SimEarth, where players could exercise their jones to be an Old Testament God—you took a dead planet and you created a breathable atmosphere and you caused volcanoes and you tried to spawn a few dinosaurs. This was a little more psychologically akimbo, but still not perverse; SimEarth was almost like an eighth-grade science project. However, The Sims broke new ground for electronic pathos. It's not a game about managing life (like *SimCity*) or even creating life (like SimEarth); it's a game about *experiencing* life, and experiencing it in the most mundane fashion possible. Whenever unimaginative TV critics tried to explain the subtle, subversive genius of *Seinfeld*, they always went back to the hack argument that "It was about nothing." But that sentiment was always a little wrong. *Seinfeld* was about nothing, but its underlying message was that nothingness still has a weight and a mass and a conflict. What seemed so new about *Seinfeld* was that it didn't need a story to have a plot: Nothing was still something. The Sims forces that aesthetic even further: Nothing is everything.

MY LIFE AS A SIM. OR (PERHAPS MORE ACCURATELY) MY LIFE AS MY LIFE.

As I had long suspected, my six-year-old niece Katie is not the former lead singer of the Talking Heads. This had been somewhat obvious for a long time, but never more so than the first time I saw a copy of The Sims, which I happened to find at her parents' house in rural North Dakota.

Since I had been fascinated by news stories about this game, I immediately tried to play The Sims when I noticed it was on the hard drive of my sister-in-law's computer. For about fifteen minutes, my seminal pre-Chuck wandered about the empty residential lots of Sim Village, trying to start conversations with inanimate objects. Young Katie couldn't help but notice my ineptitude and immediately tried to show me how the game was played (and—inadvertently—how existence works, although I doubt she would have explained it that way).

Katie displayed amazing dexterity at The Sims, effortlessly building a home and furnishing it with a cornucopia of household goods she could never operate in reality. She then instructed me to find a job and to make friends with other Sim citizens, especially the female ones (this is somewhat predictable, as Katie profoundly enjoys asking me if I have a girlfriend). However, I immediately had dozens of questions for young Katie about my new life: If I don't yet have a job, how could I afford this residence? Who put all that food in my fridge? Elves, perhaps? Can I trust them? Why don't I need a car? Where did I go to college? Don't I have any old friends I could call for moral support? *This is not my beautiful house. This is not my beautiful wife. Well, how did I get here?*

Unlike David Byrne, these questions did not interest Katie. "You just live here," she said. "That's the way it is." But where did I get all this money? "You just have money." But where did I come from? "Nobody knows. You're just here." Am I one of the 55 million Americans living without health insurance? "Be quiet! You won't get sick." This went on for several minutes, finally ending in a stalemate when Katie realized warm cookies were suddenly available in the kitchen. However, something struck me about this dialogue: It was uncharacteristic for Katie to be so unwilling to tell harmless lies. If she had been playing with her Barbie Dream House and I asked her why Barbie had four pairs of shoes but only two decent outfits, Katie would have undoubtedly spent the next half hour explaining that Barbie purchased the extra shoes while shopping in Hong Kong with Britney Spears and planned to wear them to a cocktail party in Grandma's basement. When playing with real-world toys, there's no limit to the back story Katie will create for anything, animate or inanimate. That's how little kids are. But somehow it's different when life is constructed on a sixteen-inch screen; in the world of The Sims, Katie won't color outside the lines of perception. The rules become fixed. Fabricating a Sim-human's college experience would be no different than randomly deciding that *90210*'s Brenda Walsh got a C+ in tenth-grade biology. Those facts aren't available to anyone. Clearly, video technology cages imagination; it offers interesting information to use, but it implies that all peripheral information is irrelevant and off-limits. Computers make children advance faster, but they also make them think like computers.

I tried to keep this in mind when I started my new-and-improved fake life upon my own purchase of The Sims. My hypothesis was that the game's accuracy would be dependent on my willingness to think within the confines of the game's creators; I had to think like a machine. And it's quite possible that this initial postulate was right. But I'll never really know, because I couldn't do it. As I made my little SimChuck live and work, all I could think about was what I would think about.

What makes The Sims so popular is its dogged adherence to the minutiae of subsistence, and that's where we're supposed to feel the realism. But the realism I felt was the worst kind; it was the hopeless realization that I was doomed to live in my own prison, just like the singer from Creed. The Sims makes the unconscious conscious, but not in an existential Zen way; The Sims forces you to think about how even free people are eternally enslaved by the processes of living. Suddenly, I had to remember to go to the bathroom. I had to *plan* to take a shower. Instead of eating when I was hungry, I had to anticipate an unfelt hunger that was always impending. If I didn't wake up at least an hour before work, I'd miss my ride and get fired. And though I need to do all those things in reality, the thoughts scarcely cross my mind unless I'm plugged into this game.

After playing The Sims for my first ninety minutes, I paused the action, logged off my computer, and drove to a Chinese restaurant called The Platinum Dragon. I had to pass through some road construction, and it suddenly occurred to me that there would *always* be road construction—not always on this particular road, but somewhere. There will never be a point in my lifetime when all the highways are fixed. It's theoretically plausible that my closest friend might someday abandon me for no reason whatsoever, but it's completely *impossible* to envision a day where I could drive from New York to California without hitting roadwork somewhere along the way. It will always exist, and there's nothing I can do about it. And for the first time, that reality made me sad.

CHUCK VS. CHUCK. OR (PERHAPS MORE ACCURATELY) WHY I DON'T UNDERSTAND ANYBODY.

There seems to be an inordinate number of movies about mankind going to war with machines (*Terminator*, *A.I.*, that Stephen King flick with all the AC/DC songs, etc.). That plot device always struck me as something of a cheap shot; as far as I can tell, machines have been nothing but completely civil to us. However, I can assure you that this scenario will never be a problem, even if they completely turn on us. It turns out that computers are the most gutless goddamn cowards you'll ever meet.

My SimChuck has absolutely no grit. He is constantly bummed out, forever holding his head and whining about how he's "not comfortable" or "not having fun." At one point I bought him a pretty respectable wall mirror for $300, and he responded by saying "I'm too depressed to even look at myself." As an alternative, he sat on the couch and stared at the bathroom door. Quite the drama queen, my SimChuck is.

And *why* isn't my SimChuck happy? Because he's a self-absorbed, materialistic prick. This is perhaps the most disturbing element of The Sims: The happiness of the characters is directly proportional to the shit you elect to buy them. As far as I can tell, acquiring electronic equipment and name-brand furniture is just about the only thing Sims find psychologically satisfying.

The shopping angle appears to be the part of the game its designers found most compelling, as their catalog of faux products is both massive and detailed. This is the kind of shit that would prompt Tyler Durden to hit somebody in the face. Take the on-screen description of the Soma Plasma TV, for example. Buying this item for $3,500 increases the owner's fun rating by six full points. And this is what you'd get:

Perfect form . . . perfect image conformity . . . perfect entertainment. Soma Consumer Electronics takes the 'plasma phenomenon' to a brave new level in this elegant technology statement. With its incredible image quality, unique form and super thin Flatuspective screen, the Soma Plasma TV is the undisputed leader in nanopixel technology.

It would be fun to claim that this kind of *Price Is Right* product exposition is a treacherous form of unexpected advertising, but that wouldn't be true, as all the products in The Sims are fake. And it would make me seem as astute as Chip Lambert if I suggested this game is latently attempting to brainwash children into believing that shopping is an important part of life, but I honestly don't think the wackmobile geeks at Electronic Arts have motives that sinister. It's basically just weird, and it's indisputable proof that The Sims is not a strategy game, even though that's what it calls itself. If this was somehow about strategy, all we'd need to know is that getting the biggest television gets you *x* number of fun points. But nobody cares about the math. The reason so much effort has been placed in the "promotion" of fake Sims merchandise is so that its real-life players will enjoy the experience of buying them. It's almost circular logic: If a human playing The Sims somehow enjoys pretending to buy a plasma TV that doesn't even exist, it stands to reason that my little SimChuck would profoundly enjoy watching said TV if it were somehow real. By this justification, buying high-end electronics really *should* cure depression.

And what's even more amazing is that this is kind of true, and—ultimately—it's what I'll never understand about human nature (simulated or otherwise). I never enjoy the process of buying anything, but I get the impression that most Americans love it. What The Sims suggests is that buying things makes people happy because it takes their mind off being alive. I would think this would actually make them feel worse, but every woman I've ever dated seems to disagree.

To succeed at this game, I am forced to consume like a mofo. Perhaps the greatest chasm between Chuck and SimChuck is that I don't own a bed and he can't live without one. I realize it might seem crazy for a thirty-year-old to exist without a bed, but I just can't get myself to buy one; it never seems worth it, because all I would use it for is sleeping (and once I'm unconscious, what do I care where I'm lying?). I get by fine with my "Sleeping Machine," sort of a self-styled nest in the corner of my bedroom. Oh, I can't deny that some overnight visitors to my chamber of slumber have been "disturbed" by my unwillingness to own a traditional bed, but the simple truth is that I don't need that kind of luxury in my life. My Sleeping Machine provides all the REM I require. I hope I never own a bed. But don't tell that to SimChuck. Until I got him his $1,000 Napoleon Sleigh Bed ("made with actual wood and real aromatic cedar"), all he did was cry like a little bitch.

I NEED LOVE. OR (PERHAPS LESS ACCURATELY) LOVE IS ALL AROUND, BUT *ONLY* AROUND.

Truth be told, my secret motivation for experimenting with The Sims was to see if I could sustain any kind of successful relationship within the scope of the game—essentially "playing" to "get play." I'm guessing this is a pretty big draw for all *Sims* obsessives, since it's hard to imagine how anyone regularly sitting in front of a computer for hours at a time could be having much sex. I realize that's a stereotype, but the popularity of The Sims almost irrefutably proves it to be true: This game is single-mindedly designed to be a reflection of a normal life that's filled with normal human interaction. Apparently, that notion is so far removed from gamers that it can only be pursued through a fantasy realm.

Still, there's something oddly Utopian about The Sims relationship-driven, peacenik theology. Unlike other video games I've enjoyed in the past—The Legend of Zelda, Elevator Action, the original Nintendo version of Metal Gear, etc.—The Sims does not require me to kill virtually everyone I meet. As I meet other Sims in the neighborhood, my initial options are to talk with them (understandable), joke with them (also understandable), tickle them (somewhat less understandable), or sneak up behind their back and scare the crap out of them (pretty incomprehensible, but hard to resist). Our interactions are marked by thought bubbles that contain little pictures of the conversation topic; the characters don't speak with real words. They talk in a goofy pigeon language that has been compared to the teachers in old *Peanuts* cartoons, although I tend to think it sounds like a combination of French, Ebonics, and the Japanese pop band Pizzicato Five (interestingly, *Sims* players in different counties sometimes assume that what they are hearing is real dialogue they merely can't decipher—Electronic Arts has fielded phone calls from Americans who thought they had accidentally purchased the Spanish version, Germans who suspected they had been sent the Italian version, Brazilians who thought they had the Canadian version, etc., etc., etc.).

The first two people I ("I" being "SimChuck") meet in "Simburbia" are Mortimer and Bella, a guy with a mustache and a woman wearing a tight red dress. They evidently live nearby. Mortimer is a lot like my real-world friend Dr. Dave in Akron: He's always up for anything. Bella is a tougher nut to crack; she often glances at her watch when I talk to her. But because Bella's a woman, I keep talking (and talking, and talking), and I throw a little tickling into the mix, and I talk some more, and in no time at all I am given the opportunity to select the "flirt" option whenever I meet Bella on the street.

I start calling Bella on my SimPhone several times a day, and she always comes over immediately. This SimChuck is one suave bastard. A little pink heart icon appears next to Bella's on-screen dossier, and she begins defining me as "The Sim I adore." We smooch hardcore. Yet—for some reason—I can't come up with a finishing move. It's not so much that Bella declines to sleep with me; it's more that I don't know how to ask. I stand by my

21

bed and call her name, and she runs right over : . . but then we start talking about skiing. I buy a billiard table in order to impress her (and to set the stage for some, *Penthouse Forum*, Cybill-Shepherd-in-*The Last-Picture-Show*-style shagging), but all she does is clap her hands. I mean, I *know* she's comfortable with me: She has no qualms about using the toilet while I'm standing right next to her, an experience that's light-years more intimate than most kinds of oral sex. But SimChuck remains denied.

And you know why SimChuck gets no nookie? Because Bella was lying to me all along. At the height of our relationship, I invite Bella over for a game of pool (and "maybe more"), and she says, "Sure, I'd love to come over. Can I bring a friend?" I reluctantly agree, but guess who shows up: Mortimer! It turns out he and Bella are married. Upon watching Bella's hello embrace, Mortimer immediately slaps me, and we kind of scuffle. I try to call him the next morning to apologize, but he tells me to get bent. In a matter of simulated hours, I've managed to lose my only male acquaintance by *not* having sex with his wife. This is unprecedented. Even Chuck can't compete with the problems of SimChuck. I had no choice but to buy a Zimantz component hi-fi stereo system ($650).

GOD'S GOD. OR (PERHAPS MORE ACCURATELY) WILL WRIGHT.

After seventy-two hours of Simming I had grown so despondent over the sexless, consumer-obsessed state of my fake life that I called directory assistance and got the number of Electronic Arts in Redwood, California, demanding to speak to Sims creator Will Wright. They directed me to their satellite division Maxis, and I used the Maxis company directory to leave a message with Mr. Wright, assuming he was working on the prototype for SimSoul and would most likely never call me back. However, I was wrong: He returned my call in just a few hours and tried to help me understand how I've managed to destroy my life twice.

"If there's any core question with The Sims, it's got be, 'What is the purpose of life?' Is it to be loved? Is it to be rich? Is it to be successful? They're the same questions you could ask if you never knew the game existed," Wright told me. "But it does seem like some people come to these interesting conclusions about themselves when they play. And if a game changes your perception of the world around you, it's successful."

By that definition, The Sims would, in fact, be classified as art (and art in the truest sense of the word). Wright clearly sees it as such, and he makes a good argument. A forty-two-year-old who never graduated from college (though he did log time at Louisiana State, Louisiana Tech, and the New School in New York City), Wright fell into programming and gaming as an extension of his interest in robotics, a mentality that's readily noticed in Sim behavior.

I explained the conditions of my dilemma to Wright, and—perhaps predictably—he seemed to have heard every one of my questions before. I told him what had happened with Bella. "Yeah, Bella's kind of a slut," he snickered. He explained that his larger vision with The Sims was to show how day-to-day living is—in and of itself—an ongoing strategy problem, which is why so much of The Sims is built around time constraints and the oblique pressure of responsibility. We even had a friendly chat about Abraham Maslow's Hierarchy of Needs, which probably wouldn't have happened if I had called the creator of Donkey Kong.

However, Wright bristled when I suggested that The Sims is mostly a glorification of consumerism that ultimately suggests happiness is available at the mall. He didn't necessarily seem annoyed by this accusation, but he remains baffled that everyone who plays The Sims seems to come to that same conclusion.

"Materialism is the red herring of the game," he says. "Nobody seems to pick up on that. The more you play, the more you realize that all the stuff you buy eventually breaks down and creates all these little explosions in your life. If you play long enough, you start to realize that those things won't really make you happy."

When Wright told me this, I immediately asked if what Sim-Chuck needed was a midlife crisis. Maybe if I kept playing, he'd eventually reach a point where he'd be self-actualized, even if I took away his $1,800 pinball machine. Once again, Wright bristled; he asked if I was talking about the little person in my computer or the little person in my own mind. I told him that it was hard to tell the difference, because we both seemed to be doing the same shit and neither one of us knew why.

"Well, life doesn't have a score," Wright said. "I've noticed that whenever people play The Sims for the first time, they do all these little experiments. They want to see what their power will do, so they lock a character in a room for five days and watch them starve to death. They'll try to make somebody electrocute themselves. But at some point, that power is meaningless. It stops being interesting. You need to have somebody pushing back."

That reminded me of something. Or (perhaps more accurately), that reminded me of *someone*.

I hung up the phone and went back to my computer, opening The Sims and revisiting the place I had been when I started this essay. My SimChuck was still there, frozen in space, hungry and tired and gesturing like a madman, covered in piss. Up until my discussion with Wright, I had assumed individual Sims could not be killed; I thought they were like doomed vampires from Anne Rice novels, forced to exist eternally in a world they did not create. In truth, my Sim was just a confused little guy, still waiting for a reason to live.

I clicked on the "options" key and directed my cursor to the button that said "Free Will." I deployed actualization, and Sim-Chuck was emancipated. I watched him take a shower and crawl into his Sleeping Machine, where he slept for the next fourteen hours. And then I did the same.

"I don't know how I feel about MTV's *The Real World*," he said. "I mean, is it really *real*? How real is it, really? Is it a depiction of reality, or is it a reflection of what we *perceive* to be reality? They advertise this as 'reality programming,' but isn't anything *programmed* inherently fabricated? How real is real, you know?"

She said nothing. She continued smoking a menthol cigarette. Twenty seconds passed.

"Well, what do you think?" he finally asked.

"About what," she asked, exhaling through her teeth.

"About *The Real World*," he repeated. "Do you think it's real?"

"Compared to what?"

"Well . . . to . . . I guess compared to things that are completely real."

Twenty more seconds passed.

"Is the show taped or edited in the Fourth Dimension?" she asked.

"No."

"Are the characters robots?"

"No."

"Can the episodic plotlines only be perceived by people who have ingested mind-expanding hallucinogens, such as lysergic acid diethylamide, mescaline, phencyclidine, ketamine, or psychedelic mushrooms?"

"No."

"Well then," she concluded, "it sounds real to me."

3   What Happens When People
Stop Being Polite   0:26

Even before Eric Neis came into my life, I was having a pretty good 1992.

I wasn't doing anything of consequence that summer, but—at least retrospectively—nothingness always seems to facilitate the best periods of my life. I suppose I was ostensibly going to summer school, sort of; I had signed up for three summer classes at the University of North Dakota in order to qualify for the maximum amount of financial aid, but then I dropped two of the classes the same day I got my check. I suppose I was also employed, sort of; I had a work-study job in the campus "geography library," which was really just a room with a high ceiling, filled with maps no one ever used. For some reason, it was my job to count these maps for three hours a day (I was, however, allowed to listen to classic-rock radio). But most importantly, I was living in an apartment with a guy who spent all night locked in his bedroom writing a novel he was unironically titling *Bits of Reality,* which I think was a modern retelling of *Oedipus Rex.* He slept during the afternoon and mostly subsisted on raw hot dogs. I think his girlfriend paid the rent for both of us.

Now, this dude who ate the hot dogs . . . he was an excellent roommate. He didn't care about anything remotely practical. When two people live together, there's typically an unconscious *Odd Couple* relationship: There's always one fastidious guy who keeps life organized, and there's always one chaotic guy who makes life wacky and interesting. Somehow, the hot dog eater and I both fit into the latter category. In our lives, there was no

26

Tony Randall. We would sit in the living room, drink a case of Busch beer, and throw the empty cans into the kitchen for no reason whatsoever, beyond the fact that it was the most overtly irresponsible way for any two people to live. We would consciously choose to put out cigarettes on the carpet when ashtrays were readily available; we would write phone messages on the walls; we would vomit out the window. And this was a basement apartment.

Obviously, we rarely argued about the living conditions.

We did, however, argue about everything else. Constantly. We'd argue about H. Ross Perot's chances in the upcoming presidential election, and we'd argue about whether there were fewer Jews in the NBA than logic should dictate. We argued about the merits of dog racing, dogfighting, cockfighting, affirmative action, legalized prostitution, the properties of ice, chaos theory, and whether or not water had a discernible flavor. We argued about how difficult it would be to ride a bear, assuming said bear was muzzled. We argued about partial-birth abortion, and we argued about the possibility of Trent Reznor committing suicide and/or being gay. We once got into a vicious argument over whether or not I had actually read all of an aggrandizing Guns N' Roses biography within the scope of a single day, an achievement my hot dog–gorged roommate claimed was impossible (that particular debate extended for all of July). Mostly, we argued about which of us was better at arguing, and particularly about who had won the previous argument.

Perhaps this is why we were both enraptured by that summer's debut of MTV's *The Real World*, an artistic product that mostly seemed like a TV show about people arguing. And these people were *terrible* arguers; the seven cast members thrown into that New York loft always made ill-conceived points and got unjustifiably emotional, and they all seemed to take everything much too personally. But the raw hot dog eater and I watched these people argue all summer long, and then we watched them argue again in the summer of 1993, and then again in the summer of 1994.

27

Technically, these people were completely different every year, but they were also exactly the same. And pretty soon it became clear that the producers of *The Real World* weren't sampling the youth of America—they were unintentionally creating it. By now, everyone I know is one of seven defined strangers, inevitably hoping to represent a predefined demographic and always failing horribly. *The Real World* is the real world is *The Real World* is the real world. It's the same true story, even when it isn't.

I tend to consider myself an amateur *Real World* scholar. I say "amateur" because I've done no actual university study on this subject, but I still say "scholar" because I've stopped watching the show as entertainment. At this point, I only watch it in hopes of unlocking the questions that have haunted man since the dawn of civilization. I've seen every episode of every season, and I've seen them all a minimum of three times. This, of course, is the key to appreciating *The Real World* (and the rest of MTV's programming): repetition. To really get it, you have to watch MTV so much that you know things you never tried to remember. You can't try to deduce the day-to-day habits of Jon Brennan (he was the cowboy dude) from *RW 2: Los Angeles*. That would be ridiculous. You can't consciously try to figure out what he likes and what he hates and how he lives; these are things you have to know without trying. You just have to "know" he constantly drinks cherry Kool-Aid. But you can't try to *learn* that, because that would make you a weirdo. This kind of knowledge is like a vivid dream you suddenly pull out of the cosmic ether, eight hours after waking up. If someone asks you when Montana from *RW 6: Boston* exposed her breasts, you just sort of vaguely recall it was on a boat; if someone asks you who the effeminate black guy from Seattle slapped in the face, you inexplicably know it was the chick with Lyme disease. Yet these are not bits of information you actively acquired; these are things picked up the same way you sussed out how to get around on the subway, or the way you figured out how to properly mix Bloody Marys. One day, you just suddenly realize it's something you know. And—somehow—there's a cold logic to it. It's an extension of your own life, even though you never tried to make it that way.

In 1992, *The Real World* was supposed to be that kind of calculated accident; it was theoretically created as a seamless extension of reality. But somewhere that relationship became reversed; theory was replaced by practice. During that first *RW* summer, I saw kids on MTV who reminded me of people I knew in real life. By 1997, the opposite was starting to happen; I kept meeting new people who were like old *Real World* characters. I've met at least six Pucks in the past five years. This doesn't mean they necessarily talk about snot or eat peanut butter with their hands; what it means is they play The Puck Role. In any given situation, they will provide The Puck Perspective, and they will force those around them to Confront The Puck Paradigm. If nothing else, *The Real World* has provided avenues for world views that are both specialized and universal, and it has particularly validated world views that are patently unreasonable.

Part of me is hesitant to write about cast members from *The Real World* in any specific sense, because I realize few Americans have studied (or even seen) all twelve seasons of the show. You hear a lot of people say things like they watched most of the first two seasons, or that they watched every season up until Miami, or that they never started watching until the San Francisco season, or that they've only seen bits and pieces of the last three years and tend to get the casts mixed up. For most normal TV watchers, *The Real World* is an obsession that fades at roughly the same rate as denim. I've noticed that much of the program's original 1992 audience gets especially bored whenever a modern cast starts to talk like teenage aliens.[1] Last year, an old friend told me she's grown to hate the *Real World* because, "MTV used to pick people for that show who I could relate to. Now they just have these stupid little kids who act like selfish twits." This was said by a woman—now a responsible twenty-nine-year-old soft-

1. An obvious example: White kids using the word like *phat* unironically.

ware specialist—who once threw a drink into the face of her college roommate for reasons that could never be explained. It's hard for most people to hang with a show that so deeply bathes in a fountain of youth.

However, another part of me realizes there's no risk whatsoever in pointing out specific *RW* cast members, even to people who've never seen the show once: You don't need to know the people I'm talking about, because *you know the people I'm talking about*. And I don't mean you know them in the ham-fisted way MTV casts them (i.e., "The Angry Black Militant"[2] or "The Gay One"[3] or "The Naive Virginal Southerner Who's Vaguely Foxy"[4]). When I say "you know these people," it's because the personalities on *The Real World* have become the only available personalities for everyone who's (a) alive and (b) under the age of twenty-nine.

Our cultural preparation for a *Real World* universe actually started in movie theaters during the eighties, particularly with two films that both came out in 1985: *The Breakfast Club* and *St. Elmo's Fire*. These seminal portraits were what *The Real World* was supposed to be like, assuming MTV could find nonfictional people who would have interesting conversations on a semiregular basis. Like most *RW* casts, *The Breakfast Club* broke teen culture into five segments that were laughably stereotypical (and—just in case you somehow missed what they were—Anthony Michael Hall pedantically explains it all in the closing scene). *St. Elmo's Fire* used many of the same actors, but it evolved their personalities by five years and made them more (ahem) "philosophically complex." Here is where we see the true genesis of future *Real World*ians. With Judd Nelson, we have the respected social climber doomed to fail ethically;[5] with Andrew McCarthy, the

2. Kevin from *RW 1*, Kameelah from *RW 6*, Coral from *RW 10*, etc.
3. Norman, Beth, Pedro, Dan, Chris, et al.
4. Julie, Elka, that big-toothed Mormon, the girl with perfect lips from Louisiana, and Trishelle.
5. Joe from Miami.

sensitive, self-absorbed guy who works hard at being bitter.[6] Rob Lowe is the self-destructive guy we're somehow supposed to envy;[7] Emilio Estevez is the romantic that all chumps are supposed to identify with, mostly because he's obsessed with his own obviousness.[8] Demi Moore is fucked up and pathetic,[9] but Mare Winningham is even more pathetic because she *aspires* to be fucked up.[10] Ally Sheedy is too normal to have these friends[11] (or, I suppose, to be in this particular movie).

If we were to combine these two films—in other words, if we were to throw the *St. Elmo's* kids into all-day Saturday detention—we'd have a pretty good *Real World*. It's been noted that one of the keys to Alfred Hitchcock's success as a filmmaker was that he didn't draw characters as much as he drew character *types*; this is how he normalized the cinematic experience. It's the same way with *The Real World*. The show succeeds because it edits malleable personalities into flat, twenty-something archetypes. What interests me is the way those archetypes so quickly became the normal way for people of my generation to behave.

It's become popular for *Real World* revisionists to claim that the first season was the only truly transcendent *RW*, the argument being that this was the singular year its cast members actually acted "real." In a broad sense, that's accurate: Since that first *Real World* was entirely new, no one knew what it was going to look like (or how it would be received). Nobody in the original New York loft was able to formulate an agenda *on purpose*. Logically, this

6. Judd from San Francisco.

7. Dominic from L.A.

8. Kind of like that dork from Hawaii who fell in love with the alcoholic lesbian and then dated her sister.

9. Theoretically Ruthie, the drunk chick from Hawaii—although (in truth) she was actually more reasonable than everyone else in that house.

10. Cory in San Fran, all the other girls from Hawaii, Tonya from Chicago, and every other female who spends at least two episodes of any season staring at a large body of water.

11. Julie from the first NYC cast, the blonde from New Orleans, Kevin in the second set of New Yorkers, and Frank from Vegas.

should make for great television. In practice, it doesn't translate: In truth, *RW 1* is mostly dull. It was fascinating in 1992 because of the novelty, but it doesn't stand up over time.

I'll concede that the cast on the first *Real World* were the only ones who didn't constantly play to the camera; only hunky model Eric Neis did so on an episode-to-episode basis, but one gets the impression this was just his normal behavior. While the actual filming was taking place, I have no doubt the seven loft-dwellers were clueless about what the final product would look like on television; that certainly fostered the possibility for spontaneous "reality," and there are glimpses of that throughout *RW 1*. The problem is that hard reality tends to be static: On paper, the conversations from that virgin *Real World* would make for a terrible script. In fact, the greatest moments from the first *Real World* are when nothing is going on *at all*—the awkwardness becomes transfixing, not unlike the sensation of sitting in an airport and watching someone read a newspaper. Yet if every cast of *The Real World* has been as "real" as that first New York ensemble, the show would have only lasted two seasons.

Ironically, the reason *RW* flourished is because its telegenic humanoids became less complex with every passing season. Multifaceted people do not translate within *The Real World* format. Future cast members figured this out when that initial season finally aired and it was immediately obvious that only two personalities mattered: Alabama belle Julie and angry African-American Kevin. The only truly compelling episode from the first season came in week eleven, when Julie and Kevin had an outdoor screaming match over a seemingly random race issue.[12] But the

12. I say "seemingly" because this argument appears totally superficial—until you find out the context: It happened during the Rodney King riots in Los Angeles, a fact that MTV never mentioned. As a rule, *The Real World* does not deal with the issue of context very well, consciously skewing it much of the time. When David (the black comedian in Los Angeles) was kicked out for "sexually harassing" future NBA groupie Tami in *RW 2*, the viewing audience is given the impression that he had been living in the house for weeks. In truth, it happened almost immediately after everyone moved in.

fight itself wasn't the key. What was important was the way it galvanized two archetypes that would become cornerstones for late-twentieth-century youth: the educated automaton and the likable anti-intellectual. Those two personality sects are suddenly everywhere, and they're both children of *The Real World*.

Obviously, Kevin embodies the former attitude and Julie embodies the latter. And—almost as obviously—neither designation is particularly accurate. Kevin became a solid hip-hop writer for *Vibe* and *Rolling Stone*, and he's far less robotic than he appears on *The Real World*. Meanwhile, Julie was never a backwater hick (I interviewed her in 1995, and I honestly suspect she might be the savviest person in the show's history). But within the truncated course of those thirteen original episodes, we are led to believe that (a) Kevin is obsessed with racial identity and attempts to inject his blackness into every conversation, while (b) Julie adores anything remotely new and abhors everything remotely pretentious.

Kevin's Huey Newton–like image can't be blamed entirely on him: *The Real World* is unnaturally obsessed with race. And what's disheartening is that *The Real World* is so consumed with creating racial tension that it often makes black people look terrible: If your only exposure to diversity was Coral and Nicole from the 2001 "Back to New York" *RW* cast, you'd be forced to assume all black women are blithering idiots. This is partially because the only black characters who get valuable *RW* airtime are the ones who refuse to talk about anything else. It's the same situation for homosexual cast members—their Q factor is completely dependent on how aggressively gay they're willing to act. In that first NYC season, Norman is immediately identified as bisexual, but he's not bisexual enough; he only gets major face time when he's dating future TV talk-show host Charles Perez. Future queer cast members would not make this mistake; for people like AIDS victim Pedro Zamora and Dan from *RW 5: Miami*, being gay was pretty much their *only* personality trait. Perhaps more than anything else, this is the ultimate accomplishment of *The Real*

World: It has validated the merits of having a one-dimensional personality. In fact, it has made that kind of persona desirable, because other one-dimensional personalities can more easily understand you.

If you believe *Real World* producers Mary-Ellis Bunim and Jon Murray, they don't look for troublemakers when they make casting decisions. They insist they simply cast for "diversity." But this is only true in a macro sense—they want *obvious* diversity. They want physical diversity, or sexual diversity, or economic diversity. What they have no use for is intellectual diversity. A Renaissance man (or woman) need not apply to this program. You need to be able to deduce who a given *Real World*er represents socially before the second commercial break of the very first episode, which gives you about eighteen minutes of personality. It was very easy to make *RW 1* Kevin appear one-dimensional, even if that portrayal wasn't accurate; he gave them enough "race card" material to ignore everything else. Thus, Kevin became the inadvertent model for thousands and thousands of future *Real World* applicants—these are the people who looked at themselves in the mirror and thought, "I could get on that show. I could be the _____ guy."

The "_____" became almost anything: race, gender, geographic origin, sexual appetite, etc. There was suddenly an unspoken understanding that every person in the *Real World* house was supposed to fit some kind of highly specific—but completely one-dimensional—persona. In his memoir *A Heartbreaking Work of Staggering Genius*, Dave Eggers writes about how he tried to get on *Real World 3: San Francisco*, but was beaten out by Judd. Coincidentally, both of those guys were cartoonists. But the larger issue is that they were both liberal and sensitive, and they were both likely to be the kind of guy who would fall in love with a female housemate who only perceived him as a good friend. This is exactly the person Judd became; there is now a famous[13] scene

---

13. Relatively speaking.

from that third season where Judd is rowing a boat and longingly stares at roommate Pam and her boyfriend, Christopher, as they paddle alongside in a similar watercraft. Months after the conclusion of *RW 3*, Pam broke up with Chris and fell in love with Judd, which is (a) kind of bizarre, but mostly (b) exactly what MTV dreams of having happen during any given season. Whenever I see repeat episodes of *RW 3*, I find myself deconstructing every casual conversation Judd and Pam have, because I know a secret they don't—eighteen months later, they will have sex. It's sort of like seeing old Judas Priest videos on VH1 Classic and looking for signs of Rob Halford's homosexuality.

The Judd-Pam undercurrent is part of the reason I consider *Real World 3: San Francisco* the best-ever *RW*, but that's not the only reason. Central to my affinity for *RW 3* is a wholly personal issue: The summer it premiered was the summer following my college graduation. I had just moved to a town where I knew almost no one, and my cable was installed the afternoon of *The Real World* season premiere. The first new friends I made were Cory and Pedro, and I rode with them on a train to California. And I pretty much hated both of them (or at least Cory) immediately.

In truth, there wasn't any member of *RW 3* I particularly liked, and I couldn't relate to any of them, except maybe Rachel (and only because she was a bad Catholic). But I became emotionally attached to these people in a very authentic way, and I think it was because I started noticing that the cast members on *RW 3* were not like people from my past. Instead, they seemed like new people I was meeting in the present.

Because *The Real World* has now been going on for a decade—and because of *Survivor* and *Big Brother* and *The Mole* and *Temptation Island* and *The Osbournes*—the idea of "reality TV" is now something everyone understands. Without even trying, American TV watchers have developed an amazingly sophisticated view of postmodernism, even if they would never use the word *postmodern* in any conversation (or even be able to define it).[14] However, this was still a new idea in 1994. And what's important about *RW 3* is that it was the first time MTV quit trying to pretend it wasn't on television.

Here's what I mean by that: I once read a movie review by Roger Ebert for the film *Jay and Silent Bob Strike Back*. Early in the review, Ebert makes a tangential point about whether or not film characters are theoretically "aware" of *other* films and *other* movie characters. Ebert only touches on this issue casually, but it's probably the most interesting philosophical question ever asked about film grammar. Could Harrison Ford's character in *What Lies Beneath* rent *Raiders of the Lost Ark*? Could John Rambo draw personal inspiration from *Rocky*? In *Desperately Seeking Susan*, what is Madonna hearing when she goes to a club and dances to her own song? Within the reality of one specific fiction, how do other fictions exist?

The Real World deals with an identical problem, but in a completely opposite way: They have a nonfiction situation that is supposed to have no relationship to other nonfictions. They have to behave as if what they're doing hasn't been done before. *Real World*ers always get into arguments, but you never hear them say, "Oh, you're only saying that because you know this is going to be on TV," even though that would be the best come-back 90 percent of the time. No one would ever compare a housemate to a cast member from a different season, even when such comparisons seem obvious. The kids talk directly into the camera every single day, but they are ceaselessly instructed to pretend as if they are not being videotaped whenever they're outside the confessional. Most of all, they never openly recognize that

14. This is partially because everyone who **does** use *postmodern* in casual conversation seems to define it differently, usually in accordance with whatever argument they're trying to illustrate. I think the best definition is the simplest: "Any art that is conscious of the fact that it is, in fact, art." So when I refer to something as *postmodern*, that's usually what I mean. I realize some would suggest that an even better definition is "Any art that is conscious of the fact that it is, in fact, product," but that strikes me as needlessly cynical.

they're part of a cultural phenomenon; they never mention how weird it is that people are watching them exist. Every *Real World* cast exists in a vacuum.

That illusion started to crack in *RW 3*. That's also when the show's mentality started to leak into the social bloodstream.

The reason this occurred in San Francisco is because two of the housemates, Puck and Pedro, never allowed themselves to slip into *The Real World*'s fabricated portrait of reality; they were always keenly cognizant of how they could use this program to forward their goals. Depending on your attitude, Pedro's agenda was either altruistic (i.e., personalizing the HIV epidemic), self-aggrandizing (he was doggedly focused on achieving martyrdom status), or a little of both (which is probably closest to the mark). Meanwhile, Puck's agenda was entirely negative, any way you slice it; he wanted to become the show's first "breakout star" (a *Real World* Fonzie, if you will), and he succeeded at that goal by actively trying to wreck the entire project. In a show about living together, he tried to be impossible to live with. But in at least one way, Pedro and Puck were identical: Both of these guys immediately saw that they could design their own TV show by developing a script within their head. They fashioned themselves as caricatures.

Ironically, they both attacked each other for doing this. By the ninth episode, Puck was breaking the fourth wall by suggesting that Pedro was trying to force his message down the throats of viewers; no one had ever implied something like this before. Without being too obvious, *The Real World* producers relaxed the reins and gave up on the notion that this show was somehow organic; a decision was made to let Puck and Pedro fight over the future identity of *The Real World*. Puck represented the idea of a show where everyone was openly fake and we all knew it was a sham; Pedro represented the aesthetic of a show where what we saw was mostly fake, but we would agree to watch it as if it was totally real. It was almost a social contract. To feel Pedro's pain (as Bill Clinton supposedly did), you had to suspend your disbelief— a paradoxical requirement for a reality program.

In the end, Puck's asinine subversion turned everyone against him with too much voracity. He was jettisoned from the house in episode eleven, appearing only sporadically for the remainder of the season. Pedro remained in the residence and became MTV's shining moment of the 1990s; he proved himself as an educational hero with a mind-blowing flair for the dramatic (the fact that he died the day after the final episode aired is almost as eerie as Charles Schulz dying the same day the final *Peanuts* strip ran in newspapers). Though the second half of the *RW 3* season (after Puck's departure) is considerably less entertaining than its first half, it's probably good Puck was booted. He would have destroyed the show. In fact, whenever a member of a *Real World* cast has tried to subvert the premise of the program—Puck, Seattle's Irene,[15] Hawaii's Justin[16]—they've never made it through an entire season. If they did, it would have turned something charmingly silly into a complete farce. But as long as that unspoken agreement remains between the show and the audience— they pretend to be normal people, we pretend to believe them—*The Real World* works as both bubblegum sociology and a sculptor of human behavior . . . which brings me back to what I was saying about how almost everyone I meet has suddenly turned into a *Real World* cast member.

It all became clear in 1994, during *RW 3*: I had just graduated from college the previous spring and was residing in Fargo, a town I was logistically familiar with despite knowing virtually no one who lived there. However, Fargo is only an hour's drive from Grand Forks, North Dakota (the college town where I attended school), so I drove back to "rock" every other weekend. I'd cut out of work early and arrive in G.F. around 4:30 P.M.; I'd spring for a case of Busch pounders (I was now making $18,500 a year and was therefore unspeakably rich) and I'd sit around with a revolving door of acquaintances in someone's shithole apartment. We'd

15. This was that chick with Lyme disease.
16. This was the gay law student with the spiky hair.

load up on Busch until it was time to go to the local uncool sports bar (Jonesy's) at 8:00, which was where you went before hitting the hipster bar (Whitey's) at around 10:20. Not unlike the summer of 1992, there was no real activity: We'd just sit around and listen to the dying days of grunge, fondly reminiscing about things that had happened in the very recent past. But sometimes I'd notice something weird, especially if strangers stumbled into our posse: Everyone was adopting a singularity to their self-awareness. When I had first arrived at college in 1990, one of the things I loved was the discovery of people who seemed impossible to categorize; I'd meet a guy watching a Vikings-Packers game in the TV room, only to later discover that he was obsessed with Fugazi, only to eventually learn that he was a gay born-again Christian. There was a certain collegiate cachet to being a walking contradiction. But somehow *The Real World* leaked out of those TV sets when Puck shattered the glass barrier between his life and ours. People started becoming personality templates, devoid of complication and obsessed with melodrama. I distinctly recall drinking with two girls in a Grand Forks tavern while they discussed their plan to "confront" a third roommate about her "abrasive" behavior. How did that become a normal way to talk? Who makes plans to "confront" a roommate? To me, it was obvious where this stuff came from: It came from *Real World* people. It was *Real World* culture. It's a microcosm of the United Nations, occupied by seven underdeveloped countries trying to force the others to recognize their right to exist.

During that very first summer of *The Real World*, everyone kept telling me I should try to get on *RW 2*. They gave the same advice to my hot dog–eating roommate. I suspect this was meant to be a compliment to both of us; when people tell you that you should be on a reality program, they're basically saying you're crazy enough to amuse total strangers. I was always flattered by this suggestion, and I used to fantasize about being cast on *The Real World*, imagining that it would make me famous. What I failed to realize is that being a former member of *The Real World* is the worst kind of fame. There is no financial upside; it offers no artistic credibility or mainstream adoration or easy sex. Basically, the only reward is that people will (a) point at you in public, and (b) ask you about absolutely nothing else until the day you die, when your participation in a cable television program becomes the lead item in your obituary. You will be the kind of person who suddenly gets recognized at places like Burger King, but you will still be the kind of person who eats at places like Burger King.

Once you've been on TV, nothing else matters. If Flora from Miami wrote the twenty-first-century version of *Anna Karenina*, she'd still be known as the loud-mouthed bitch who fell through the bathroom window. Almost a dozen ex–*Real World*ers have pursued careers in music, all with a jump-start from MTV. None have succeeded; their combined album sales would be dwarfed by Arrested Development's live album. Eric Neis and Puck managed to stay in the spotlight for a few extra milliseconds, but they both went bankrupt. It appears that the highest residual success one can achieve from a *Real World* stint is that of being asked to compete in a *Real World/Road Rules* challenge All these people are forever doomed to the one-dimensional qualities that made them famous nobodies. The idea that they could do anything else seems impossible.

This is why I could never be on *The Real World*, no matter how much I love watching it. I could never filter every experience through my singular, self-conscious individuality. Yet part of me fears this will happen anyway; I fear that *The Real World*'s unipersonal approach will become so central to American life that I'll need a singular persona just to make conversation with whatever media-saturated robot I end up marrying. Being interesting has been replaced by being identifiable. I guess my only hope is to find myself an Alabama Julie, whose wonderfully one-dimensional naïveté will be impressed by the unpretentious way I vomit out the window.

When I initially heard CBS was creating the quasi-Orwellian reality program *Big Brother,* I was wildly enthusiastic. It sounded like a better version of *The Real World,* because the premise seemed to guarantee emotional confliction: Not only were they going to force total strangers to live together, but these poor chumps wouldn't even be allowed to leave the room. I imagined it would be like jamming Puck and Pedro and Amaya and that drunk Hawaiian girl into Anne Frank's annex and forcing them to emote at gunpoint. This would be perfect television.

However, *Big Brother* was a failed experiment, and I know why: They don't use music. I never knew what was going on. During key moments on *The Real World,* we are always instructed how to feel; if two people are playing chess to Soundgarden's "Black Hole Sun," I know their relationship is doomed; if they're playing along with Sheryl Crow's "Everyday Is a Winding Road," I know they are mending fences and exploring a new level of companionship. But on *Big Brother,* there is never a musical subtext; in this particular instance, we'd merely see two hollow stoics moving rooks and knights, wholly devoid of sentiment.

Without a soundtrack, human interaction is meaningless. I once spent an evening chatting about the complexity of modern relationships with a male acquaintance, his ex-girlfriend, and her roommate. When I went to bed that night, I thought our conversation had been wonderful. Twelve hours later, I was informed that the ex-girlfriend spent the entire evening "in a rage," apparently because the other male in our foursome had been "brooding and surly," creating a tension that subsequently made the ex-girlfriend's roommate "completely uncomfortable" with the nature of our dialogue. I never noticed any of this. I never have any idea how other people feel; they always appear fine to me. But if somebody had pointedly played Pat Benatar's "Love Is a Battlefield" that night, I'm sure I could have constructed some empathy.

4 Every Dog Must Have His Every Day, Every Drunk Must Have His Drink 0:42

Several months before nineteen unsmiling people from the Middle East woke up early on a Tuesday in order to commit suicide by flying planes into tall New York office buildings, I sent out a mass e-mail to several acquaintances that focused on the concept of patriotism. At the time, "patriotism" seemed like a quaint, baffling concept; it was almost like asking people to express their feelings on the art of blacksmithing. But sometimes I like to ask people what they think about blacksmithing, too.

So ANYWAY, here was the content of my e-mail: I gave everyone two potential options for a hypothetical blind date and asked them to pick who they'd prefer. The only things they knew about the first candidate was that he or she was attractive and successful. The only things they knew about the second candidate was that he or she was attractive, successful, and "extremely patriotic." No other details were provided or could be ascertained.

Just about everyone immediately responded by selecting the first individual. They viewed patriotism as a downside. I wasn't too surprised; in fact, I was mostly just amused by how everyone seemed to think extremely patriotic people weren't just undateable, but totally fucking insane. One of them wrote that the quality of "patriotism" was on par with "regularly listening to Cat Stevens" and "loves Robin Williams movies." Comparisons were made to Ted Nugent and Patrick Henry. And one especially snide fellow sent back a mass message to the entire e-mail group, essentially claiming that any woman who loved America didn't *deserve* to date him, not because he hated his country but because patriotic people weren't smart.

That last response outraged one of my friends, a thirty-one-year-old lawyer who had been the only individual in the entire group who claimed to prefer the extremely patriotic candidate to the alternative. He sent me one of the most sincerely aggravated epistles I've ever received, and I still recall a segment of his electronic diatribe that was painfully accurate: "You know how historians call people who came of age during World War II 'the greatest generation'? No one will ever say that about us," he wrote. "We'll be 'the cool generation.' That's all we're good at, and that's all you and your friends seem to aspire to."

What's kind of ironic about this statement is that I think my lawyer friend was trying to make me reevaluate the state of my life, but it mostly just made me think about Billy Joel. Nobody would ever claim that Billy Joel is *cool* in the conventional sense, particularly if they're the kind of person who actively worries about what coolness is supposed to mean. Billy Joel is also not cool in the kitschy, campy, "he's so uncool he's cool" sense, which also happens to be the most tired designation in popular culture. He has no intrinsic coolness, and he has no extrinsic coolness. If cool was a color, it would be black—and Billy Joel would be sort of burnt orange.

Yet Billy Joel is *great*. And he's not great *because* he's uncool, nor is he great because he "doesn't worry about being cool" (because I think he kind of does). No, he's great in the same the way that your dead grandfather is great. Because unlike 99 percent of pop artists, there is absolutely no relationship between Joel's greatness and Joel's coolness (or lack thereof), just as there's no relationship between the "greatness" of serving in World War II and the "coolness" of serving in World War II. What he does as an artist wouldn't be better if he was significantly cooler, and it's not worse because he isn't. And that's sort of amazing when one considers that he's supposedly a rock star.

For just about everybody else in the idiom of rock, being cool is pretty much the whole job description. It's difficult to think of rock artists who are great without being cool, since that's precisely why we need them to exist. There have been countless bands in rock history—T. Rex, Jane's Addiction, the White Stripes, et al.—who I will always classify as "great," even though they're really just spine-crushingly "cool." What they *are* is more important than what they *do*. And this is not a criticism of coolness; by and large, the musical component of rock isn't nearly as important as the iconography and the posturing and the *idea* of what we're supposed to be experiencing. If given the choice between hearing a great band and seeing a cool band, I'll take the latter every single time; this is why the Eagles suck. But it's the constraints of that very relationship that give Billy Joel his subterranean fabulousity, and it's why he's unassumingly superior to all his mainstream seventies peers who got far more credit (James Taylor, Carole King, Bruce Springsteen, etc.). Joel is the only rock star I've ever loved who I *never* wanted to be (not even when he was sleeping with Christie Brinkley). Every one of Joel's important songs—including the happy ones—are ultimately about loneliness. And it's not "clever lonely" (like Morrissey) or "interesting lonely" (like Radiohead); it's "lonely lonely," like the way it feels when you're being hugged by someone and it somehow makes you sadder.

Now, I know what you're thinking: What about that godawful current events song that seemed like a rip-off of R.E.M. (1989's "We Didn't Start the Fire")? What's lonely about that, you ask? Well, my response is simple—I don't count that song. I don't count anything that comes after his *An Innocent Man* album, and I barely count that one. And aesthetically, this is totally acceptable. Unless they die before the age of thirty-three, nobody's entire career matters, and we all unconsciously understand this. If you're trapped in a Beatles-Stones debate, it's not like anybody tries to prove a point by comparing *Help!* to *Steel Wheels*. Black Sabbath is the most underrated band in rock history, and that designation isn't weakened by 1994's *Cross Purposes*. Even guys who make relatively important albums in the twilight of their artistic life—most notably Bob Dylan and Neil Young—are granted unlimited lines of critical credit simply for *not* making albums that are completely terrible. The unspoken (though much-denied) conceit of everybody who loves rock 'n' roll is that nobody old and rickety can be relevant *at all*, so anything remotely close to social consequence is akin to genius; that's why *Love and Theft* was classified as "classic" in 2001, even though it would have been nothing more than "solid" in 1976. So no one is denying that Billy Joel has put out crap for as many years as he put out quality. But it doesn't matter, because he never had the responsibility of staying cool. His crappiest albums (*The Bridge*, *River of Dreams*, etc.) can just be separated out and ignored entirely. Unlike Lou Reed or David Bowie, "Billy Joel" is not a larger pop construct or an expansive pop idea. Billy Joel is just a guy. And that's why—unlike someone like Jeff Buckley—his records wouldn't seem any better if he was dead.

What I'm saying is that there are no conditions for appreciating Billy Joel. I'm not sure loving an album like *Glass Houses* says anything about me (or about anyone). And in theory, this should make it a bad record, or—at best—a meaningless artifact. It should make liking *Glass Houses* akin to liking mashed potatoes or rainy afternoons. You can't characterize your self-image through its ten songs. I was eight when that record came out in 1980, and I vividly recall both my sister Teresa (who was nineteen) my brother Paul (who was eighteen) playing *Glass Houses* constantly, which was normally unthinkable; Teresa liked the Police and Elton John, and Paul liked Molly Hatchet and Foreigner. The only albums they could play when they were in the same room were Cheap Trick's *At Budokan* and *Glass Houses*. Retrospectively, the unilateral Cheap Trick fixation made perfect sense: Cheap Trick was good at being cool *for everybody*. They rocked just hard enough to be cool to metal kids, they looked just cool enough to be New Wave, and Robin Zander had the kind of hair that semimature teenage girls wanted to play with. Even today, the Cheap Trick logo stands as the coolest-looking font in the history of rock. But none of those qualities can be applied to *Glass Houses*, now or then; in theory, there is no way that record should have mattered to anyone, and certainly not to everyone.

However, even I liked that record, and I was eight. And I didn't like records when I was eight; I mostly liked dinosaurs and math. This was all new. But what's even weirder is that *I could relate* to this album. And I can still relate to it—differently, I suppose, but maybe less differently than I realize. What I heard on *Glass Houses* (and what I still hear) is somebody who's bored and trapped and unimpressed by his own success, all of which are sentiments that have never stopped making sense to me.

It's always difficult to understand what people think they're hearing when they listen to the radio. This was especially true in the 1970s, when there seemed to be no difference between what was supposedly "good music" and what was supposedly "bad music." WMMS, the premiere radio station in Cleveland during the Carter administration, was famous for playing Springsteen's "Born to Run" every Friday afternoon at exactly 5:00 P.M. For years, that was the station's calling card. And this was done without irony; this song was supposed to serve as the anthem and the spirit for working-class Northeast Ohioans. Eventually, that's what "Born to Run" became. But what nobody seemed to notice is that this song has some of the most ridiculous lyrics ever recorded. Half the time, Springsteen writes like someone typing a PG-13 letter for *Penthouse Forum*: The lines *"Just wrap your legs round these velvet rims / And strap your hands across my engines"* is as funny as anything Tenacious D ever recorded, except Bruce is trying to be deep.

Now, it's not like this song is necessarily terrible, and it's certainly better than everything on *Born in the U.S.A.* (except "Glory Days" and maybe "I'm Goin' Down"). But it's difficult to understand why "Born to Run" is considered a higher poetic achievement than Meat Loaf's "Paradise by the Dashboard Light" or Van

46

Halen's "Runnin' with the Devil," two equally popular songs from the same period that expressed roughly similar themes while earning no cred whatsoever. So the real question becomes: Why did this happen? Part of it is probably based in fact; I suppose Springsteen is "more real" (or whatever) and took a legitimately emotive risk with his earnest eighth-grade poetry; referring to your guts as "my engines" may be idiotic, but I have little doubt that Bruce really thinks of his rib cage in those terms. However, Springsteen's sincerity only mattered if you had a predetermined opinion about what he was trying to accomplish. David Lee Roth might have been sincere, but he was just a cool kid trying to get laid; Meat Loaf might have been sincere, but he was just a fat goofball who was cool in spite of himself. *But Bruce was trying to save you.* He appealed to the kind of desperate intellectual who halfway believed that—when not recording or touring—Springsteen actually went back to New Jersey to work at a car wash. Before he even utters his lyrics, people accept his words as insights into their version of existence. Had Bruce written "Paradise by the Dashboard Light," people would play it at weddings.

Once again, I want to stress that I have no qualms with how this process works. I'm not interested in trying to convince anyone that they should (or shouldn't) adore whichever denim-clad icon they choose. However, this abstract relationship between the perception of the artist and the appreciation of his product unfairly ghettoized Billy Joel while he was making the best music of his career (and some of the best music of the late seventies and early eighties). Because Billy is not "cool," like Elvis Costello—and because he's not "anticool," like Randy Newman—Joel was perceived as edgeless light rock. All anybody noticed was the dulcet plinking of his piano. Since his songs were so radio-friendly, it was assumed that he was the FM version of AM. This is what happens when you don't construct an archetypical persona: If you're popular and melodic and faceless, you seem meaningless. The same thing happened to Steely Dan, a group who served as the house band for every 1978 West Coast singles bar despite being more lyrically subversive than the Sex Pistols and the Clash combined. If a musician can't convince people that he's cool, nobody cool is going to care. And in the realm of rock 'n' roll, the cool kids fucking *rule*.

In fact, I sometimes suspect that if I had first heard *Glass Houses* five years later than I did—when I was, say, thirteen—I might have hated it before I even put the needle down. The whole metaphor behind the cover shot ("Look! I'm self-reflexively throwing rocks at my identity!") might have seemed forced, and the skinny tie he's wearing on the back cover would have seemed like something from the Knack's closet, and everybody hated the Knack in 1985 (including, I think, the actual members of the Knack). But because I was too young to understand that rock music was supposed to be cool, I played *Glass Houses* in my basement ad nauseam and—in that weird, second-grade way—I studied its contents. My favorite song was "All for Leyna" at the conclusion of side one, where Billy claimed to be, *"Kidding myself / Wasting my time."* However, I mostly listened to side two, which included "I Don't Want to Be Alone Anymore" (where Billy enters a relationship only because his female acquaintance is bored with dating), "Sleeping with the Television On" (where Billy expresses regret for being a "thinking man," which is already how I viewed myself at the age of eight), and the pseudo-metal "Close to the Borderline"[1] (where Billy suddenly becomes Frank Serpico). Certainly, it's not as if Billy Joel was the first artist who ever sang about being inexplicably depressed. But he might be the first artist who ever sang about getting yelled at *by his dad* for being depressed, which is less a commentary on his father and more an illustration of how Joel couldn't deny that he had no valid

---

1. "Close to the Borderline" was also the inadvertent cause of the funniest thing anyone has ever said to me. I was playing *Glass Houses* at college—this was like 1991—and my roommate Mike Schauer walked into our dorm room at the exact moment Joel was singing the lines, *"Another night I fought the good fight / But I'm getting closer to the borderline."* Mike made a very strange face and said, "Is this Stryper unplugged?"

reason to be unhappy (yet still was). When I eventually learned that Joel tried to kill himself in 1969 by drinking half a bottle of furniture polish (how Goth!), I wasn't the least bit surprised. Joel's best work always sounds like unsuccessful suicide attempts.

Glass Houses sold seven million records, mostly on the strength of its singles "You May Be Right" and "It's Still Rock and Roll to Me." These songs are okay, I guess, although they never struck me as being particularly reflective of anything too important. They felt (and still feel) a tad melodramatic. They seem like they're *supposed* to be "hit singles," which means they sound like they're supposed to be experienced in public. Because Joel has no clear connotation as a public figure, these songs don't gain any significance by being popular. That paradox is even more evident on Joel's 1982 follow-up album *The Nylon Curtain*, an opus with three decent songs that lots of people know by heart—"Allentown," "Pressure," and "Goodnight Saigon"—and six amazingly self-exploratory songs that almost no one except diehard fans are even vaguely familiar with.

Granted, I realize that I'm making a trite, superfan-ish argument: I constantly meet people who love some terrible band (usually the Moody Blues) and proceed to tell me that the reason I fail to understand their greatness is because I only know what I've heard on the radio. Most of the time, these people are completely wrong; while the finest Led Zeppelin songs (for example) are all obscure, the most important Zep songs are "Whole Lotta Love," "Immigrant Song," and "Stairway to Heaven." These are the tracks that define what Zeppelin was about, beyond their tangible iconography as a loud four-piece rock band. *Houses of the Holy* is a great (small *g*) album, but those aforementioned three songs are why Led Zeppelin is Great (big G). This is true for most artists. So that being the case, it seems strange to advocate Billy Joel's Greatness (big G) by pointing to unheralded songs off *The Nylon Curtain*, an album that only sold one million copies and was widely seen as a commercial disappointment. Logically, I should be talking about

1973's "Piano Man," his bread-and-butter tour de force and the one Joel song that's forever part of the cultural lexicon. But that deconstructive angle wouldn't work in this particular case; to argue for Joel's import on the strength of "Piano Man" would make him no more consequential than Don McLean or Dexy's Midnight Runners. "Piano Man" now belongs to everybody, and most of that everybody couldn't care less about its source. Saying you like "Piano Man" doesn't mean you like Billy Joel; it means you're willing to go to a piano bar if there's nothing else to do.

Meanwhile, saying you like "Immigrant Song" (or even just saying that you don't *hate* "Stairway to Heaven") means you like Led Zeppelin—and to say you "like Led Zeppelin" means you like their highly stylized version of cock-rock cool. It means you accept a certain kind of art. Pretty much everybody agrees that Zeppelin is—at the very least—cool to mainstream audiences, so their timelessness and significance is best defined by their best-known work. That's how it works with cool artists (Miles Davis, Iggy Pop, whoever). But—as I've stated all along—Billy Joel is not cool.[2] Even though "Piano Man" is autobiographical, it's not important that he's the guy who wrote the words and sang the song; I'm sure it would be just as popular if Bernie Taupin had come up with those lyrics and Elton John had released it as the second single off *Madman Across the Water*. Because there's nothing about Joel's personage that's integral to his success, he's one of the only hyper-mainstream pop artists who's brilliant for reasons (and for songs) that almost no one is aware of.

Which brings me back to *The Nylon Curtain*. The reason I generally dismiss the popular songs on this record is because they seem like big ideas that aren't about any specific person, and Joel is better when he does the opposite. "Allentown" has a likable structure, but it's just this big song about why baby boomers sup-

---

2. It just now occurred to me that—if Billy Joel were to actually read this— he must hate how every attempt at advocating his genius is prefaced with a reminder of how cool he *isn't*.

posedly have it rough. "Pressure" is the big keyboardy *Bright Lights, Big City* coke song; "Goodnight Saigon" is the big retrospective Vietnam song that's critical of the war but supportive of the people who fought there, a distinction nobody seemed to put forward until they starting reading Time-Life books in the early 1980s. All of this is fine and painless, and my assumption is that these three songs are the tunes conventional Joel proponents adore. But it's two other songs—"Laura" and "Where's the Orchestra"—that warrant a complete reinvention of how hipsters should look at Joel as a spokesman for the disaffection of success.

Joel wanted *The Nylon Curtain* to be like a mid-period Beatles record, which would be like me wanting this book to be as good as *Catch-22*. But "Laura" and "Where's the Orchestra" really *are* as good as most of what's on *The White Album*. This is because the first song says things so directly that its words shouldn't make sense to anybody else (and yet they do), while the latter is so metaphorically vague that anybody should be able to understand what he's implying (yet I've listened to this song for twenty years and still feel like I'm missing something).

"Laura" is about a relentlessly desperate woman (possibly his ex-wife, possibly someone else, possibly somebody fictional)[3] who is slowly killing the narrator by refusing to end a relationship that's clearly over. Making matters worse is the narrator's inability to say "no" to Laura, a woman who continues to sexually control him.

Now, the reason I keep using the term *narrator* (as opposed to *Billy*) is because this amazingly personal song never makes me think of the person who's singing it. Whenever I hear "Laura," I

3. Actually, it turns out I was completely wrong about this: When I eventually had the opportunity to interview Joel (months after the completion of this essay) I asked him about "Laura," and he said it was about a family member. He noted, "There's a complete giveaway line where I sing, 'How can she hold an umbilical cord so long.' Now, who the hell could that be about?" Obviously, I can't argue about the meaning of a song with the person who wrote it. But I still think my interpretation is more interesting than his truth.

immediately put myself in Joel's position, and he sort of disappears into the ether. It's almost as if Joel's role in the musical experience is just to create a framework that I can place myself into; some of Raymond Carver's best stories do the same thing. The Laura character has specific—but not exclusionary—traits (her behavior seems unique, but still somewhat universal), and the mood of Joel's piano playing has a quality that jams hopelessness into beauty. This is a song about someone whose life is technically and superficially perfect, but secretly in shambles. It's about having a dark secret, but—once again—not a *cool* secret. This is not a sexy problem (like heroin addiction), or even an interesting one (like the entanglements expressed in Rufus Wainright's "Instant Pleasure" or Sloan's "Underwhelmed"). It's mostly just exhausting, and that's how it feels.

"Where's the Orchestra" reveals the same sentiments, only sadder. The lyrics are one long allusion to watching a theatrical production that isn't satisfying, and virtually anyone can figure out that Joel is actually discussing the inexplicable emptiness of his own life. The words are not subtle. But it paints a worldview that I have never been able to see through, and there has never been a point in my life—be it junior high, college, or ten minutes ago—when this song didn't seem like the single most accurate depiction of my feelings toward the entire world. In fact, sometimes I tell people that they will understand me better if they listen to "Where's the Orchestra?" And you know what? They never do. They never do, and it's because they all inevitably think the song is actually about *them*.

That's what all of *The Nylon Curtain* is really about, I think: the New Depression, which started around the same time this album came out. People have always been depressed, but—during the early eighties—there just seemed to be this overwhelming public consensus that being depressed was the most normal thing anyone could be. In fact, being depressed sort of meant you were smart. And in a larger sense, Joel's music was documenting that idea from the very beginning. A song like "Honesty" (on

1978's *52nd Street*) implies that the only way you can tell whether someone really cares about you is if they tell you you're bad. "So It Goes" (a ballad released in 1990 but actually written in 1983) has Joel conceding that every woman who loves him will eventually decide to leave; "Scenes from an Italian Restaurant," off *The Stranger*, is about how the most perfect relationships are inevitably the most doomed. Joel's music always has an undercurrent railing against the desire for perfection. Another song off *The Stranger*—"Just the Way You Are"—proves that sentiment twice (once cleverly, and once profoundly).

To this day, women are touched by the words of "Just the Way You Are," a musical love letter that says everything everybody wants to hear: You're not flawless, but you're still what I want. It was written about Joel's wife and manager Elizabeth Weber, and it outlines how he doesn't want his woman to "try some new fashion" or dye her hair blond or work on being witty. He specifically asks that she "don't go changing" in the hopes of pleasing him. The short-term analysis is that this is a criticism of perfection, but in the best possible way; it's like Billy is saying he loves Weber *because* she's not perfect, and that he could never leave her in times of trouble.

The sad irony, of course, is that Joel divorced Elizabeth three years after "Just the Way You Are" won a Grammy for Song of the Year. Obviously, some would say that cheapens the song and makes it irrelevant. I think the opposite is true. I think the fact that Joel divorced the woman he wrote this song about makes it his single greatest achievement.

When I hear "Just the Way You Are," it never makes me think about Joel's broken marriage. It makes me think about all the perfectly scribed love letters and drunken e-mails I have written over the past twelve years, and about all the various women who received them. I think about how I told them they changed the way I thought about the universe, and that they made every other woman on earth unattractive, and that I would love them unconditionally even if we were never together. I hate that those letters still exist. But I don't hate them because what I said was false; I hate them because what I said was completely true. My convictions could not have been stronger when I wrote those words, and—for whatever reason—they still faded into nothingness. Three times I have been certain that I could never love anyone else, and I was wrong every time. Those old love letters remind me of my emotional failure and my accidental lies, just as "Just the Way You Are" undoubtedly reminds Joel of his.

Perhaps this is why I can't see Billy Joel as cool. Perhaps it's because all he makes me see is me.

Last year I had to go to one of those "adult" parties. I think you know the kind of party I mean: People brought their screaming children and someone inexplicably served fresh cornbread, and half the house stood around and watched the local news affiliate when it came on at 11:00 P.M. I spent the whole evening in the kitchen with the two guys I came with; we tried to have an exclusionary conversation despite the fact that we consciously drove to this party in order to be social. Most of the guests began to exit at around midnight, which is the same time some odd fellow I'd never seen before suddenly appeared next to the refrigerator and pulled out a Zippo lighter and a little wooden box.

The gathering took a decidedly different turn.

Ten minutes later, I found it necessary to mention that Journey was rock's version of the TV show *Dynasty*. This prompted a spirited debate we dubbed "Monkees = *Monkees*." The goal is to figure out which television show is the closest philosophical analogy to a specific rock 'n' roll band, and the criteria is mind-blowingly complex: It's a combination of longevity, era, critical acclaim, commercial success, and—most important—the aesthetic soul of each artistic entity. For example, the Rolling Stones are *Gunsmoke*. The Strokes are Kiefer Sutherland's *24*. Jimi Hendrix was *The Twilight Zone*. Devo was *Fernwood 2-Night*. Lynyrd Skynyrd was *The Beverly Hillbillies,* which makes Molly Hatchet *Petticoat Junction*. The Black Crowes are *That '70s Show*. Hall & Oates were *Bosom Buddies*. U2 is *M*A*S*H* (both got preachy at the end). Dokken was Jason Bateman's short-lived sitcom *It's Your Move*. Eurythmics were *Mork & Mindy*. We even deduced comparisons for solo projects, which can only be made to series that were spawned as spin-offs. The four Beatles are as follows: John = *Maude,* Paul = *Frasier,* George = *The Jeffersons,* and Ringo = *Flo*. David Lee Roth's solo period was *Knots Landing*.

So there's proof: Marijuana makes you smarter.

5 Appetite for Replication   0:56

She is not a beautiful woman.

She is not necessarily repulsive, I suppose, but no one is going to suspect this woman is an upstart actress or an aspiring model. One assumes there aren't a lot of actresses or models in White Sulphur Springs, West Virginia, and one assumes even fewer would be working in a roadside café at 5:55 A.M. on Saturday morning. But for the next ten minutes, this aging red-haired woman is being treated like the foxiest rock chick in Appalachia. For a few post-dawn moments on this particular Saturday, she might as well be Tawny Kitaen.

"Do you like Guns N' Roses?" asks Randy Trask, the bespectacled twenty-eight-year-old who talks more than the other five people at the table combined. "We're a Guns N' Roses tribute band. I'm Axl. We're doing a show tonight in Harrisonburg. You gotta come. It's only like four hours away. Bring all your girlfriends. It's going to be *insane*. They love us in Harrisonburg. But I need to see you there. I'm the singer. I play Axl."

The waitress blushes like a middle-school crossing guard and calls Trask a sweetheart. She tells us that she can't come to the show because her grandfather is dying, and you can tell she's not lying. In a weird way, this might be flirting. When she leaves to fetch our pancakes, Trask glows like the MTV logo, circa 1988. Before we leave the restaurant, he will give this not-so-anorexic waitress a hug and aggressively declare that we will stop back to see her on our way home tomorrow afternoon.

"Exit 175. Remember that. This restaurant is off Exit 175," he says when we crawl back into the pickup. "What did I tell you? There's just something about me and redheads."

• • •

In truth, Mr. Trask should *be* a redhead. His overt blondness—along with the fact that he's six-foot-four—makes him look more like David Lee Roth than W. Axl Rose, and he knows it. "I am going to dye my hair red. That is definitely in the works," he says. "It's just that the last time I tried, it turned sort of pink. And for some reason, people get scared of you when you have red hair. I don't know why that it is, but it's true. They just don't warm up to you the way they do if you're blond."

Trask tells me this at ten minutes to midnight while we sit in his 1997 extended-cab Ford Ranger pickup, which we will drive from Cincinnati to northern Virginia for tomorrow night's rock show. It's roughly a ten-hour drive, so leaving in the middle of the night should get us to town just in time to check into the Hampton Inn for an afternoon nap. There is some concern about this, because the last time Trask and his band mates in Paradise City were in Harrisonburg they were banned for life from the Econo Lodge. This weekend, they need to make sure things go smoothly at the Hampton; there just aren't that many hotels in Harrisonburg.

Our pickup is sitting outside the home of Paul Dischner, and the engine is idling. Like Trask, Dischner is striving to be someone else; he's supposed to be Izzy Stradlin, Guns N' Roses original rhythm guitar player. In the band Paradise City, everybody is supposed to be someone else. That's the idea.

"I initially had a problem with the idea of doing a Guns N' Roses tribute, because I didn't want anyone to think I was discrediting Axl. That was always my main concern. If Axl was somehow against this, I'd straight up quit. I would never do this if he disapproved," Trask says. "But I really think we can do his songs justice. People constantly tell me, 'You sound better than Axl,' but I always say, 'Whoa now, slow down.' Because I like the way I sing Axl's songs, but I *love* the way Axl sings them. That's the main thing I'm concerned about with this article: I do not want this to say anything negative about Guns N' Roses. That's all I ask."

I am the first reporter who has ever done a story on Paradise City. This is less a commentary on Paradise City and more a commentary on the tribute band phenomenon, arguably the most universally maligned sector of rock 'n' roll. These are bands mired in obscurity and engaged in a bizarrely postmodern zero-sum game: If a tribute band were to completely succeed, its members would no longer have personalities. They would have no character whatsoever, beyond the qualities of whomever they tried to emulate. The goal is not to be somebody; the goal is be somebody else.

Though the Beatles and Elvis Presley were the first artists to spawn impersonators, the modern tribute template was mostly set by groups like Strutter, Hotter than Hell, and Cold Gin, all of whom toured in the early nineties by looking, acting, and singing like the 1978 version of KISS. It worked a little better than anyone could have expected: People would sooner pay $10 to see four guys pretending to be KISS than $5 to see four guys playing original songs nobody had ever heard before. And club owners understand money. There are now hundreds—probably thousands—of rock bands who make a living by method acting. There's the Atomic Punks, a Van Halen tribute that celebrates the band's Roth era. Battery is a tribute to Metallica. Planet Earth are L.A.-based Duran Duran clones. Bjorn Again claims to be Australia's finest ABBA tribute. AC/DShe is an all-female AC/DC cover group from San Francisco. There are tributes to groups who never seemed that popular to begin with (Badfinger, Thin Lizzy, Dream Theater), and there are tributes to bands who are not altogether difficult to see for real (The Dave Matthews Band, Creed). And though rock critics deride Stone Temple Pilots and Oasis for ripping off other artists, drunk people in rural bars pay good money to see tribute bands rip off Stone Temple Pilots and Oasis as accurately as possible.

And being consciously derivative is not easy.

Trask and Dischner can talk for hours about the complexity of feeding their appetite for replication. Unlike starting a garage band, there are countless caveats that must be fulfilled when auditioning potential members for a tribute. This was especially obvious when Paradise City had to find a new person to play Slash, GNR's signature lead guitarist. It is not enough to find a guy who plays the guitar well; your Slash needs to sound like Slash. He needs to play a Les Paul, and he needs to tune it like Slash. He needs to have long black hair that hangs in his face and a $75 top hat. Preferably, he should have a dark complexion, an emaciated physique, and a willingness to play shirtless. And if possible, he should drink Jack Daniel's on stage.

The Slash in Paradise City fulfills about half of those requirements.

"Bobby is on thin ice right now, and he knows he's on thin ice," says Trask, referring to lead guitarist Bobby Young. "I mean, he's an okay guy, and he's a good guitar player. But we have ads out right now for a new Slash, and he knows that. I want someone who is *transfixed* with being Slash. We want someone who is as sick about Slash as I am about Axl."

What's ironic about Young's shortcomings as Slash is that—in a traditional band—his job would likely be the most secure: He is clearly the most skilled musician in Paradise City, having received a degree from Cincinnati's Conservatory of Music in 1987 (that was the same year GNR debuted with the album *Appetite for Destruction*). "I was classically trained, so I'm used to everything being built around minor chords," he tells me. "But Slash plays almost everything in a major chord, and his soloing is very different than mine. It's not in chromatic keys. I really thought I could learn all of these Guns N' Roses songs in two days, but it took me almost two weeks."

Unfortunately, Young can't learn how to look like a mulatto ex-heroin addict, and this is the only occupation in America for which that is a job requirement. He only vaguely resembles Slash, and his band mates tease him about being akin to an Oompa Loompa from *Willy Wonka and the Chocolate Factory*.

There's a similar problem with Paradise City's bassist; he's portrayed by an affable, laidback blond named Spike, but Spike is built a little too much like a farmer. His shoulders are broad, and he actually looks more like Larry Bird than Duff McKagan. Amazingly, Spike is also partially deaf from playing heavy metal for so many years (he can't hear certain frequencies, including feedback), but—somehow—that doesn't pose a problem.

Visually, the rest of Paradise City succeeds at varying degrees. Drummer Rob "The Monster" Pohlman could pass for Steven Adler if Pohlman hadn't just shaved his head and dyed his remaining locks orange, a move that completely baffles Dischner.[1] The fact that he hides behind a drum kit, however, substantially mitigates this problem. Trask is eight inches too tall, but he has the voice and—more importantly—the desire. He wills himself into Axlocity.

Dischner is the only Paradise City member who naturally looks like a GNR doppelgänger. He's also the guy who makes the trains run on time; he handles the money, coordinates the schedules, and generally keeps his bandmates from killing each other. All of these guys are friendly, but Dischner is the most relentlessly nice. He's also mind-blowingly idiosyncratic. Prior to Paradise City, Dischner played in an Yngwie Malmsteen–influenced band called Premonition, a group whose entire existence was based on the premise that the Antichrist is Juan Carlos, the King of Spain.[2] To this day, Dischner adheres to this theory and claims it can be proven through biblical prophecy. He lives with his wife (an aspiring vampire novelist) in a small suburb of Cincinnati, and he peppers his conversation with a high-pitched, two-note laugh that sounds like "Wee Hee!" Over the next

1. Three days before Pohlman's haircut, Dischner had told me that "What sets us apart from the other twenty-two Guns N' Roses tribute bands in America is that we don't wear wigs." This new development with Pohlman's scalp was not to his liking.
2. Premonition's two singles, "He Is Rising" and "Mr. Heroin," were both (presumably) about Carlos and allegedly charted in Greece.

thirty-six hours, he will make that sound approximately four hundred times.

When we leave from Dischner's house at 12:30 A.M., it has already been an incredibly long day for Trask. He awoke Friday morning at 2:00 A.M. at his home in Ravenna, Ohio, and immediately drove four hours to the outskirts of Cincinnati, where he spent the day cutting down a troublesome tree in Dischner's front yard; Trask's father runs a tree service in Northeast Ohio, so his son knows how to handle a chainsaw. After a brief afternoon nap, the band hooked up for a few hours of rehearsal before supper. Now it's midnight, and Trask is preparing to drive the entire way to Virginia, nonstop. I have never met anyone who needs sleep less. Trask once drove twenty-two hours straight to Hayes, Kansas, and played a show immediately upon arrival. If the real Axl Rose had this kind of focus, Guns N' Roses would have released fifteen albums by now.

There was a time when Paradise City had a tour bus, but they lost it last summer. This is not a euphemism; they literally can't find it. It broke down on a trip to Kansas City, and they had to leave it in a Missouri garage to make it to the club on time. Somehow, they lost the business card of the garage and have never been able to recall its location. Dischner tells me this story three times before I realize he's not joking.

"We drove back through Missouri a bunch of times, we put up a picture on our Web site, and we even called the Highway Patrol," Dischner says. "But we lost the bus. And I guess there's some law that states you only have thirty days to find your bus."

As it is, the band is now traveling in two vehicles. Axl/Randy will pull the Haulmark trailer that contains their gear; he'll drive the truck, I'll ride shotgun, and Izzy/Paul will curl up in the extended cab. A friend of the band—some dude named Teddy— will follow in his Ford Mustang, which will also hold Slash/Bobby and Steven/Rob. The pickup box is covered with a topper, so Duff/Spike will lay back in the truck bed with Punky.

Trask and Dischner do not know who Punky is.

They've only met Punky a few times, and they don't know his last name (or his real first name). They are told that Punky is friends with Teddy and Young, all of whom are evidently long-time running buddies. Young is thirty-six, which is a little older than Trask (twenty-eight), Dischner (thirty-one), and Pohlman (twenty-nine). Nobody knows how old Spike is and he refuses to say; a good guess might be forty.

Our last stop before hitting the highway is Spike's home in Clifton, Ohio, a few scant miles from the site of Cincinnati's recent race riots. Spike's house is terrifying. It appears completely dilapidated, but—supposedly—it's actually being renovated. The home contains a python, several large birds, two alligators in the bathtub, and the most bloodthirsty Rottweiler in North America (Dischner gives me four full minutes of instruction about how to safely *walk past* this animal). Spike deals exotic animals in his spare time; nobody but me seems to find this unusual.

At departure time, only 40 percent of the band is not under the influence of some kind of chemical. Twenty minutes into the trip, that percentage will fall to zero. Even before we get on the road, this Punky character looks drunk enough to die; amazingly, he's just getting started. They're *all* just getting started. Everyone is smoking pot, and it's the second-strongest dope I've ever inhaled: I keep looking through the windshield, and the vehicle seems to be moving much faster than it should be. It feels like we're driving down an extremely steep incline, but the earth remains flat. I am not the type who normally gets paranoid, but this is a bit disturbing. I'm trying very hard to act cool, but I start thinking too much; in order to relax, I smoke another half joint, which (of course) never works. I start imaging that we're going to crash and that my death is going to be reported as some sort of predictable irony—I will forever be remembered as the guy who wrote a book about heavy metal bands who were mostly fake and then died while touring with a heavy metal band that was *com-*

pletely fake. I start having hallucinations of elk running out in front of the vehicle, and I notice that Trask isn't even watching the road when he talks to me. Finally, I can't take it anymore. I politely turn to Trask and Dischner and make the following announcement: "Okay—now, don't take this the wrong way, because I'm probably just nuts, and I'm probably just too fucked up to know what's going on, and I'm probably overreacting for no valid reason, and I hate to sound unreasonable or immature, and I don't want to sound pretentious, but elks are prevalent. And perhaps this is out of line and I'm certainly open to debate on this issue, but I need to go on record and say that I am not 100 percent comfortable with the situation regarding this truck at the moment, because I have a feeling that we are all going to die."

"Dude," Trask tells me. "I *totally* wish I could trade bodies with you right now."

It remains to be seen if these guys can sound like Guns N' Roses, but they clearly have their self-destructive aspirations deftly mastered.

Our vehicles barrel into the darkness of Kentucky, loaded like a freight train and flyin' like an aero-plane. Spike and Punky are freezing in the box of the pickup, and they try to stay warm by drinking more Bud Lite. Inside the toasty cab, faux-Axl and faux-Izzy have straightened up (slightly), and we're discussing the question most people have about tribute bands, which is "Why do you possibly do this?" It seems antithetical to the whole concept of art; the notion of creativity has been completely removed from the equation. Wouldn't the members of Paradise City be happier if they could write their own songs, dress however they want, and—quite simply—be themselves?

No.

"Obviously, being in an original band is the ultimate dream, but it mostly sucks," Dischner says. "You don't get to tour. You don't get no money. You have to beg your own friends to come to the show. But being a mock star is awesome."

Paradise City will earn $1,100 for the Harrisonburg show. After their manager takes his 15 percent and they pay for gas and promotions, they will be left with $655, which—split between five people—ends up being $131 each. This is almost nothing. But the operative word is "almost." If these same five guys in Paradise City performed their own material, they would have to pay to play in most reputable clubs; as a tribute band, they can live as "professional musicians." Relatively speaking, $1,100 is good money.

"The thing about being in a tribute band is that your fans already exist," Trask says. "You show up at the bar, and there's immediately a few hundred people who love Guns N' Roses and therefore love you."

This is not always true. A month later, Paradise City will play a show at a club called Dr. Feelgood's in the desperate lake town of Conneaut, Ohio, and virtually no one will notice; the bar's billiard tables will have more spectators than the stage, and the owner won't even give them free beer until they finish the first set. It's a bit uncomfortable for everyone involved, but not really humbling or tragic: No one in Paradise City seems confused about the social significance of this group.

"I never think of myself as Axl Rose, and we don't think of ourselves as Guns N' Roses," Trask says. "Our fans are Guns N' Roses fans—they're not really fans of Paradise City. We're not deluding ourselves."

And in a way, somber nights in ghost towns like Conneaut validate their cred; Paradise City almost seems to enjoy adversity. They love talking about how "life on the road" is a hard-yet-satisfying experience. They give "tribute quotes" that sound like outtakes from VH1's *Behind the Music*: It's all about the fans, it's all about the music, it's all about the awe-inspiring majesty of rock; it's all about something, and then it's all about something else entirely. But they're never lying—in tribute bands, all those clichés are true. Paradise City cares more about Guns N' Roses than the original members of Guns N' Roses care about the song "Paradise City."

In fact, the guys in Paradise City seem to care about *all* music with more enthusiasm than any group of musicians I've ever encountered. There is no elitism. As we roll toward West Virginia, the truck's stereo never plays an artist they dislike. They have positive things to say about Aerosmith, Nickelback, Celine Dion (!), Black Sabbath, White Lion, Pink Floyd, and Alabama. When Jewel's "You Were Meant for Me" comes on the radio, Dischner mentions that the song always makes him wish it were raining; ten minutes later, he tells me that Rush is "just about the greatest three-piece band ever," and then gives a similar compliment to the Rush tribute band 2112.

We fly through the West Virginia border at 4:04 A.M. This is a strange part of the country, but perhaps an ideal place for a group trying to re-create 1988: On the same FM station that played Jewel and Rush, two early morning DJs are unironically joking about Julia Roberts's relationship with Lyle Lovett.

After getting breakfast from the aforementioned redhead in White Sulphur Springs, we get back on the road (doomed to complete the voyage while driving into the rising sun). After hitting the Virginia state line, Trask begins scanning all the radio stations in the hope of hearing "The Commercial." This is a radio spot promoting Paradise City's concert at the Mainstreet Bar & Grill. The band gets excited about hearing "The Commercial" in the same way normal bands get excited about hearing their first single on the radio; for a tribute group, exposure equals success. When we finally hear said advertisement, it refers to Paradise City's "triumphant return" to Virginia. High-fives are exchanged all around.

I want to talk about the real Guns N' Roses for a while, and Trask is more than willing to oblige. Though he admits that his first musical love was Mötley Crüe (before Paradise City, he fronted a Mötley tribute called Bastard), one cannot deny his sincere adoration for GNR, a band whose legacy is—to be fair—problematic. Guns N' Roses debuted as L.A.'s most dangerous band in 1987, blowing the doors off pop metal with *Appetite for*

Destruction, arguably the strongest debut album in rock history. They followed with an EP titled *GNR Lies*, which is best remembered for the ballad "Patience" and the controversial "One in a Million,"[3] a track that managed to be racist, homophobic, and xenophobic in just over six scant minutes. Two years later, the Gunners released two massive albums on the same day, *Use Your Illusion I* and *II*, cementing their place as the biggest band in the world. Yet by 1997, all had collapsed; one by one, every member— except the mercurial Axl Rose—either quit or was fired. Rose became a virtual recluse for almost a decade, endlessly working on his alleged masterpiece, *Chinese Democracy*, and earnestly growing dreadlocks.

I ask my traveling partners if they're concerned about what will happen when *Chinese Democracy* eventually hits stores. It's a paradoxical problem: If the album does well and Rose tours, it could decrease the demand for a GNR tribute; if the album flops, it might make the concept of a GNR "tribute" vaguely ridiculous. But Trask and Dischner aren't worried. They're confident there will always be a demand for the original incarnation of Guns N' Roses, and that can only be experienced through their show. History is not an issue for these people; for them, the past is not different than the present, and the future will be identical. Every year, Axl Rose grows a little older, but Paradise City never ages beyond the summer of '91.

We arrive at the Hampton Inn parking lot just before 11 A.M. The girl at the front desk is a little overweight, but she has a nice smile. Trask is impressed. "Do you like Guns N' Roses?" he asks her. "We're a Guns N' Roses tribute band. I'm Axl. You should come to the show tonight at the Mainstreet. It's going to be crazy. They love us here."

---

3. The last time Paradise City performed in Harrisonburg, they received a death threat from two Middle Eastern patrons after playing "One in a Million." Over the course of the weekend, this story is breathlessly recounted to me six times.

In a few hours, members of the Paradise City entourage will have lunch at a nearby Long John Silver's. A total stranger will ask Punky if they're in a band. When Punky replies "Sort of," the man will ask him, "Are you guys Molly Hatchet?"

There are no "fashion don'ts" inside the Mainstreet Bar & Grill in downtown Harrisonburg. You want to inexplicably wear a headband? Fine. You want to wear a FUBU sweatshirt with a baseball hat that features the Confederate flag? No problem. This is the kind of place where you will see a college girl attempting to buy a $2.25 glass of Natural Light on tap with her credit card— *and have her card denied*.

Certainly, the Mainstreet is not trendy. But it's still cool, or at least interesting, and Paradise City has sold it out. Almost five hundred people (mostly kids from nearby James Madison University) have paid $12 to get inside, which is as many as the Mainstreet will draw for next week's Dokken show. One can only wonder how the real guys in Dokken feel about being as popular as five fake guys in Guns N' Roses.

The opening act is a local collegiate jam band called Alpine Recess; they look like they'd rather be opening for a Phish tribute, but the crowd is polite. Meanwhile, Paradise City is dressing downstairs in the basement,[4] drinking free Budweiser in the storeroom, and leaning against the water heater. They have decided to open with the song "Night Train," even though the tune includes an extended five-minute guitar solo that Young fears might anesthetize the audience.

Unlike the real GNR, Paradise City hits the stage exactly on time. However, things are not perfect: There are sound problems

4. During the Paradise City set, Punky will lay on the dressing room's concrete floor after falling down a flight of stairs. Though he will continue to post-party with the band for most of the night, Punky will need to be rushed to the hospital by ambulance the following morning when—upon finally sobering up—he will realize he has broken his wrist. Oddly (or perhaps predictably), the band will simply leave him in Harrisonburg and drive back to Ohio.

on "Night Train" that can only be described as cataclysmic, and Trask glares at the soundman. But things get better. Things get tighter. Trask moves his hips in Axl's signature snakelike sway, and the crowd sings along with everything. Paradise City may not always look like Guns N' Roses, but they certainly sound like them; when I go to the bathroom and hear the music through a wooden door, it's impossible not to imagine that this is how it would have sounded to urinate on the Sunset Strip in 1986.

"This next song is dedicated to everybody who ever told you how to live," Trask tells us as he prowls the twenty-five-foot-stage in his kilt. "This is for everybody who told you not to smoke weed or not to drink beer every day. There are just too many people who make life too hard."

This soliloquy leads into the bubbling bass intro of "It's So Easy," the angriest three minutes off *Appetite for Destruction*. Girls begin crawling on stage to dance on top of the amplifiers, and the band couldn't be happier. Ultimately, this is why they do this: They're literally paying tribute to the music of Guns N' Roses, but they're figuratively paying tribute to the Guns N' Roses Lifestyle. They're totally willing to become other people, as long as those people party all the time, live like gypsies, and have pretty girls dancing on their amplifiers. This is precisely why guys create rock bands; Paradise City just created somebody else's.

"I'm not pretending to be a Guns N' Roses fan," says Kelly Gony, a stunning twenty-two-year-old history major who danced on stage in her cut-off denim skirt for the last forty-five minutes of the show. "I just think they did an excellent job. Maybe some of the people in the crowd were clapping for Guns N' Roses, but there also might have been some people clapping about the fact that these guys can act exactly like Guns N' Roses. I mean, look at me—I'm dressed like it's 1988. It's just fun, you know?"

This blue-eyed girl is correct—it *is* fun, although not so fun that she accepts the band's offer to go back to their hotel. Gony goes home. However, a few females (most of whom seem *very* young) agree to go back to the Hampton for a few dozen night caps and more weed. I assume the goal is to have sex with them, although I don't think this works out for anybody, except possibly Spike. Punky sporadically asks these girls to remove their tank tops, and—although they never actually do—they don't seem particularly offended by the request.

I hang with Paradise City until around 3:30 A.M.. Part of me thinks that I should really try to party with them all night, because perhaps that's when things will truly get insane. Maybe there will be a transcendent moment, complete with speedballs and hookers and an albino musk ox. But the larger part of me is tired and drunk and stoned, so I go to bed (luckily, I have my own room). The next morning, I see Dischner in the lobby and ask him how the rest of the night went; he tells me nothing really happened. I ask the same question when I run into Bobby Young, and he spends ten minutes telling me how the girls who came back to the hotel were nothing but "brain-dead cock teases." He thought the evening sucked.

But not Randy.

Trask is sitting at the wheel of his truck, ready to drive us home on three hours rest. His version of the night is quite different. "It was a madhouse," he tells me unspecifically, neither lying nor telling the truth. "You should have stayed up with us, Chuck. It was unbelievable. I'm serious. I wouldn't even know where to begin."

I nod. I agree. One way or the other, we all use our illusions. And I'm sure Axl would completely approve.

As America's best-loved semipro freelance conversationalist, I am often queried about my brazen humorousity. "How is it possible," I am asked, "that you are able to extemporaneously lecture so effortlessly on such a myriad of complex topics? What is the key to your incisive, witty repertoire?"

It's a valid question.

Certainly, there *is* a formula to being relentlessly dynamic. There's a shockingly simple equation to being *über*-interesting, and it works with every subject imaginable.

The formula is as follows: When discussing any given issue, always do three things. First, make an intellectual concession (this makes the listener feel comfortable). Next, make a completely incomprehensible—but remarkably specific—"cultural accusation" (this makes you insightful). Finally, end the dialogue by interjecting slang lexicon that does not necessarily exist (this makes you contemporary). Here are a few examples . . .

When talking about sports: "I mean, come on—you just know that Rodney Rogers is sitting in the locker room before every game reading Nietzsche, and he's totally thinking to himself, 'If Ron Artest tries to step to me one more time, I'm gonna slap jack his brisket, Philly style.'"

When talking about music: "Oh, let's face it—we all know that if Rivers Cuomo makes one more album about the Cubism didactic, he might as well just give up completely and turn Weezer into a hobo-core three-piece."

When talking about film: "Everybody in this room has seen Peter Bogdanovich at his worst, and everybody in this room already suspects that he probably sits in his gazebo and beats off to *Pet Sounds* five nights a week, so I think it's safe to assume this whole era of the 'Scarecrow Thriller' is as dead as the diplodocus."

When talking about politics: "That crazy Condoleeza Rice—who does she think she's fooling with all that neo-Ventura, post-Dickensian welfare state pseudo-shit? If that's supposed to be the future, she may as well stick the Q like the salt queen that she is."

Do you understand? Do you see the forest through the trees? Do you not see what I am no longer not saying to you? If so—congratulations! Prepare to have sex constantly.

6 Ten Seconds to Love 0:71

"Merry Christmas, Juggalo."

This is what he scrawled on the card, a little one-flap piece of construction paper featuring a picture of a Clydesdale standing next to a snow-capped conifer. It was attached to a Fuji videotape and handed to me in my favorite bar. I immediately knew what it was. "Thanks, Ninja," I replied to the dashing twenty-four-year-old doctor who gave it to me. "You are my stone cold elf." My doctor friend returned to his dart game; I proceeded to have four more drinks while listening to Dean Martin on the jukebox before getting into my car and driving home, traversing the empty, frozen streets of downtown Fargo. Winter nights in urban North Dakota are fascinating, because they resemble overcast summer afternoons: The painfully white snow has such a high albedo that it reflects the glow from streetlights with a remarkable intensity. You can drive without headlights at midnight, which is exactly what I did. It was beautiful. "I love Christmas," I thought to myself when I arrived home from Duffy's Tavern, just drunk enough to wrap myself in a terry-cloth robe and watch Pamela Anderson perform oral sex on Tommy Lee.

Every holiday season, I rewatch my illegally dubbed Pamela-Tommy sex tape. It's sort of my version of *It's a Wonderful Life*. There is no thrill in seeing it anymore, and certainly no prurient rush: It is probably the least arousing videotape I own, with the possible exception of *Walking with Dinosaurs*. However, it's also the only "important" videotape I own, and it's important because it shows how unsexy oral sex can represent what we want as a society (or maybe what we're afraid to want). Everyone is willing to classify Pamela Anderson as a bimbo and a whore and an idealized version of why half the women in America loathe their bodies, and all of that might be true—but what nobody seems willing to admit is that she's the most crucial woman of her generation, partially because we hate to think about what Pam Anderson's heaving bosom means to our culture.

People freak out whenever you attempt to compare Anderson to Marilyn Monroe. In fact, I used to freak out when others have made that comparison, even though I had no idea why. I was unironically watching the E! network a few years back, and some forgettable bozo kept insisting that Pamela was a Marilyn for the nineties (this was either a retrospective on *Baywatch* or a promotional special for *V.I.P.*, but I can't remember which). Somehow, this bozo's assertion made me vaguely angry, which is how I used to react whenever someone claimed Metallica was my generation's Led Zeppelin.

My desire to protect Marilyn Monroe is inexplicable; I have no idea why I would feel territorial about the legacy of a woman who died ten years before I was born. Marilyn died young and lonely, so (I suppose) it's impossible not to feel a certain sense of compassion for her—but it's also hard to imagine anyone who benefited more from an early death. James Dean comes close, but it's entirely possible he might have made a handful of good films in his forties, and beyond; it's unlikely Monroe could have had any long-term career. Film revisionists have taken to insisting she was an underrated actress (mostly because of *Some Like It Hot, Bus Stop,* and *Niagara*), but it's actually the other way around: So many people have retrospectively declared her acting to be "underrated" that she's become *overrated,* simply because she didn't make enough important films to vindicate her advocates' claims.

However, Monroe was the most significant female figure of the middle twentieth century (cinematically or otherwise), and that had almost nothing to do with acting. Both physically and philosophically, Norma Jean was the incarnation of the early fifties sexual archetype. And ironically, that's why that forgettable bozo on

E! was right when he compared Monroe to Pamela Anderson, even though he'd never be able to explain why. Pam *is* the contemporary Marilyn Monroe, inadvertently illustrating which aspects of human desire can evolve (and which aspects never will).

I can't seem to find a definitive source for Anderson's physical dimensions. The numbers once ran at 36–24–34, but those obviously changed after her 1999 breast reduction. Her height is listed as either five-foot-seven or five-foot-five (although—oddly—never five-foot-six), and her weight is generally placed at 107 pounds. She has what women refer to as an "impossible body," a claim that's only partially contradicted by the fact that her body actually exists. There are scientists (goofball sociobiologists, mostly, and also Desmond Morris) who argue that men are visually (and one assumes unconsciously) attracted to the "two-thirds ratio" in nature, which is why the cliché dimensions for ideal women somehow became 36–24–36. Man's affinity for this ratio supposedly shows up in everything he creates—architecture, auto chassis, the circumference of an Absolut vodka bottle in relation to its height, etc., etc., etc. This is an interesting theory, especially since it would seem to explain why male artists in the sixteenth century were attracted to obese women (one could argue that they were interested in the same 2/3 body ratio and simply inverted the modern-day proportions). Of course, this is a very male-o-centric theory to advocate: Guys would love to somehow prove they want to have sex with Pamela Anderson because of *math*.

Still, I can't help but partially believe in this hypothesis, probably because I'm secretly ashamed to be attracted to Pamela Anderson. Somehow, it makes me feel stupid. It's almost like desiring Pam Anderson is like admitting that—sexually—you have no creativity. I would feel much better about myself if I would prefer to go down on Kim Deal or Ellen Barkin. I would somehow feel smarter if what I wanted was even just a model with a mantis-like skeleton body, like Kate Moss. I profoundly prefer to be turned on by any woman who looks vaguely fucked-up; that's much more intellectually satisfying. And I know dozens of men who have completely talked themselves into this way of thinking, so much so that they don't even realize they're overcompensating; these are the same people who insist they prefer Mary Ann to Ginger. In fact, I once worked with a guy who told me that he thinks Pamela Anderson is a fundamentally ugly, plastic woman who's "antisexy." His claim is that it's not just that Anderson doesn't excite him—she actually makes him want to recoil. And every woman in our office seemed to like him more after he said that.

What I've come to realize is that a remarkably high percentage of everyday citizens—and this applies to both men and women—actively despise Pam Anderson. Moreover, their dislike for this woman is a completely conscious decision: They've decided to hate Anderson on principle. But what they really hate is the modern world; what they hate is that Pamela Anderson is the incarnation of the perfect, idealized icon we all sort of concede is supposed to be impossible. We've established this unrealistic image of what we want from the human race, but it angers people to see that image in real life. It sort of shows why most Americans hate themselves.

Every so often I stumble across *The Man Show* on Comedy Central, a program where two semi-charming jerks insist that men are brilliant because men are idiots.[1] It's the apex of that whole "we men are magnificent bastards" movement that began in roughly 1992—I think Tim Allen probably spawned it—and it suggests that true guys can only like beer and football and pork ribs and strippers. Now, granted—these *are* things that many men

1. It's possible that *The Man Show* might be off the air by the time this book is released, mostly because Jimmy Kimmel seems like something of a rising cultural force. Of course, it's entirely plausible that Comedy Central would replace *The Man Show* with an innovative new series featuring two guys sitting in a beer garden each week and comparing their wives' vaginas to that of a Hereford heifer.

genuinely adore—but not in the rote, unilaterally Sasquatchian manner this kind of shtick always implies. A program like *The Man Show* is legitimately negative for society, but not because it's misogynistic; *The Man Show* is socially negative because it actively tries to prove an inaccurate hypothesis that too many women already believe: The premise of *The Man Show* is that all men think exactly the same way. And that consensus makes it difficult to write about Pam Anderson, because everyone assumes you're just a perv who adores tits. And that's not true (at least not for me). In truth, you can adore tits *and* you can love Pamela Anderson—and without necessarily associating the former with the latter.

Am I physically attracted to Pamela Anderson? Of course. But the more I see her, the more I realize I'm not looking at a person I'd like to sleep with; I'm looking at America. And I'm sure a lot of guys who masturbated to black-and-white photos of Marilyn Monroe during the Korean conflict had the same experience, even though they probably didn't think about it in those terms.

Answer this question. Let's say you were given two options: You can either (a) have sex with the world's most attractive person, but you can tell no one and no one will ever know, or (b) you can walk through life with that person hand-in-hand, creating the illusion to everyone alive that this individual is your lover—even though you will never so much as kiss.

Which would you pick?

If you're like most people, your immediate gut reaction is to take option "a" Everyone seems to say this at first blush, mostly because we all want to imagine ourselves as visceral beings (this is especially true of men, who *always* pick "a" immediately). However, if you keep talking to someone about this question, and you start pointing out the specifics of what these two scenarios mean, you'll find that everybody eventually admits that the second alternative would be more satisfying. And this query always makes me think about Marilyn Monroe and her 1954 marriage to Joe DiMaggio.

Despite lasting only nine months, the Monroe-DiMaggio union was probably the most perfect marriage in American history. In a way, it seemed like an example of how life is supposed to work: The sexiest, most desirable woman on the planet fell in love with the coolest, most beloved stud of the Greatest Generation. Yet this marriage was doomed; in fact, my suspicion is that the relationship was even more of a nightmare than we know. The more we learn about DiMaggio, the more he seems like a cold, sullen badass who was always alone (even in a roomful of people).[2] And as for Marilyn . . . well, she personifies every beautiful/crazy/sexy/suicidal woman I've ever met (and you know the type of person I'm referring to—this is the kind of girl who's depressed by the irrational notion that men only want her for her physical appearance but who still cannot shake the equally irrational fear that she is somehow overweight and repulsive). I am certain that having sex with Marilyn Monroe was four minutes of ecstasy followed by five hours of frustration. This is one of the reasons why DiMaggio couldn't make his marriage work, yet still felt compelled to decorate her crypt with roses for the next four decades. Remember that question I posed two paragraphs ago? Joltin' Joe is just about the only man in history who faced this hypothetical *for real* and somehow picked *both* options. And it's that second option—the lonely, painful option "b"—that matters metaphorically. What's compelling about the idea of the Monroe-DiMaggio relationship—and the Monroe–Arthur Miller relationship, and the Monroe-JFK relationship—is not the idea of them being together. It's the idea of them not being together. It's the hollow reality of things not working out. It's about Monroe being unattainable to everyone—world-class athletes, brilliant playwrights, and the only movie star president of the twentieth century. She was above them all.

Oh, I know: Every one of those guys had sex with Marilyn, so

2. Although the fact that he never missed a cut-off man in his entire career somehow makes this seem acceptable.

it's kind of a naive notion to think of her as pure. But it's not so much that Monroe seemed virginal; it's more like she seemed too overtly sexual to actually participate in the unseemly process of intercourse. Trying to picture Norma Jean (ahem) "getting her freak on" is like trying to imagine Bruce Lee getting into a bar fight: Even in my mind, I can't conceive anything that doesn't seem like cinema. It's impossible to think of Monroe having sex like a normal person. I always imagine a breeze blowing the curtains over the bedpost, and all her naughty bits are hidden; her hair is perfect, and she's sorta smiling with her eyes half closed. It's even PG-13 *in my brain*. Norman Mailer used to tell a (possibly) apocryphal story that claims—upon signing her first lucrative contract with Twentieth Century Fox—Monroe sardonically said, "Well, that's the last cock I eat." I really hate that story, even if it's true. Marilyn Monroe is the definition of the old-school American sex symbol, and part of that definition is that it's unfathomable to picture her giving anyone a blow job.

Conversely, it is not particularly difficult to envision Pamela Anderson doing this. It's actually happening on the TV in my living room as I type this very sentence.[3] But what's weird is that my ability to experience Pam enjoying an act I can't even imagine Marilyn performing is not an illustration of how they are different; it somehow makes them more alike. And I think this is because we all unconsciously identify iconic figures with whatever social philosophy they represent (I suppose this is what makes them "iconic"). Monroe and Anderson might suggest totally different worldviews, but they both seem like victims. They're both sexually tragic figures. Looking at the life of Pam Anderson in the present tense tells us as much about ourselves as looking back on Marilyn Monroe tells us about our fathers and mothers.

Monroe's men were generally the kind of people I wanted to be until I turned about fourteen: a great athlete, a president, a

3. And—as I mentioned earlier—it's surprisingly unsexy (it's sort of like watching that cow get butchered at the end of *Apocalypse Now*).

writer, etc. Anderson's men are the kind of people I want to be whenever I watch documentaries about KISS. But both Marilyn and Pam desired what their world valued: Men in the fifties wanted Monroe because she made love to the men they respected; modern men want Anderson because she makes love to the concept of celebrity.

There's no way the modern-day version of Marilyn could date the modern-day version of DiMaggio. Today, there is too much of a chasm between sexuality and "classic greatness." DiMaggio wasn't necessarily the finest baseball player on the planet in a technical sense, but he was always the *greatest* player, inasmuch as he defined what was beautiful and noble about the art of the game. He was classically great. Even when Ted Williams was hitting better than Joe, Ted was only striking a leather projectile with a wooden stick; DiMaggio was defining what Americans loved about democracy. Through the 1990s, the closest thing there was to a DiMaggio-esque figure was Michael Jordan; M.J. is the DiMaggio of his age, just as Pam is the Marilyn of hers. But it goes without saying that Michael Jordan could never date Pamela Anderson. That would cause the apocalypse.

If Jordan dated Pamela Anderson, it would destroy him. He'd still be remembered as the greatest two-guard who ever lived, but his iconography would never be the same. In the eyes of people who obsess over celebrities without really thinking about why they care—in other words, in the eyes of 90 percent of America—Jordan would be dating a slut. It would be like the rich, big-toothed high school quarterback showing up at the prom with a Goth chick who'd dropped out of community college to buy a used IROC. America's greatest athletes can no longer date America's greatest sex symbols unless said athletes are willing to become freaks (case in point: José Canseco and Dennis Rodman). But back in Monroe's day, it was normal for vixens to date dashing sports stars; Jane Russell was married to Bob Waterfield, and they slept in a Murphy bed in downtown Cleveland. That seemed normal and kind of sweet. Today, that would seem unnatural (and not just because of the Murphy bed). There are a few exceptions, but none of them matter. Yankees shortstop Derek Jeter used to date Mariah Carey, but nobody cared; she's crazy and he's not crazy enough. Chris Webber hits it with Tyra Banks, but C-Webb refuses to talk about it and T-Banks evidently can't speak. Canadian hoopster Steve Nash supposedly dated Elizabeth Hurley, but she's about ten times more famous than he is, even in Canada.[4]

The reason Pam Anderson can't date M.J. is because being the modern Monroe means there is nothing understated about your sexuality. At all. That's what I mean when I say the gap between sexuality and classic greatness has expanded beyond recognition; there is something inherently understated about the term *classical*, and there's obviously nothing understated about Pammy. Sleeping with Pam would destroy Jordan's ethos; you can't be the hero to an eight-year-old boy in Duluth *and* the paramour to 107-pound public orgasmatron. But the larger problem is that dating the Michael Jordans of the world is not part of Pam Anderson's job description. Since Pam is the hyperaccelerated manifestation of contemporary sexuality, she is socially obligated to deliver her most intimate gifts to those who represent contemporary America. That's what Marilyn did; she gave her body to the post–World War II archetypes of sport, art, and politics. She was the lover of—at least *for*—classic greatness. Pam's in the same position, but she has to be the lover of post-modern greatness. That's why we all had to watch her give a blow job to the drummer from Mötley Crüe.

The newfangled postmodern sex goddess can't just sleep with a cool guy; she needs to sleep with the entire "concept" of

4. However, you gotta give Steve Nash this: On December 11, 2001, Nash scored 39 points against the Portland Trail Blazers on 12 of 16 shooting. He scored 17 points over the final 6:23 of regulation, including two free throws with 3.9 seconds remaining that gave Dallas the win. And then he went back to his hotel room AND PROBABLY HAD SEX WITH ELIZABETH HURLEY. Nice night, dude.

celebrity. For people born in the seventies and eighties, the "concept" of celebrity has replaced people like Joe DiMaggio. On the surface, this probably seems paradoxical, since DiMaggio *was* a celebrity. But DiMaggio was a celebrity when "celebrity" wasn't a concept; it was merely a designation. If you asked anyone in 1951 why DiMaggio was a celebrity (or even if you asked someone that question today), they could undoubtedly give a satisfactory answer. However, it's impossible to explain why Tommy Lee is a celebrity. You can't say "because he's a rock star," because he's not; the last record Tommy Lee made that lots of people liked was *Dr. Feelgood,* which came out in 1989. Yet Tommy is far more famous now than he was in 1989, and it's because he's directed his energy into being a celebrity in the conceptual sense. He is famous for being famous, and for behaving famously, and for taking drugs, and for having his relationship with Pam Anderson available on the pay-per-view menu of most hotels (which makes him *more* famous, but which only happened because he *was* famous). And he is exactly the type of man Pam Anderson should be with. This is not a criticism of Pam or a backhanded compliment to Tommy; it's just sort of true.

Pam is the embodiment of modern female sexuality, and that embodiment is a Barbie Doll. But that's not necessarily bad; it's what intellectual men want (because she can be appreciated lecherously *and* ironically), and it's what intellectual women want (because it provides the opportunity to rail against Barbie dolls). She's an intellectual symbol of what every forward-thinking feminist has warned us about, and she's a physical symbol of all the things men find alluring (some of which are rudimentary, some of which are complex). Society's relationship with Pam Anderson is exactly like its former relationship with Monroe. What's different is how they respond back.

Ultimately, both women serve the same role, and that role is both shallow and profound. People use Monroe and Anderson as a kind of cultural shorthand for understanding the most important sexual mores of entire generations. Marilyn and Pam succeed in that capacity because they're *not* complicated; they're sexual for reasons that are *only* about sex. Everything else just muddles the equation. I mean, there's probably never been a sexier woman than Elizabeth Taylor in *Cat on a Hot Tin Roof,* but that wasn't just because she looked incredible—that was "acting." She made herself sexier. Monroe never needed to act. In a sense, Taylor was too complex to be an icon of this magnitude. The same thing happened to former MTV personality Jenny McCarthy, a peer of Anderson's, who—for roughly seven weeks in the summer of 1995—was everyone's Woman of the Moment. But her problem was that she became too normal; McCarthy seemed completely aware of who she was and what her breasts could be extrapolated to say about society. That self-awareness killed her career. At this point, Jenny McCarthy is a likable bombshell who's only slightly more interesting than a bucket of shark chum. She could have been a supernatural pictogram of the new sensuality, but elected to merely become a "person."

Not Pammy, though. She's never been a person, and I'm glad. Pam doesn't just have sex with guys; Pam fucks reality. As I type this, she has divorced Lee and is involved with mook musician Kid Rock.[5] Here again, Pam has made the perfect romantic decision. Here's a guy who actually named himself after youth and rock 'n' roll. Here's a guy who openly aspires to be the new David Lee Roth. Here's a guy who operates within the idiom of rap

5. And here's something you only notice if you're as obsessive as I am: Kid Rock likes to mention in interviews how he hates Radiohead; in his video for "You Never Met a Motherf**ker Quite Like Me," he actually wipes his arse with toilet paper that has the word *Radiohead* embossed on every tissue. On the surface, that might seem like a statement against pretension and elitism, almost as if Rock is saying he's the anti–Thom Yorke. However, it actually has to do with Mötley Crüe. On page 358 of the Crüe biography *The Dirt,* Tommy Lee mentions that Pamela threw a massive birthday party for him when he turned thirty-three, and Lee says she "cranked our favorite band, Radiohead, on the sound system." I have no doubt that Pam has told Kid how she and Tommy used to adore *OK Computer,* and it drives him crazy. Kid Rock hates Radiohead for the same reason I hate Coldplay (as described on page 4).

metal, an art form that critics despise and normal people adore. Here's an underrated antigenius who represents the redneck renaissance and what's great about music, pot, and popular culture (and, I suppose, America). Kid Rock's not a person either. I sure hope those crazy kids make it!

My eyes have drifted back to my TV just now, and I spent a few moments looking at Tommy Lee's penis. I realize this is no brilliant insight, but Tommy Lee's genitalia is stupidly huge. In the scene I'm watching right now, he appears to be beating his penis against the steering wheel of a boat. It's oddly reassuring. In fact, it's making me think about Joe DiMaggio again: DiMaggio used his 36-inch, 36-ounce bat to hit safely in fifty-six straight games, and Tommy used his 10-inch, 13-ounce bat[6] to hit Heather Locklear, Bobbi Brown, and the single-most important woman of our times. World-class sex kittens no longer date sports heroes because modern sports heroes have joined heavy metal bands. Tommy Lee is our "Joltin' Joe." Most of the guys I know would much rather have sex with three of the world's most beautiful women than hit .325 career against American League pitching. Now, it's possible this was always the case (perhaps young men in 1953 felt the same way). But the difference is that admitting that choice in the 1950s meant you were profoundly honest and a little pathetic. In the twenty-first century, it still means you're pathetic, but that's considered normal.

That's the weird irony that makes Pam Anderson so essential to our times: She's not a real person, but she's still more real than any sexual icon we've ever had. Pam Anderson is a mainstream, nonsubversive porn star who actually does all the dirty things her disciples fantasize about. Marilyn Monroe was the perfect vessel for an age where it was wrong to want wild, easy sex; Pam is the perfect vessel in an age where not wanting wild, easy sex makes you a puritanical, born-again weirdo. It's not enough just to talk like Mae West. Anybody can do that. *We need proof.* Pam has the

6. Approximate.

proof. In the short-term, the Tommy-Pamela videotape sullied her already sketchy reputation. But it was probably the greatest thing that could have happened to her long-term legacy—it made her transcendent and organic in the same breath.

Whenever I hear intellectuals talk about sexual icons of the present day, the name mentioned most is Madonna. That seems like a good answer, and it's the kind of answer Madonna has worked very hard to perpetuate. Earning that title was her only career goal. But Madonna's not even close to representing contemporary sexuality in any important fashion. She tries way too hard, and it never seems honest. It's very telling that the two best songs in Madonna's catalog—"Like a Virgin" and "Like a Prayer"—are titled after similes. Her whole career is a collection of similes: Madonna is *like* a sexual idol, but that's just the plot for her self-styled promotional blitz. When she overtly attempted to embody Marilyn Monroe in the video for "Material Girl," Madonna got the dance steps perfect but completely missed the message: That song suggests that sex is about money, and that sex is about power, and that sex is about getting what you want. Well, fine. That's how it is with Madonna. But with the original Monroe, sex was about *sex*. It was completely without guile or intellect. Being a sexual icon is sort of like being the frontman for an Orange County punk band: As soon as you can explain why you're necessary, you're over.

Madonna is an unsuccessful sexual icon because she desperately wants to be a sexual icon. Pamela Anderson is the perfect sexual icon because she wants to have sex. You think that makes her dumb? Well, maybe you're right. But how smart are *you* while you're having sex? What part of sex is "intellectual"? Certainly none of the good parts.

There are a lot of interesting moments on my Pam 'n' Tommy Fuji videotape, several of which are so weird that its authenticity can't be doubted. Pam and Tommy listen to MC Hammer and Soul Asylum. They try to write a cookbook for dope smokers. Tommy uses the word *rad* in casual conversation. Pam tells

Tommy, "You're the best fucking husband on the planet," and they get married with the aid of a spaceman. But if you had a transcript of this film, you'd find that there's one phrase that appears more often than all others: *"Where are we?"*

This question is asked over twenty times, and it's never answered. They're on a boat, they look at the horizon, and they say, "Where are we?" And if someone wanted to use Pam as a metaphor for the decline of American morality and the vapidity of modern relationships, they could point out that phrase as an illuminating example of a lost generation. "Where are we, indeed," such a critic might write in the last paragraph of an essay. But that kind of snarkiness is more negative than necessary, and it misses the point. We don't need Pam to know where she is; she helps us understand where *we* are.

"You're missing the point," she said. "What you're saying makes sense in theory, but not in practice. You're trying to compare apples and oranges."

"Why do you keep saying that?" he asked in response. "Apples and oranges aren't that different, really. I mean, they're both fruit. Their weight is extremely similar. They both contain acidic elements. They're both roughly spherical. They serve the same social purpose. With the possible exception of a tangerine, I can't think of anything *more* similar to an orange than an apple. If I was having lunch with a man who was eating an apple and—while I was looking away—he replaced that apple with an orange, I doubt I'd even notice. So how is this a metaphor for difference? I could understand if you said, 'That's like comparing apples and uranium,' or 'That's like comparing apples with baby wolverines,' or 'That's like comparing apples with the early work of Raymond Carver,' or 'That's like comparing apples with hermaphroditic ground sloths.' Those would all be valid examples of profound disparity. But not apples and oranges. In every meaningful way, they're virtually identical."

"You're missing the point," she said again, this time for different reasons.

7 George Will vs. Nick Hornby 0:86

Like many U.S. citizens, I spend much of my free time thinking about the future of sports and the future of our children. This is because I care deeply about sports.

In the spirit of both, I've spent the last fifteen years of my life railing against the game of soccer, an exercise that has been lauded as "the sport of the future" since 1977. Thankfully, that future dystopia has never come. But people continue to tell me that soccer will soon become part of the fabric of this country, and that soccer will eventually be as popular as football, basketball, karate, pinball, smoking, glue sniffing, menstruation, animal cruelty, photocopying, and everything else that fuels the eroticized, hyperkinetic zeitgeist of Americana. After the U.S. placed eighth in the 2002 World Cup tournament, team forward Clint Mathis said, "If we can turn one more person who wasn't a soccer fan into a soccer fan, we've accomplished something." Apparently, that's all that matters to these idiots. They won't be satisfied until we're all systematically brainwashed into thinking soccer is cool and that placing eighth[1] is somehow noble. However, I know this will never happen. Not really. Dumb bunnies like Clint Mathis will be wrong forever, and that might be the only thing saving us from ourselves.

My personal war against the so-called "soccer menace" probably reached its peak in 1993, when I was nearly fired from a college newspaper for suggesting that soccer was the reason thousands of Brazilians are annually killed at Quiet Riot concerts in Rio de Janeiro, a statement that is—admittedly—only half true. A few weeks after the publication of said piece, a petition to have me

1. And losing to Poland!

removed as the newspaper's sports editor was circulated by a ridiculously vocal campus organization called the Hispanic American Council, prompting an "academic hearing" where I was accused (with absolute seriousness) of libeling Pelé. If memory serves, I think my criticism of soccer and Quiet Riot was somehow taken as latently racist, although—admittedly—I'm not completely positive, as I was intoxicated for most of the monthlong episode. But the bottom line is that I am still willing to die a painful public death, assuming my execution destroys the game of soccer (or—at the very least—convinces people to shut up about it).

According to the Soccer Industry Council of America, soccer is the No. 1 youth participation sport in the U.S. There are more than 3.6 million players under the age of nineteen registered to play, and that number has been expanding at over 8 percent a year since 1990. There's also been a substantial increase in the number of kids who play past the age of twelve, a statistic that soccer proponents are especially thrilled about. "These are the players that will go on to be fans, referees, coaches, adult volunteers, and players in the future," observed Virgil Lewis, chairman of the United States Youth Soccer Association.

Certainly, I can't argue with Virgil's math: I have no doubt that battalions of Gatorade-stained children are running around the green wastelands of suburbia, randomly kicking a black-and-white ball in the general direction of tuna netting. However, Lewis's larger logic is profoundly flawed. There continues to be this blindly optimistic belief that all of the brats playing soccer in 2003 are going to be crazed MSBL fans in 2023, just as it was assumed that eleven-year-old soccer players in 1983 would be watching Bob Costas provide play-by-play for indoor soccer games right now. That will never happen. We will never care about soccer in this country. And it's not just because soccer is inherently un-American, which is what most soccer haters (Frank Deford, Jim Rome, et al.) tend to insinuate. It's mostly because soccer is inherently geared toward Outcast Culture.

On the surface, one might assume that would actually play to soccer's advantage, as America has plenty of outcasts. Some American outcasts are very popular, such as OutKast.[2] But Outcast Culture does not meld with Intimidation Culture, and the latter aesthetic has always been a cornerstone of team sports. An outcast can be intimidating in an individual event—Mike Tyson and John McEnroe are proof—but they rarely thrive in the social environment of a team organism (e.g., Duane Thomas, Pete Maravich, Albert Belle, et al.). Unless you're Barry Bonds, being an outcast is antithetical to the group concept. But soccer is the one sport that's an exception to that reality: Soccer unconsciously rewards the outcast, which is why so many adults are fooled into thinking their kids love it. The truth is that most children don't love soccer; they simply hate the alternatives more. For 60 percent of the adolescents in any fourth-grade classroom, sports are a humiliation waiting to happen. These are the kids who play baseball and strike out four times a game. These are the kids who are afraid to get fouled in basketball, because it only means they're now required to shoot two free throws, which equates to two air balls. Basketball games actually *stop* to recognize their failure. And football is nothing more than an ironical death sentence; somehow, outcasts find themselves in a situation where the people normally penalized for teasing them are suddenly urged to *annihilate* them.

This is why soccer seems like such a respite from all that mortification; it's the one aerobic activity where nothingness is expected. Even at the highest levels, every soccer match seems to end 1–0 or 2–1.[3] A normal eleven-year-old can play an entire sea-

2. And also Jake Gyllenhaal.
3. My statistically obsessed compadre Jon Blixt once made a brilliant deduction about World Cup soccer: It must be a nightmare for gamblers. "I cannot comprehend how casinos could set the point spread for these games, as it appears the favored nation wins every single match—yet never by a margin of more than a single goal," he wrote me while watching Italy defeat Bulgaria 2–1 in a 1994 World Cup semifinal, a contest that was immediately followed by Brazil's 1–0 win over Sweden. "Perhaps they only bet the over-under, which must always be 2½."

son without placing toe to sphere and nobody would even notice, assuming he or she does a proper job of running about and avoiding major collisions. Soccer feels "fun" because it's not terrifying—it's the only sport where you can't fuck up. An outcast can succeed simply by not failing, and public failure is every outcast's deepest fear. For society's prepubescent pariahs, soccer represents safety.

However, the demand for such an oasis disappears once an outcast escapes from the imposed slavery of youth athletics; by the time they reach ninth grade, it's perfectly acceptable to just quit the team and shop at Hot Topic. Most youth soccer players end up joining the debate team before they turn fifteen. Meanwhile, the kind of person who truly loves the notion of sports (and—perhaps sadly—unconsciously *needs* to have sports in their life) doesn't want to watch a game that's designed for losers. They're never going to care about a sport where announcers inexplicably celebrate the beauty of missed shots and the strategic glory of repetitive stalemates. We want to see domination. We want to see athletes who don't look like us, and who we could never be. We want to see people who could destroy us, and we want to feel like that desire is normal. But those people don't exist in soccer; their game is dominated by mono-monikered clones obsessed with falling to their knees and ripping off their clothes. I can't watch a minute of professional soccer without feeling like I'm looking at a playground of desperate, depressed fourthgraders, all trying to act normal and failing horribly.

In short, soccer players kind of remind me of "my guys."

Now, when I say "my guys," I don't mean kids who are actually *mine,* as I am not father material (or human material, or even Sleestak material). When I say "my guys," I am referring to a collection of scrappy, rag-tag, mostly unremarkable fourth- and fifth-graders I governed when I was sixteen years old. During the summer in 1988, I worked as a totally unqualified Little League baseball coach. This is noteworthy for one reason and one reason only: I remain the only youth sports instructor in the history of my town who was ever fired, a distinction that has made me both a legend and an antihero (at least among "my guys"). And even though I happened to be coaching the game of baseball that summer, this was the experience that galvanized my hatred for the game of soccer—and particularly my hatred for the ideology that would eventually become the Youth Soccer Phenomenon.

Between my sophomore and junior year of high school, I applied to coach Pee Wee and Midget baseball in Wyndmere, North Dakota, the tiny farming town (pop. 498) where I lived and breathed and listened to Guns N' Roses. The competition for this position was not intense: There were twenty-three kids in my class and only fourteen in the grade ahead of me, and almost all of the other boys had to spend the summer working on their family farms. Theoretically, I should have been in the same position. However, I was too clever to farm and too lazy to work, and I simply had no interest in shit like cultivating (or in cultivating shit, for that matter). Instead, I decided to spend my summer coaching Pee Wee and Midget baseball for $250 a month. I had to deliver my job application to the Wyndmere Park Board, and—since this job was always given to local high school boys—one of the questions on the application asked who my role models were. I wrote "Bobby Knight and George Orwell," and I wasn't joking. But it really didn't matter what I wrote, since I was the only applicant. "We're excited by your enthusiasm," said the vaguely blonde Park Board president.

We had practice three times a week. The Pee Wee kids worked out from 9 A.M. to 10 A.M., and this was always a horrifically boring sixty minutes. These were really little kids (like, under four feet tall), and they hit off a batting tee. As long as nobody broke their clavicle or vomited, I viewed practice as a success. Only one kid had any talent (a left-handed shortstop!), but aptitude was pretty much a nonfactor: I played everybody the same amount and generally tried to act like that black dude from *Reading Rainbow*. I mostly just tried to convince them to stop throwing rocks at birds.

The Midgets, however, were a different story. Though not vastly dissimilar in age (the Pee Wees were eight- and nine-year-olds and the Midgets were ten and eleven), the Midgets were "my guys," and I intended to turn them into a war machine. At the Midget level, there was real pitching. There was base stealing. There was bunting. And—at least in my vision—there was hitting and running, double switching, outfield shading, middle-relieving, and a run-manufacturing offensive philosophy modeled after Whitey Herzog's St. Louis Cardinals. I'm convinced we were the only Midget League team in North Dakota history to have a southpaw closer. I even implemented the concept of physical conditioning to my preseason regime, which immediately raised the eyebrows of some of the less-competitive parents. However, my explanation for making ten-year-olds run wind sprints was always well-founded. "The running is not important, in and of itself," I told one skeptical mother. "What's important is that 'my guys' realize that success doesn't come without work." Weeks later, I would learn that this mother respected my idealism but disliked the way I casually used the phrase "in and of itself."

To be honest, I was merely coaching these kids the way I had wanted to be coached when I was in fourth grade. I was a pretty fucking insane ten-year-old. I was the kind of kid who hated authority—but sports coaches were *always* an inexplicable exception. For whatever the reason, a coach could tell me anything and I'd just stand there and listen; he could degrade me or question my intelligence or sit me on the bench to prove a point that had absolutely nothing to do with anything I did, and I always assumed it was completely valid. I never cared that much about winning on an emotional level, but winning always made sense to me intellectually; it seemed like the logical thing to want. Mostly, I just wanted the process of winning to be *complicated*. I was fascinated by anything that made sports more cerebral and less physical; as a consequence, my coaching style became loosely patterned on the life of Wile E. Coyote. We'd practice conventionally from 10:00 to 11:00, but then we'd spend forty-five minutes memorizing a battery of unnecessary third-base signals (I recall that tugging on my "belt" meant "bunt," because both words start with the letter *b*). I also assaulted their fifth-grade cerebellums with dozens of strategic hypotheticals: "Let's assume our opponent has runners on first and third with no outs, and they send the trail runner to second with the count at 0–2," I would theorize. "What is our objective?" One frail kid with eyeglasses answered pretty much everything; most of the others just discussed their favorite flavors of Big League Chew. I constantly questioned their commitment to excellence.

Still, four or five of "my guys" were oddly enthusiastic about my Pyramid of Success, and that was enough to kill (or at least scare) most of our early season opponents. But what I kept noticing was that the other fifteen kids on my squad didn't care if we won or lost. They didn't seem to care about *anything*, really, or at least nothing that had an application to baseball. I couldn't tell what they found more excruciating: when they didn't get to play (because sitting on the bench was boring), or when they *had* to play (because that meant another two strikeouts and an hour of praying that no fly balls would be hit in their general direction). In fact, some of "my guys" started complaining to their mothers. And near the end of June, I was told to attend the next Wyndmere Park Board meeting for a "free-form discussion about my coaching style."

Now, it should be noted that Wyndmere didn't really need a park board, because Wyndmere doesn't have a park. Wyndmere does have the Rock Garden (not *a* rock garden, but *the* Rock Garden), which is a stone enclosure that's as big as a city block and augmented by a forty-foot replica of a Scottish castle (it also has a basketball court and several uncomfortable picnic tables). When, who, or why the Rock Garden was built remains a mystery on par with Stonehenge, so living in Wyndmere always made you feel a little like Leonard Nimoy on *In Search Of*. And what's even crazier is that the Wyndmere Park Board had no clear jurisdiction over the Wyndmere Rock Garden; the Wyndmere Park Board seemed to exclusively serve as a legislative body for Little League athletics. When the secretary read the minutes from the May meeting, the only item was, "Board approves motion to hire Chuck Klosterman as baseball coach."

Now, had I only been meeting with the actual park board members, I suspect the whole affair would have gone smoothly: I would have outlined my goal-oriented mission statement and expressed deep affinity for the future of "my guys," and I would have exited the meeting with nothing more than a gentle reminder to keep everyone's best interest in mind. I have no problem pretending to be conciliatory if the ends justify the means. Unfortunately, a few mothers showed up at the meeting that night as well. And—as we all know—there is nothing more frustrating than a mother who cares about her children.

Predictably, these were the mothers of kids who really had no interest in baseball, or in sports, or in competing against other children in any meaningful way. And that's fine; these kids were great people (possibly), and have gone on to fine careers (perhaps) and wonderful families (I assume). There's nothing admirable about having the kind of killer instinct that always felt normal to a weirdo like me. I mean, these little guys didn't want to spend two months chasing a stupid leather sphere through the stupid green grass in stupid right field; they just wanted to do something that kept them under the radar until they got to tenth grade, when they could quit pretending they cared about sports and start listening to Replacements cassettes. I'm sure my guys would have *loved* youth soccer.

But ANYWAY, suffice it to say the mothers of these kids didn't see it that way. They seemed to believe their sons actually adored baseball and were being discriminated against, apparently for being crappy baseball players. I decided to prove them wrong by grabbing a dictionary and reciting the exact Webster definition of "discrimination," which inadvertently proved their point entirely. But—somehow—this still felt like a draw. Their second argument was that I was setting a bad example by starting the same nine kids in every game, and that the starters should either be selected randomly or alphabetically; I argued that this was like giving every student the same grade on a test no matter how many questions they answered correctly (not a flawless analogy, I realize, but I was always good at rhetorical misdirection). They went on to propose that every player should get to try every position over the course of the season, a suggestion I deemed "unprofessional." And when they finally demanded that I had to stop keeping score and that I needed to play every future contest as an exhibition, I casually made the kind of statement sixteen-year-olds should not make to forty-six-year-old Midwestern housewives: "Why are you telling me how to do my job?" I asked. "It's not like I show up in your kitchen and tell you when to bake cookies."

In my defense, I did not mean to imply that these women were *only* suited for cookie-oriented purposes, and I was fully aware that the particular person I told this to worked in a bank (which actually might have made things worse). My statement was to be taken at face value and as a point of fact. However, the park board found this "exchange of ideas" rather damaging to my case and immediately adopted all of the mothers' suggestions, all of which I unabashedly ignored in our very next game (a 16–6 drubbing of our hated rivals from Fairmount). When I jumped into my father's pickup truck after the contest, I noticed an envelope under the windshield wiper: I had been terminated for "insubordination." This did not strike me as an especially brave way to fire a sixteen-year-old, but I knew that was how the industry operated; one year later, the same thing would happen to Tom Landry.

Now, perhaps you're curious as to how my ill-fated experience as a baseball coach has anything to do with my maniacal distaste for soccer; on the surface, probably nothing. But in that larger, deeper, "what-does-it-all-mean?" kind of way, the connection is clear. What those anti-cookie-baking mothers wanted me to do was turn baseball into soccer. They wanted a state-sponsored Outcast Culture. They wanted to watch their kids play a game where their perfect little angels could not fuck up, and that would somehow make themselves feel better about being parents.

Soccer fanatics love to tell you that soccer is the most popular game on earth and that it's played by 500 million people every day, as if that somehow proves its value. Actually, the opposite is true. Why should I care that every single citizen of Chile and Iran and Gibraltar thoughtlessly adores "futball"? Do the people making this argument also assume Coca-Cola is ambrosia? *Real sports aren't for everyone.* And don't accuse me of being the Ugly American for degrading soccer. That has nothing to do with it. It's not xeno-phobic to hate soccer; it's socially reprehensible to support it. To say you love soccer is to say you believe in enforced equality more than you believe in the value of competition and the capacity of the human spirit. It should surprise no one that Benito Mussolini loved being photographed with Italian soccer stars during the 1930s; they were undoubtedly kindred spirits. I would sooner have my kid deal crystal meth than play soccer. Every time I pull up behind a Ford Aerostar with a "#1 Soccer Mom" bumper sticker, I feel like I'm marching in the wake of the Khmer Rouge.

That said, I don't feel my thoughts on soccer are radical. If push came to shove, I would be more than willing to compromise: It's not necessary to wholly outlaw soccer as a living entity. I con-cede that it has a right to exist. All I ask is that I never have to see it on television, that it's never played in public (or supported with public funding), and that nobody—and I mean *nobody*—ever utters the phrase "Soccer is the sport of the future" for the next forty thousand years. Outcasts may grow up to be novelists and filmmakers and computer tycoons, but they will never be the ath-letic ruling class. Your hopeless dystopia shall never befall us, Mr. Pelé. Now get back in that Aerostar and return to the killing fields.

On the last day of May in 2002, the Los Angeles Lakers defeated the Sacramento Kings in the sixth game of the Western Conference Finals in one of the worst officiated games in recent memory (the Lakers shot a whopping twenty-seven free throws in the fourth quarter alone, and Kings guard Mike Bibby was whistled for a critical phantom foul after Kobe Bryant elbowed him in the head).

Obviously, this is not the first time hoop zebras have cost someone a game. However, people will always remember this particular travesty, mostly because the game was publicly protested by former Green Party presidential candidate Ralph Nader.

"Unless the NBA orders a review of this game's officiating, perceptions and suspicions, however presently absent any evidence, will abound," wrote the semi-respected consumer advocate in a letter to NBA commissioner David Stern. "A review that satisfies the fans' sense of fairness and deters future recurrences would be a salutary contribution to the public trust that the NBA badly needs."

As usual, Nader's argument is only half right. Were the Kings jammed by the referees? Yes. Was Game Six an egregious example of state-sponsored cheating? Probably. But this is what sets the NBA apart from every other team sport in North America: Everyone who loves pro basketball assumes it's a little fixed. We all think the annual draft lottery is probably rigged, we all accept that the league aggressively wants big market teams to advance deep into the playoffs, and we all concede that certain marquee players are going to get preferential treatment for no valid reason. The outcomes of games aren't predetermined or scripted, but there are definitely dark forces who play with our reality. There are faceless puppet masters who pull strings and manipulate the purity of justice. It's not necessarily a full-on conspiracy, but it's certainly not fair. And that's why the NBA remains the only game that matters: Pro basketball is exactly like life.

8   33   0:97

Every time I watch a Spike Lee movie on HBO, I get nervous. That probably happens to a lot of white people, and I suppose that's sort of the idea. But my reason for getting nervous has nothing to do with the sociocultural ideas that Spike expresses, nor does it have anything to do with fear that a race riot is going to break out in my living room, nor is it any kind of artistic apprehension. My fear is that I know there's a 50 percent chance a particular situation is going to occur on screen, and the situation is this: A black guy and a white guy are going to get into an argument over basketball, and the debate will focus on the fact that the black guy loves the Lakers and the white guy loves the Celtics. And this argument is going to be a metaphor for all of America, and its fundamental point will be that we're all unconsciously racist, because any white guy who thought Larry Bird was the messiah is latently denying that Jesus was black. The relative blackness and whiteness of the Los Angeles Lakers and the Boston Celtics (circa 1980–1989) is supposed to symbolize everything we ever needed to know about America's racial cold war, and everyone who takes sports seriously seems to concede that fact.

But this metaphor is only half the equation.

To say the 1980s rivalry between the Celtics and the Lakers represents America's racial anguish is actually a short-sighted understatement. As I have grown older, it's become clear that the Lakers-Celtics rivalry represents absolutely *everything*: race, religion, politics, mathematics, the reason I'm still not married, the Challenger explosion, *Man vs. Beast*, and everything else. There is no relationship that isn't a Celtics-Lakers relationship. It emerges from nothingness to design nature, just as Gerald

97

Henderson emerged from nothingness to steal James Worthy's errant inbound pass in game two of the 1983 finals. Do you realize that the distance between Henderson and Worthy at the start of that play—and the distance between them at the point of interception—works out to a ratio of 1.618, the same digits of Leonardo da Vinci's so-called "golden ratio" that inexplicably explains the mathematical construction of the universe?[1] Do not act surprised. It would be more surprising if the ratio did not.

AM I SERIOUS?

Yes. How could I not be? For ten years—but for *only* ten years— you had two teams that were (a) clearly the class of their profession, and (b) completely and diametrically opposed in every possible respect. This is no accident. For at least one decade, God was obsessed with pro basketball. And as I stated earlier, everyone always wants to dwell on the fact that (a) the Celtics started three Caucasians in a league that was 80 percent black and (b) the Lakers never had a white player who mattered (the only exception being Kurt Rambis, a role player who seemed artless on purpose, going so far as refusing to purchase contact lenses). But what made this rivalry so universal was that it wasn't about black and white people; it was about black and white philosophies. Americans have become conditioned to believe the world is a gray place without absolutes; this is because we're simultaneously cowardly and arrogant. We don't know the answers, so we assume they must not exist. But they *do* exist. They are unclear and/or unfathomable, but they're out there. And—perhaps surprisingly—the only way to find those answers is to study NBA playoff games that happened twenty years ago. For all practical purposes, the voice of Brent Musburger was the pen of Ayn Rand.

Perhaps you're curious as to why we must go back two decades to do this; obviously, pro basketball still exists. The answer is sim-

1. This is probably not true.

ple: necessity. I mean, you certainly can't understand the world from the way the NBA is now. Two years ago, I watched an over-time game between the Philadelphia 76ers and the Toronto Raptors: Allen Iverson scored 51 points and Vince Carter scored 39. As I type those numbers into my keyboard, it looks like I'm painting the portrait of an amazing contest (and exactly the kind of *mano-a-mano* war NBC wanted to show me on a Sunday afternoon). But it was an abortion. It was like watching somebody commit suicide with a belt and a folding chair. Iverson took 40 shots; Carter was 15 for 36 from the field. It was like those excruciating NBA games from the late 1970s, where collapsing super-novas such as World B. Free and John Williamson would shoot the ball on every possession and David Thompson would try to score 70 points against the New Orleans Jazz before blowing two weeks' pay on Colombian nose candy. Guys like Iverson and Carter are mechanically awesome, but they don't represent any-thing beyond themselves. They're nothing more than good bas-ketball players, and that's depressing. Watching modern pro basketball reminds me of watching my roommate play Nintendo in college. In order to remedy this aesthetic decline, the league decided to let teams play zone defense, which has got to be the least logical step ever taken to increase excitement. This is like try-ing to combat teen pregnancy by lowering the drinking age.

The NBA doesn't need to *sanction* zone defense; the smart guys were playing zone when it was still illegal. Larry Bird played zone defense every night of his career. What the NBA needs to do is provide a product that will help us better understand ourselves and foster self-actualization. Granted, this is not an easy goal to legislate. But that's the only solution that can save this dying bra-chiosaurus. I didn't need Michael Jordan to come back; I need to watch a game that tells me who to vote for.

Here's what I mean: I never understood partisan politics until I watched the last epic Lakers-Celtics war, which happened in the summer of 1987. The contest everyone remembers is game four, which I watched as a high school sophomore at a summer basketball camp on the campus of North Dakota State University. You probably remember this game, too: It's June 9 at the Boston Garden, and the Lakers lead the series 2–1. Boston has the ball with under thirty seconds left, down one; they dump it to McHale on the right block, who kicks it out to Ainge, who reverses to Bird in the far corner for a three. Twine. Celtics by two. The Lakers come down on offense and Kareem gets hacked; he makes one and misses the second, but it bounces off Parish and goes out of bounds under the rack. Magic takes the inbounds pass, blows by McHale and hits that repulsive running hook across the lane. Lakers lead by one. After the obligatory timeout moves the rock to halfcourt, the Celtics have two seconds to get a shot. Bird's forty-footer is dead-on, but two inches deep. L.A. wins 107–106; they go up three games to one and win the rings five days later.

This, of course, was like a ten-inch stiletto jammed into my aorta. Magic Johnson is one of my favorite players of all time, but I hate him. I once interviewed Johnson about all those stupid, civic-minded, state-of-the-art movie theaters he's putting into depressed urban areas, and I was caught between feeling impressed by his suit, nervous about his stature, and overcome by the desire to punch him in the face. However, my personal feeling toward Earvin can't negate the larger meaning of his heroics, and that meaning is political. Because what I really remember most about that game was that I was just about the only kid at this camp who wanted Boston to win. The only other people who liked the Celtics were the camp's coaches; I was the only Bird apostle under the age of thirty-five. If you liked the Celtics, it meant you liked your dad's team. And this is when I came to understand that I was actually rooting for the Republican party.

Regardless of how liberal Massachusetts may seem, the Celtics were totally GOP. Like Thomas Jefferson, K. C. Jones did not believe in a strong central government: The Celtic players mostly coached themselves. They practiced when they felt like practicing and pulled themselves out of games when they deemed it appropriate, and they wanted to avoid anything taxing. They wanted to avoid *taxes*. And they excelled by attacking the world in the same way they had been raised to understand it: You pick-and-roll, you throw the bounce pass, you make your free throws. If it worked in the 1950s, it can work now. Meanwhile, the Lakers were like late sixties Democrats: They *seemed* liberal and exhilarating, but Pat Riley controlled the whole show. There were no state's rights within the locker room of the Fabulous Forum. Government was seen as the answer to all problems, including the problem of keeping Robert Parish off the offensive glass. Riley was a tyrant—a dashing tyrant, but a tyrant nonetheless—and arguably the strongest singular governing force since LBJ. I once heard an apocryphal story about Lyndon Johnson and a military helicopter: After addressing some Vietnam-bound troops, he was supposed to get on a chopper and leave the Air Force base, so one of his sycophants asked him, "Sir, which of these helicopters is yours?" Johnson supposedly said, "Son, *all* these helicopters are mine." That's how Riley looked at James Worthy.

Perhaps you think this kind of sweeping generalization is insane. Most people do. If you ask almost anyone about the cultural ramifications of a series of basketball games (some of which happened twenty-one years ago), they will inevitably scoff. I know this, because I've tried. "I'm really very hesitant to buy into any theories of this nature," says longtime *Boston Globe* writer Bob Ryan, generally considered America's foremost media expert on the NBA and someone who's known for buying into illogical theories. "I just think that's reaching beyond any reasonable limit of logic." Of course, immediately after making that statement, Ryan spent the next ten minutes explaining why these two teams represented "the conflict between speed and convention."[2] The fact of the matter is that everyone who truly cares about basketball subconsciously knows that Celtics vs. Lakers reflects every fabric of male existence, just as everyone who loves rock 'n' roll knows that the difference between the Beatles and the

2. Two entities that—to the best of my knowledge—are not in conflict.

Stones is not so much a dispute over music as it is a way to describe your own self-identity. This is why men need to become obsessed with things: It's an extroverted way to pursue solipsism. We are able to study something that defines who we are; therefore, we are able to study ourselves. Do you know people who insist they like "all kinds of music"? That actually means they like *no kinds* of music. And do you know guys who didn't care who won when the Celtics played the Lakers? That means they never really cared about anything.

THE CORE PRINCIPLE OF OUR METAREALITY, AND/OR PAT RILEY'S HEAD

I called the Miami Heat's front office to see if Riley would talk to me about my hypothesis. Much to my surprise, he called back in only two days; much to his surprise, the first thing I asked him about was his hair. What I wanted to know was whether he realized that his hair symbolized the hypermodern, antitraditional paradigm the Lakers used to mock the Celtics' archetypical simplicity and Greatest Generation morality.

Oddly, Riley acted like he had heard this question before.

"Oh, I was totally aware of that," he said. "I knew I was being packaged by CBS and everybody else in the media. But I didn't pay attention to it. If you play in the finals seven times, somebody is going to notice you slick your hair back, and sportswriters make a big deal about things like that. And as those teams go down in history, the myths become more important than anything that actually went down for real."

I suppose that detached mythology is really what I'm writing about. In truth, these teams didn't play each other as often as it seems retrospectively. Though there wasn't an NBA championship series in the eighties that didn't include either L.A. or Boston, they only played each other three times. They only faced each other in a seventh game once, and the star that night was forgotten antihero Cedric "Cornbread" Maxwell. The greatest

Celtic team—the 1985–86 squad that used Bill Walton as the sixth man—never played L.A. in the finals, because the Lakers were upset in the playoffs by an inferior Houston team led by underachiever Ralph Sampson. The era's best Laker squad was probably the one from 1986–87 (Jabbar's last decent season and Byron Scott's first good one), but Boston was so devastated by injury that year they essentially played with only five guys (their best reserve was Jerry fucking Sichting). In a way, the rivalry is akin to memories from keg parties from your freshman year at college—it all sort of runs together into one hazy image that never technically occurred, yet somehow feels to have occurred all the time.

But in so many ways, that kind of mythology is the only thing that keeps us alive. Remember when Danny Ainge bit Tree Rollins's hand in the 1984 Eastern conference play-offs? If you do, you shouldn't: Rollins is actually the guy who bit Ainge. For some reason, everyone recalls the opposite. This is a big part of why so many people hated the greatest Mormon in league history—because someone bit *him*. Life is rarely about what happened; it's mostly about what we *think* happened.

Riley knew this, too. When I asked him what the ultimate key to beating Boston was, I assumed (and kind of hoped, actually) that he'd start talking about the way Michael Cooper matched up with Bird defensively. Instead, he went into a bunch of crap about the fifteenth-century Boers.

"We had to get over the psychological element of the Celtic mystique," Riley insisted. "After we choked in '84, I had to teach my guys exactly who the Celtics were in a historical sense. I mean, the Celts were a cult who did sinister things in secret places. That's where I took it. I had to teach them who their opponent was originally, because that's exactly who they were playing in 1987. I don't know if the Celtic players knew about Celt history, but that's how those guys played."

This is probably true, although a bit comical (I like to imagine Riley handing out scouting reports that included such insights as, "Dennis Johnson: no range beyond twenty-one feet, initiates contact on drives to the hole, may have aspirations to sack Iberia"). But it proves that Riley understood that sport (or least the transcendent moments of sport) has almost nothing to do with the concept of a *game*. Scrabble is a game. Popomatic Trouble is a game. Major League Baseball is a game. But any situation where Bird is boxing out Magic for a rebound that matters is not. That is a conflict that dwarfs Dante. That is the crouching tiger *and* the hidden dragon.

So this is how I have come to make every decision in my life: I suss out the Celtics and Lakers dynamic in any given scenario, and then I go with Larry. I'm a Celtic Person; for me, life is simple. And just in case you're blind to the abundantly obvious, here are ten examples of how you can construct a green and gold humanity:

QUESTION # 1—"What kind of car should I drive?"
If you're a Laker Person, buy a two-door car, preferably something made in America. I'd go with a Camaro IROC or possibly a Ford Probe. These are fast, domestic vehicles, just as the "Showtime" automaton was a sleek, streamlined machine that came from the streets of Michigan (which is where Magic was raised). Meanwhile, Celtic People are four-door sedan owners. I lean toward the Chrysler LeBaron and the Chevy Cavalier, the veritable D.J. and Ainge of the automotive universe.

QUESTION # 2—"Whom should I marry?"
If you're a Celtic Person, you should try to marry the most beautiful woman willing to sleep with you. In all likelihood, you are not attractive, Celtic Fan. Your haircut is ridiculous. You need to marry the equivalent of a model, lest your kids will almost certainly be repulsive. It is the Celtic Way to find that middle ground between the beautiful (i.e., the rotation on Bird's release) and the ugly (i.e., Kevin McHale's skeletal structure). If you're a Laker Person, you need to marry the most understanding, forward-

thinking, unconventional female you can possibly find. This is because (a) you will only enjoy a creative relationship, and (b) you will undoubtedly cheat on her, and probably with a hooker.

QUESTION # 3—"What should I have for breakfast?"
There's sort of a gut reaction to insist that Celtic People should eat pancakes and bacon while they read the newspaper, but nobody does that except lumberjacks and maybe Mark Cuban. A Celtic Person eats cereal, but nothing bland; Cap'n Crunch or Frosted Flakes are the best options, because the empty sugar represents M. L. Carr and the ample riboflavin represents Scott Wedman (i.e., something that is good for you, even though you have no idea what it does). Laker People consume Kellogg's Pop-Tarts, which heat up in a hurry—a lot like Bob McAdoo.

QUESTION # 4—"Who Should I Believe Killed John F. Kennedy?"
Laker People side with the conspiracy that implicates the military-industrial complex, although they also suspect this is why nobody turned on the air conditioners during game five at the Garden in 1984. Celtic People think Oswald acted alone and without justification, just like Philadelphia 76er Andrew Toney.

QUESTION # 5—"What should be my favorite sexual position?"
I don't want to get too graphic, but here's a hint: Look at the way Danny Ainge shot his jumper. Then look at the way Jamaal Wilkes shot his. Enough said.

QUESTION # 6—"What kind of drugs should I take?"
Remember the first game of Magic's career, when Kareem hit a skyhook at the buzzer against the Clippers and Johnson hugged him like a grizzly? The only people I know who behave like that are usually on Ecstasy. Meanwhile, Celtic People smoke pot, just like the Chief.

QUESTION # 7—"David Lee Roth or Sammy Hagar?"
This is a tricky one, because Dave was the ultimate California boy
and Sammy's heaviest solo record is titled *Standing Hampton*,
which I think is in New Hampshire (the Red Rocker also looks a
bit like Bill Walton, sans headband). Yet upon further review, it's
all too obvious: Celtic People are Roth People, because that's the
original, definitive incarnation of a classic archetype. Laker People are Hagar People, because Sammy was in the band longer and
ultimately sold more albums (just as L.A. ultimately won five
titles to Boston's three, while Magic won twenty-two of his thirty-
seven head-to-head meetings with Bird). Hell, the Lakers weren't
as cool, but they were better, you know?

QUESTION # 8—"Should capital punishment be legal?"
Laker People say no, as Kareem Abdul-Jabbar is a human rights
activist who would question the validity of any practice that
essentially replicates the original crime. Celtic people say yes,
because anybody who's ever looked into Larry Bird's eyes knows
he's killer.

QUESTION # 9—"Is Adam Sandler funny?"
No.

QUESTION # 10—"What socially irresponsible rap music
should I support?"
According to N.W.A., life ain't nothin' but bitches and money,
and James Worthy (arrested for soliciting a Texas prostitute in
1990) would undoubtedly agree. Therefore, Laker People dig Ice
Cube. Celtic People go with Eminem, the only white guy who
can keep up.

Now, I know what you're saying: Question #10 is just a race
thing, which is exactly what you refuted four thousand words ago.
And I'll admit this is a slippery slope, and something that's hard
to avoid. Bob Ryan was very up front about this. "When the sub-

ject of race does come up, there's one thing you can be sure of," he told me. "The Celtics were clearly the favorite team of *blatant* racists. And that's a sorry commentary on the world, and no fault of the Celtics. But the fact that they had so many great white players made them heroes to racists and people in the Deep South. Even in Boston, there was an element of their fandom that was very happy they had white superstars. Anybody who would deny that is naive."

So perhaps that's me; perhaps I'm naive. Perhaps it seems like the Lakers and the Celtics represent everything in life simply because they represent the psychological war between black and white, the only things just about everybody in America can seem to understand. Perhaps the only real reason I worshiped Larry Bird was because he was a God I could create in my own image.

But part of me knows this was really about Pop-Tarts. And about Oswald. And about voting for Bob Dole.

David Halberstam has noted that Larry Bird and Magic Johnson were actually raised with paradoxical pathologies: Halberstam insists Magic's middle-class upbringing was a traditional white experience, while Bird's impoverished, screwed-up childhood (his father committed suicide when Larry was nineteen) was more stereotypically black. Perhaps this is part of the reason both men could so successfully represent people who have absolutely nothing to do with them. I am not a white person; not really. I am a Celtic Person. That's my identity, and I'm never going to try to pretend I'm some sort of eclectic iconoclast. This does not mean I'm always right and you're always wrong, nor does it mean I subconsciously need other people to feel the same way I do about anything. You don't need to side with the Boston Celtics to be a good person. But you should definitely side with *somebody*. Either you're with us or you're against us, and both of those options is better than living without a soul.

In every episode of *Happy Days,* Arthur Fonzarelli was surrounded by adoring teenage girls. The Fonz would snap his fingers and they would rush to his embrace. This phenomenon was central to all *Happy Days*–related discourse. We (as viewers) were constantly regaled with stories of his remarkable exploits at the popular makeout locale Inspiration Point; these tales often involved twin sisters. This was just an accepted part of life. Richie Cunningham would periodically wander up to the Fonz's spartan apartment over the garage, and—inevitably—Fonzie would be with a buxom (and strangely mute) high school junior.

This forces us to pose an ethical question: Are we to assume the Fonz was having sex with all of these girls? I mean, this was the 1950s, and Milwaukee is a conservative Midwestern city. It's hard to believe that such a staid community would be supersaturated with so many sexually aggressive teenage girls. Moreover, we are supposed to perceive the Fonz as a "good guy," correct? Oh, he's a bit of a rogue (what with all the bull riding and shark jumping and whatnot), but he's certainly not the type of guy who would sexually corrupt dozens—perhaps hundreds!—of virginal high school females, many of whom would have undoubtedly been under the legal age of consent in the state of Wisconsin (currently eighteen years of age). That scenario is unthinkable. We cannot exist in a society where someone like Fonzie would be lionized for being an insatiable sexaholic, a statutory rapist, and a potential child molester. This is not the behavior of a "good guy." And since Fonzie never seemed to have a long-term rapport with any of these girls, it's unlikely that he ever experienced a loving, mutually satisfying, logically advancing relationship (the lone exception being Pinky Tuscadero, who did not seem to reside in the immediate Milwaukee area).

That being the case, there is only one conclusion to draw. For the entire 255-episode duration of *Happy Days,* the Fonz was a virgin.

9   Porn   1:09

When exactly did every housewife in America become a whore?[1]

Now, this is not an attack on housewives. I can't say I *support* the idea of every housewife in America being a whore, but I suppose things could be worse; a loose army of housewife whores is obviously preferable to 2 million housewife serial killers, or 3 million housewife crackheads, or 10 million housewife crossbow enthusiasts. Still, the fact that we have so many whorific housewives is mildly unsettling and profoundly inexplicable. It's hard to wrap your mind around the motivations of a forty-four-year-old mother smiling while someone takes a series of photographs that prominently feature her birth canal.

Yet according to the affable robots at google.com, there are 6,250 sites on the Internet that prominently include the phrase "naked housewives." There are also 7,110 that include the phrase "nude housewives," which I suppose is technically classier. We have 586 that promote "housewife whores," while a solid 2,600 offer a more generic alternative ("housewife sluts"). I could only find 51 that contain the phrase "my wife is a whore," although that number is somewhat offset by the 6 sites specifically promoting that "my wife is a *fucking* whore," not to mention the semiofficial domain name housewifewhore.com. Since one can assume all of these sites have—conservatively—50 whores apiece, that's a little over 830,000 domestic sexaholics in English-speaking countries alone, all of which can be located in roughly ninety seconds.

Considering how few women are still stay-at-home moms, that's quite an accomplishment.

1. Except, of course, my mom.

109

Everyone knows that the Internet is changing our lives, mostly because someone in the media has uttered that exact phrase every single day since 1993. However, it certainly appears that the main thing the Internet has accomplished is the normalization of amateur pornography. There is no justification for the amount of naked people on the World Wide Web, many of whom are clearly (clearly!) doing so for non-monetary reasons. Where were all these people fifteen years ago? Were there really millions of women in 1986 turning to their husbands and saying, "You know, I would love to have total strangers masturbate to images of me deep-throating a titanium dildo, but there's simply no medium for that kind of entertainment. I guess we'll just have to sit here and watch *Falcon Crest* again."

This phenomenon blows my mind, but—apparently—nobody else is the least bit surprised. It has been my experience that people who are especially obsessed with Internet technology (HTML designers, "new media" pundits, *Lord of the Rings* fans, etc.) tend to become extremely agitated when you start to talk about Internet pornography, typically because they think that it degrades the social import of the Web and insults all the bespectacled geniuses who create it.[2] The argument they make in response is usually something along the lines of this: "Okay, sure—there's porn on the Internet. But who cares? There are some perverts on computers who spend all day looking at Teri Hatcher's ass, but there are just as many perverts in public libraries looking at medical journals and playing with themselves under the table. You wouldn't judge the merits of literature by the actions of those losers, and it's equally shortsighted to study the Internet through the prism of its lowest common denominator. People who obsess about Internet porn are missing the point."

The first time I heard that argument, it seemed savvy. However,

---

2. One Web designer actually told me that focusing a discussion around the topic of porn sites "insults" the Internet, prompting me to ask him if the Internet gets jealous when I use the microwave.

I've grown to realize that the opposite is true. People who *aren't* obsessing about Internet porn are missing the point, because that sleaze was the catalyst for everything else. I doubt that pornography has been good for the advancement of society, but I suspect it's done wonders for the advancement of computer technology.

People always forget how new the Internet truly is. I was a senior in college during the spring of 1994, and I knew exactly two people who had e-mail addresses. They wrote e-mails *to each other*. It seemed completely impractical and a total waste of time. From what I could tell, the only people who were sending e-mail were people who drank Zima, and they mostly used the Internet to discuss properties of calculus or to send Steven Wright jokes to other weirdos in Canada. They were mostly CompuServe users. I can recall an extremely antisocial MC Hammer fan in my dormitory who had a Macintosh in his room and once tied up the phone line for five hours while he downloaded the Batman logo for no apparent reason; soon after, he unsuccessfully tried to commit suicide by taking an overdose of Ibuprofen. This did not seem like the future.

However, I can also vividly recall my friend Robert showing me something in the fall of 1994 that seemed legitimately amazing—and while it didn't prompt me to get an e-mail address, it did reinvent my image of how prevalent the Internet was going to become. Robert had always been a ground-floor computer nerd, and I asked him if there truly was an avalanche of porn online (which was something I had read about in the newspaper). Robert said, "I could show you lesbians having sex in two seconds." Now, I assumed he meant "two seconds" figuratively, as in "I just have to wash my hair and put on my makeup—I'll be ready to go in two seconds." Obviously, I was wrong. Robert meant two seconds as in 00:02. And the actual image of two vacant blond girls with serpentine tongues was not nearly as mind-blowing as the fact that *someone* has designed a hypercomplicated network to show me lesbian smut. I could not fathom why this technology—*for this particular purpose*—would even exist.

Almost a decade later, I still sort of feel that way. Internet porn has replaced going to the moon as the explanation for all that is unexplainable. Here's what I mean by that: People used to ask rhetorical questions like, "How is it that we can put a man on the moon, but I still can't get a good martini in downtown Seattle?" Neil Armstrong made everything less complicated than a lunar landing seem plausible. Meanwhile, Internet porn makes everything more reasonable—once you've realized there is a massive subculture of upwardly mobile people who think it's erotic to see an Asian woman giving a hand job to a javelina, nothing else in the world seems crazy.

We all like to talk about how the Internet is such a groundbreaking educational tool, but we're missing what it can teach us about ourselves. Porn sites are the window to the modern soul; they're glimpses into the twisted minds of a faceless society. All the deviancy Freud tried to deduce through decades of analysis is now completely exposed in seconds (or milliseconds, if you have DSL). When Carl Jung introduced the concept of the "collective unconscious," he was trying to explain why all humans are inherently scared of things like darkness and vampires—but net porn is the collective conscious. It's where we all see the things people would never admit to wanting.

And what is it that we want? From what I can tell, that answer is twofold: We want imperfection, and we want heightened reality. The pornography everyone wants to see on the Internet focuses on (a) amateurs and (b) celebrities. We either want a truck stop waitress who's a little overweight and sort of freakish, or we want voyeuristic shots of Britney Love Aguilera[3] on a private beach in Italy. And some would say that's simply human nature, but they're wrong; that's a reflection of how we're still trying to understand how this technology works. Ironically—or perhaps predictably—we need porn to do this. It's what keeps us interested.

3. Best known for her role as the teenage werewolf slayer.

Let's say a guy is sitting in a bar in Des Moines and two women walk in. One of these girls is clearly a model/actress, and she has fake boobs and luxurious hair and a perfectly sculpted body; meanwhile, her companion is just a totally normal, decent-looking person. Who will our hard-drinking Iowan immediately want to see naked? The answer is obvious—he would want to see the model. And if there are twenty-five women in the bar that night and he's given the opportunity to see any one of them nude, he will pick whoever he thinks is the most attractive. Yet this would not be the case if these women were 2-D thumbnail pics on a Web site called nakedtavern.com. The first female selected would be whoever seemed the *most* normal (i.e., neither ideal nor repulsive), or maybe the woman with the nicest smile who seemed just a tier below gorgeous. And porn sites are completely aware of this phenomenon. You often see banner advertisements that scream things like, TIRED OF SITES WITH MODELS CLAIMING TO BE AMATEURS? WE GUARANTEE REAL UNPROFESSIONAL SLUTS! This is one of those bizarre paradoxes that could only have been created by the acceleration of culture: Within the realm of their Gate-ways, men prefer to look at nude images of women they'd nor-mally ignore in real life.

Now, I realize phrases like "the acceleration of culture" tend to be frustrating terms, mostly because there's a certain segment of the population that throws around this term too often (and usu-ally incorrectly), and there's another segment that only vaguely understands what it means (they can define the individual words, but the larger concept still seems fuzzy). However, it's the best explanation as to why amateur porn is more popular than pro-fessional porn, which is only the case in the on-line idiom. Before the Net devastated the smut mag industry, success had always been directly tied to professionalism: In the 1990s, *Playboy* was forever the front-runner, followed by *Penthouse*, followed by *Hus-tler*, followed by *Perfect 10*. The same still goes for live erotica: Whenever I hear guys talking about their favorite strip clubs, they always talk about how unbelievably hot the dancers are; I've never heard anyone raving about how unbelievably ordinary the dancers look. Yet with computer pornography (much of which is still free), the key is normalcy—the surfer is hoping to see the girl next door in an almost literal sense. This is the product of a technology that has accelerated faster than its user can comprehend.

In less than a decade, millions of Americans went from (1) not knowing what the Internet was, to (2) knowing what is was but not using it, to (3) having an e-mail address, to (4) using e-mail pretty much every day, to (5) being unable to exist professionally *or socially* without it. For 98 percent of the world, the speed and sweep of that evolution was too great to fathom. Consequently, we learned how to use tools most of us don't understand. This has always been the case with technology, but not quite to this extent. I mean, I drive a car that I can't fix and that I could certainly never build, but I still understand how it works in a way that goes (slightly) beyond the theoretical. I could explain how a car works to a ten-year-old. Conversely, I don't understand *anything* about the construction of the Internet, beyond those conventional *Newsweek* factoids that everyone knows (and which still seem borderline impossible). I have no practical knowledge of the "information superhighway."[4] And I'm not interested in how it works; I just want to feel like I vaguely grasp its potential and vaguely understand how to use that potential to my advantage.

This is why amateur pornography became so integral to the adoption of Internet technology: It not only made people *excited* about using the Web (because sex is prurient and arousing), but it also made people *comfortable* with using the Web (because it's organic and unsophisticated). Sex is so undeniably visceral that anyone can relate to it, assuming what they're seeing does not appear to be an untouchable, unworldly fantasy. Imperfect, unpaid nudity tightened the parameters of the virtual world; it's proof that this futuristic electronic network is still operated by humankind. This is not a pixeled construction of some Never-

4. Are people (besides Al Gore) still using this term? Probably not.

Neverland character from *Tron*; this is some girl you saw at Pizza Hut. Amateur pornography grounds us in our reality.

Of course, it should go without saying that our reality is profoundly fucked-up. Twenty minutes on the Internet cum trade is all it takes to realize that the sexual peccadilloes of modern people are clichéd, sad, incomprehensible, and/or a combination of all three. If you are to take "real" porn at face value, you would be forced to conclude that women rarely have pubic hair, except for those who are advertising as having *more* pubic hair than normal. There seems to be an unabated demand for naked teenage girls, although there also seems to be a tacit understanding that any moderately small-breasted thirty-one-year-old woman can pass for a teenager if she has pigtails and a lollipop. There is an inordinate amount of bandwidth focused on girls urinating on themselves and/or licking their own nipples (is this fun?), and there's a big demand for interracial sex, first-time anal sex, public flashing, and the ham-fisted implication of incest. What's most disturbing is the amount of Internet porn that has absolutely nothing to do with sexual desire and everything to do with cartoonish misogyny, most notably the endless sites showing men ejaculating on women's faces while the recipients pretend to enjoy it; this has about as much to do with sex as hitting someone in the face with a frying pan.

And—of course—there is also a pocket of men who masturbate to images of women getting hit in the face with frying pans. I guess there's no accounting for taste. But there's really no purpose in complaining about pornography, either. Yes, it's socially negative; no, it's not nearly as negative as Ted Bundy claimed before his execution. The tangible effect of pornography is roughly the same as the tangible effect of Ozzy Osbourne's music on stoned Midwestern teenagers: It prompts a small faction of idiots to consider idiotic impulses, which is why we have the word *idiocy*. Arguing about the psychological merits (or lack thereof) of watching intercourse on a Presario 700Z doesn't interest me. What interests me is how that habit changes the way people think about their own existence—and that brings me back to that second type of image porn surfers want to see: naked celebrities.

You'd think naked Hollywood actresses and naked West Virginia hairdressers would exist on opposite poles, but they're closer than you think. They're closer because—in a technical, physiological sense—they're identical. There are certainly differences between the nipples of Alyssa Milano and the nipples of an Olive Garden waitress in Sioux Falls, South Dakota, but the similarities of those nipples greatly outweigh the disparities. Here again, Internet pornography provides a bizarre sense of stability; it reminds us that we're working in a hard reality; naked from the neck down, your wife and Gwen Stefani have a lot in common. What people want to see with nude celebrities is proof that these superstars are not gods. Web surfers are robbing celebrities of their privacy and—in effect—stealing back power. Psychologically, the Internet is very Marxist: Everyone with a modem has access to the same information, so we all get jammed into a technological middle class. You don't need to be Lenny Kravitz to know what Lisa Bonet looks like when she steps out of the shower. You don't even need to wear hemp pants. All you need is a modem and a phone jack.

Now, is aspiring to be as sexually informed as Lenny Kravitz a sad commentary on modern ambition? Perhaps.[5] But that's not the issue. The issue is that something that's probably bad (i.e., porn) is helping us achieve something that's probably good (i.e., delivering a technological notion to the common man).

Yet one question remains:

Why don't women need this?

If this theory is all true, why are 99 percent of porn sites directed toward heterosexual men? Wouldn't this imply that females can't fathom the difference between the real and the virtual, even though they all obviously do? Why can women comprehend the power of the Internet without masturbating to

5. Well, actually, "yes."

JPEG images of dehumanizing sex acts? And why would no intelligent woman ever feel the need to rationalize her own weakness by arguing that her perversion actually expands her mind?

I can only assume it has something to do with licking your own nipples.

I'm pretty careful when it comes to my socks. Certain philosophers (Emilio Estevez in *St. Elmo's Fire,* for example) have speculated as to why socks so often get lost whenever people do laundry, but—until recently—that had never happened to me. In the span of fourteen years, I never lost a single sock. But then I lost a sock in October of 2001. And then I lost another two weeks later, and then a third around Thanksgiving. And it slowly dawned on me that something was afoot. "What in the name of Andrew W.K. is going on?" I asked aloud while sorting my freshly cleaned garments. Why were my socks suddenly disappearing like Chinese panda bears? What had changed?

The answer: Mr. Smokey.

It occurred to me that the only aspect of my laundering that had changed in recent weeks was my newfound affinity for petting a feline of unknown origin. Accessing the public laundry room in my apartment complex required that I briefly walk outside of my building's back door, where I consistently encountered a large gray cat I liked to call "Mr. Smokey." Despite our initial differences, I struck up an amicable relationship with Mr. Smokey; whenever I saw him, I would scratch his kitty ears and his kitty tummy, much to his kitty delight.

Or so it seemed.

Evidence began to mount suggesting that Mr. Smokey was using this weekly exchange as a diversion to steal my socks, one at a time. It's still not clear why he wanted my socks, since it had always been my assumption that kittens wanted mittens (in order to acquire pie).

However, there was no other explanation for these disappearances. In fact, I have reason to believe there was a whole network of cats involved in this: Perhaps Mr. Smokey stole my attention while a second cat (or cats) pounced into my laundry basket, snaring the best available footwear and fleeing into the darkness. I'm convinced an even larger cat ("Mr. Orange") from a neighboring building was part of this conspiracy.

"How often have I said," asked coke-addict Sherlock Holmes in *The Sign of Four,* "that when you have eliminated the impossible, whatever remains, however improbable, must be the truth?" This is true; I am nothing if not logical.

Mr. Smokey must die.

It's no secret that cold cereal was invented to help nineteenth-century Victorians stifle their rampant sexual desires. Any breakfast historian can tell you that. Sylvester Graham (1794–1851), a so-called "philosopher and nutrition crusader," was the kind of forward-thinking wackmobile who saw an indisputable connection between a person's decadence and their eating habits; this was partially augmented by his perception that the medical profession was wicked. "Disease is never the legitimate result of the normal operations of any of our organs," he wrote, a sentiment that would eventually spawn the creation of Quisp.

Mr. Graham suspected that bad food and inappropriate sexual desires—particularly masturbation—were the true cause of every major illness. This made the cure for all sickness relatively simple: sexual moderation (i.e., less than thirteen orgasms a year for married couples, which actually seems reasonable), daily exercise, and a proper diet.

By 1840, Graham's career was in shambles; this does not seem altogether surprising, considering he was insane. However, his well-argued insanity influenced a New Yorker named James Caleb Jackson, and Jackson embraced Graham's philosophy on his way toward creating a bad-tasting wafer out of graham flour and water. He called his food "Granula" (a precursor to Granola). Jackson was force-feeding his wretched Granula in his Dansville, New York, sanitarium when it was discovered by Ellen Harmon White, a Seventh-Day Adventist. She adopted the idea and started her own sanitarium in Battle Creek, Michigan, in 1866. In need of a staff doctor, White hired a scrappy young physician named John Harvey Kellogg. John hired his brother, William, as clerk of the institute.

John Kellogg was also a disciple of the Graham philosophy and agreed that a flavorless, grain-based food was precisely what America needed. By 1902, he had conjured a way to produce flake cereal—the ideal medium for a crunchy, soulless pabulum. He tried to make wheat flakes, but the technology for such a innovation did not yet exist. Corn flakes, however, worked swimmingly.

Initially developed for scientific purposes, corn flakes struck the brothers Kellogg as a savvy business opportunity. This crispy treat seemed perfect for a society assumedly filled with oversexed, disease-ridden lunatics. And while selling cereal made money, it also raised ethical dilemmas: The angelic White was devastated that the Kelloggs were making money from a food designed to improve human purity. Meanwhile, John Kellogg was upset that his brother added sugar to the flake recipe to improve sales, a supplement he believed would liberate the public libido and turn every corn flake aficionado into a raging sexaholic. The Kellogg brothers eventually sued one another. After winning the lawsuit, William Kellogg took control of the enterprise; his puritan brother remained a stockholder.

Years later, a trio of Rastafarian elves would promote puffed rice.

Today, few members of the scientific community see a close connection between cold cereal and sex, although advertisers still did in the 1950s. Early Corn Flakes commercials showed Superman eating cereal with Jimmy Olsen, but never with Lois Lane; this was to keep viewers from inferring that Superman and Lois Lane had spent the night together (evidently, the notion of Superman and Jimmy Olsen having a homosexual relationship was not a concern). However, sex is not the central theme to modern cereal advertising. In fact, selling cereal is not the central theme to cereal advertising. Saturday morning commercials for all the best cereals are teaching kids how to figure out what's cool.

They're the first step in the indoctrination of future hipsters: Cereal commercials teach us that anything desirable is supposed to be exclusionary.

An inordinate number of cereal commercials are based on the premise that a given cereal is so delicious that a fictional creature would want to steal it. We are presented with this scenario time and time again. The most obvious is the Trix Rabbit, a tragic figure whose doomed existence is not unlike that of Sisyphus. Since the cereal's inception, the rabbit—often marginalized as "silly"—has never been allowed to enjoy even one bowl of his favorite foodstuff, and the explanation for this embargo smacks of both age discrimination and racism (we are to accept that Trix is reserved exclusively "for kids").[1]

An even sadder illustration of cereal segregation is Sonny the Cuckoo Bird, arguably the most tortured member of the advertising community. Sonny is plagued with self-loathing; though outspokenly *otaku* for Cocoa Puffs, he doesn't feel he deserves to consume them. Sonny will do anything to escape from his jones, including (but not limited to) locking himself into a primitive skycycle and shooting himself into outer space. To make matters worse, he is bombarded by temptation: Random children endlessly taunt him with heaping bowls of C-Puffs, almost like street junkies waving heroin needles in the face of William S. Burroughs. The kids have cereal, and Sonny does not. Translation: The kids are cool, and Sonny's an extremist and a failure. And as long as they possess what he does not, Sonny shall remain a second-class phoenix, doomed by his own maniacal ambition for breakfast.

Commercials for Lucky Charms star a leprechaun who replaced the pot of gold at the end of the rainbow with a bowl of

---

1. Proof that America is ultimately a sympathetic nation surfaced in 1976, when a consumer election sponsored by General Mills indicated that over 99 percent of Trix eaters felt the flamboyant six-foot rabbit deserved a bowl of Trix, which places his approval rating on par with Colin Powell in 1996.

marshmallow-laden cereal, a narrative device that slightly over-
stated the value of the actual product. The Cookie Crisp[2] mascot
was a masked rapscallion named "Crook," whose whole self-
identity was built on stealing cereal. In ads for both Cocoa and
Fruity Pebbles, Barney Rubble went to ridiculous lengths in the
hope of shoplifting Fred Flintstone's breakfast, occasionally
dressing like a woman and/or rapping like Ghostface Killah.
Time and time again, commercials for cereal assault children with
the same theme: A product's exclusivity is directly proportional
to its social cachet, which is the definition of calculated adult
coolness.

When I say *calculated adult coolness*, I'm referring to the
kind of coolness that generally applies to people between the
ages of nineteen and thirty-six. This is different than *mainstream teen coolness* and *aging hipster default coolness*, both of
which reflect an opposing (and sort of pathetic) consumer aesthetic. Cereal ads are directed at kids, but they barely work on
young people; the kind of advertising that works on a teenager
are bandwagon spots for things like Trident and khaki Gap pants.
Those ads imply that these are products everybody else already
owns. Teenagers claim they want to be cool, but they mostly just
want to avoid being uncool. It's the same for aging hipsters, an
equally terrified class of Americans who slowly conclude that the
key to staying relevant is by exhibiting default appreciation for
the most obvious youth culture entities; this is why you often
hear forty-seven-year-old men with ponytails saying things like,
"Oh, I'm totally into the new stuff. That new Nickelback record
is just terrific." Aging hipsters and corduroy-clad high school
sophomores are both primarily concerned with dodging lame-
ness. However, there is a stretch in everyone's early adulthood
where they can choose (or choose against) creating their own
personalized version of nonpopulist cool, which may (or may

2. This is not to be confused with the short-lived Oatmeal Cookie Crisp, a
cereal fronted by the good-natured wizard "Cookie Jarvis."

not) succeed. This is accomplished by embracing semioriginal, semielitist cultural artifacts that remain just out of reach to those who desire them—the so-called "Cocoa Puffs of Power."

We all relate to Sonny the Cuckoo Bird. We pursue that which retreats from us, and coolness is always a bear market. Coolness is always what others seem to have naturally—an unspecific, delicious, chocolately paradigm we must pilfer through subterfuge. It drives us, for lack of a better term, coo coo. And part of the reason we struggle is because there is no hard-and-fast clarity about what qualifies anything as *cool*. It needs to be original, but only semioriginal: It would be legitimately inventive (and kind of "out there") to casually walk around with the petrified skull of a orangutan under your arm for no obvious reason, but this would only seem cool to a select class of performance artist. A better choice would be a T-shirt featuring the cast of *After M*A*S*H*. A cool image also needs to be semielitist, but it can't be *wholly* elitist: What you display should be extremely hard to find, yet could have been *theoretically* found by absolutely *anyone* six months ago (had they possessed the foresight). This is why calculated adult coolness would reward the possession of, say, a can of Elf soda pop, yet frown upon the possession of, say, four ounces of weapons-grade uranium.[3]

The impact of this understanding comes later in life, usually at college, and usually around the point when being "weird" starts to be periodically interpreted by others as "charming" and/or "sexually intriguing." As noted earlier, kids don't really understand the nuance of cereal advertising until they reach their twenties; this is when characters like the Trix Rabbit evolve into understated Christ figures. And though the plot is not purposeful on the behalf of cereal makers, it's also not accidental. Cereal mascots are generally associated with sugared cereals—while a box of Wheaties might feature anyone from Bruce Jenner to Michelle Kwan, Count Chocula sticks with its mischievous vampire. Super

3. Although this would make you very cool in Syria.

Golden Crisp sells itself with the portrait of a laid-back bear wearing a mock turtleneck; Grape Nuts sells itself with a photograph of Grape Nuts. And this is more proof of cereal's overlooked relationship to American cool: Being cool is mostly ridiculous, and so is sugared cereal. That's why we like it.

I eat sugared cereal almost exclusively. This is because I'm the opposite of a "no-nonsense" guy. I'm an "all-nonsense" guy. Every time I drive a long distance, I'm hounded by the fear that I will get a flat tire and be unable to change it. When a button falls off one of my dress shirts, I immediately throw away the entire garment and buy a new one. I can't swim; to me, twelve feet of water is no different than twelve feet of hydrochloric acid (it will kill me just as dead). However, I *can* stay awake for seventy-two straight hours. I *can* immediately memorize phone numbers without writing them down. When flipping channels during commercial breaks in televised sporting events, I *can* innately sense the perfect moment to return to what I was watching originally. So the rub is that I have these semicritical flaws and I have these weirdly specific gifts, and it seems like most Americans are similarly polarized by what they can (and cannot) do. There are no-nonsense people, and there are nonsense people. And it's been my experience that nonsense people tend to consume Cocoa Krispies and Lucky Charms and Cap'n Crunch ("nonsense food," if you will). Consequently, we nonsense types spend hours and hours staring at cardboard creatures like the Trix Rabbit and absorbing his ethos, slowly ingesting the principles of exclusionary coolness while rapidly ingesting sugar-saturated spoonfuls of Vitamin B-12.

The desire to be cool is—ultimately—the desire to be rescued. It's the desire to be pulled from the unwashed masses of society. It's the desire to be advanced beyond the faceless humanoid robots who will die unheralded deaths and never truly matter, mostly because they all lived the same pedestrian life. Without the spoils of exclusionary coolness, we're just cogs in the struggle. We're like a little kid trying to kayak (or perhaps freestyle rock climb), and all the older kids keep mocking our efforts, openly implying that we cannot compete. But if we can just find that one cool thing that nobody else has—that gregarious, nine-foot animated jungle cat who can provide a glimmer of hope and a balanced breakfast—we can be better than ourselves. *We can be tigers*. 'Atta boy.

The three questions I ask everybody I meet in order to decide if I can love them:

1. Let us assume you met a rudimentary magician. Let us assume he can do five simple tricks—he can pull a rabbit out of his hat, he can make a coin disappear, he can turn the ace of spades into the Joker card, and two others in a similar vein. These are his only tricks and he can't learn any more; he can only do these five. HOWEVER, it turns out he's doing these five tricks with real magic. It's not an illusion; he can actually conjure the bunny out of the ether and he can move the coin through space. He's legitimately magical, but extremely limited in scope and influence.
Would this person be more impressive than Albert Einstein?

2. Let us assume that a fully grown, completely healthy Clydesdale horse has his hooves shackled to the ground while his head is held in place with thick rope. He is conscious and standing upright, but completely immobile. And let us assume that—for some reason—every political prisoner on earth (as cited by Amnesty International) will be released from captivity if you can kick this horse to death in less than twenty minutes. You are allowed to wear steel-toed boots.
Would you attempt to do this?

3. Let us assume that there are two boxes on a table. In one box, there is a relatively normal turtle; in the other, Adolf Hitler's skull. You have to select one of these items for your home. If you select the turtle, you can't give it away and you have to keep it alive for two years; if either of these parameters are not met, you will be fined $999 by the state. If you select Hitler's skull, you are required to display it in a semi-prominent location in your living room for the same amount of time, although you will be paid a stipend of $120 per month for doing so. Display of the skull must be apolitical.
Which option do you select?

11   Being Zack Morris   1:27

Sometimes I'm a bad guy, but I still do good things. Ironically, those good things are often a direct extension of my badness. And this makes me even worse, because it means my sinister nature is making people unknowingly smile.

Here's one example: I was once dating a girl in a major American city, and I was also kind of pursuing another girl in another major American city. I had just received one of those nifty "CD burners" for my computer, so I started making compilation albums for friends and particularly for lady friends. Like most uncreative intellectual men, almost all of my previous relationships had been based on my ability to make incredibly moving mix cassettes; though I cannot prove it, I would estimate that magnetic audiotape directly influenced 66 percent of my career sexual encounters. However, the explosion of CD burning technology has forced people like me to create CDs instead of cassettes, which is somewhat disheartening. The great thing about mix tapes was that you could anticipate the listener would have to listen to the entire thing at least once (and you could guarantee this by not giving them a track listing). Sequencing was very important. The strategy was to place specific "message" songs in-between semimeaningless "rocking" songs; this would transfix, compliment, and confuse the listener, which was always sort of the goal. However, once people starting making their own CDs, the mix tape suddenly seemed cheap and archaic. I had no choice but to start making CDs, even though they're not as effective: People tend to be more impressed by the packaging of the jewel case than the songs themselves, and they end up experiencing the music no differently than if they had thoughtlessly purchased the disc at

Best Buy (i.e., they skip from track to track without really studying the larger concept behind the artistic whole).

ANYWAY, I was making a mix disc for one of these women (I will never admit which), and it was my intention to find eighteen songs that reflected key elements of our relationship, which I thought I did. But as I looked at the track selection, it suddenly dawned on me that these songs were just as applicable to my *other* relationship. My feelings for "Woman A" were completely different than my feelings for "Woman B," but the musical messages would make emotional sense to both, despite the fact that these two women were wildly dissimilar. So I ended up making two copies of this album and sending one to each woman, using all the same songs and identical cover art (computers make this entirely too easy). I expressed identical romantic overtures to two different people with one singular movement. And they both received their discs on the same day, and they both loved them.[1]

Part of me will always know this was a diabolical thing to do. However, I'm mostly struck by the fact that all my deepest, most sincere feelings are so totally stereotypical that they pretty much apply to every girl I find even vaguely attractive. My feelings toward every woman I've ever loved can be completely explained by Paul McCartney's "Maybe I'm Amazed," Rod Stewart's "You're in My Heart," and either Matthew Sweet's "Girlfriend" or Liz Phair's "Divorce Song" (depending on how long we've known each other). My feelings about politics and literature and mathematics and the rest of life's minutiae can only be described through a labyrinthine of six-sided questions, but everything that actually matters can be explained by Lindsey fucking Buckingham and Stevie fucking Nicks in four fucking minutes. Important things are inevitably cliché, but nobody wants to admit that. And that's why nobody is deconstructing *Saved by the Bell*.

Saved by the Bell is like this little generational secret that's hyperfamiliar to people born between 1970 and 1977, yet gen-

1. Until now, I suppose.

erally unremarkable to anyone born after (and completely alien to all those born before). It was an NBC sitcom that ran for four years (1989 to 1993) after an initial thirteen-episode season on the Disney Channel (where it was originally titled *Good Morning, Miss Bliss*). The show spawned two spin-offs—*Saved by the Bell: The College Years* and *Saved by the Bell: The New Class*—and also included a six-episode summer run (usually referred to as the "Malibu Sands" miniseason) and two made-for-TV movies (one set in Hawaii, the other in Las Vegas).

It was a program about high school kids.

I realize that is not much expository information. Typically, one tries to explain TV shows in terms of "context"—if someone asked me to describe *The X-Files*, for example, I would seem like a moron if I said, "It was a program about two people who mostly looked for aliens." That would never qualify as a significant description. I would have to write about how the supernatural religiosity of *The X-Files* personified a philosophical extension of its audience, and how the characters represented two distinct perspectives on modern reality, and how the sexual chemistry between Mulder and Scully was electrified by their lack of physical intimacy. All this abstract deconstruction is necessary, and it's necessary because *The X-Files* was artful. However, I have never watched even one episode of *The X-Files*, because I'm not interested. I'm not interested in trying to understand culture by understanding that particular show, and that's part of the social contract with appreciating *anything* artful. You can't place something into its aforementioned "context" unless you know where (and how) to culturally file it, and I honestly don't care where *The X-Files* belongs in the American zeitgeist. Dozens of smart people told me how great this show was, and I'm sure they were right. But I'm satisfied with assuming that program was about two people who mostly looked for aliens, so—as a consequence—the show meant nothing to me. I "don't get it."

That's not the case with *Saved by the Bell*. *Saved by the Bell* wasn't artful at all. Now, that doesn't mean it's bad (nor does it mean it's good). What it means is that you don't need to place *Saved by the Bell* into any context to experience it. I didn't care about *Saved by the Bell* any more than I cared about *The X-Files*, but the difference is that I could watch *Saved by the Bell* without caring and still have it become a minor part of my life, which is the most transcendent thing any kind of art can accomplish (regardless of its technical merits).

When I first saw *Saved by the Bell*, I was a senior in high school. It was on Saturday mornings, usually right when I woke up (which I think was either 11:00 or 11:30 A.M.). It was supposedly the first live-action show NBC ever broadcast on a Saturday morning, an idiom that had previously been reserved for animation. I would watch *Saved by the Bell* the same way all high school kids watch morning television, which is to say I stared at it with the same thoughtless intensity I displayed when watching the dryer. I watched it *because it was on TV*, which is generally the driving force behind why most people watch any program. However, I became a more serious *Saved by the Bell* student when I got to college. I suspect this kind of awakening was not uncommon, as universities always spawn little cultures of terrible TV appreciation: When I was a sophomore, the only non-MTV shows anyone seemed to watch were *Saved by the Bell*, *Life Goes On* (that was the show about the retarded kid), *Quantum Leap*, the Canadian teen drama *Fifteen*, and *Days of Our Lives*. And what was interesting was that everybody seemed to watch them together, in the same room (or over the telephone), and with a cultic intensity. We liked the "process" of watching these shows. The idea of these programs being entertaining never seemed central to anything, which remains the most fascinating aspect of all televised art: consumers don't demand it to be good. It just needs to be watchable. And the reason that designation can be applied to *Saved by the Bell* has a lot to do with the fundamental truth of its staggering unreality.

Saved by the Bell followed the lives of six kids at a California high school called Bayside. Architecturally, the school was comprised of one multipurpose classroom, one square hallway, a very small locker room, and a diner owned by a magician. The six primary characters were as follows:

> **Zack Morris (Mark-Paul Gosselaar):** Good-looking blond kid with the ability to talk directly to the camera like Ferris Bueller; possessed a cell phone years before that was common; something of an Eddie Haskell/James Spader type, but with a heart of gold.
>
> **Samuel "Screech" Powers (Dustin Diamond):** Über-geeky Zack sycophant.
>
> **Albert Clifford "A.C." Slater (Mario Lopez):** Good-looking ethnic fellow; star wrestler; nemesis of Zack—except in episodes where they're inexplicably best friends.
>
> **Kelly Kapowski (Tiffani-Amber Thiessen):** Sexy girl next door; love interest of Zack.
>
> **Jessica "Jessie" Spano (Elizabeth Berkley):** Sexy 4.00 overachieving feminist; love interest of A.C.
>
> **Lisa Turtle (Lark Voorhies):** Wildly unlikable rich black girl; vain clotheshorse; unrequited love interest of Screech.

Every other kid at Bayside was either a nerd, a jock, a randomly hot chick, or completely nondescript; it was sort of like Rydell High in *Grease*. There were several noteworthy kids from the *Good Morning, Miss Bliss* era who simply disappeared when the show moved to NBC (this is akin to what happened to people like Molly Ringwald and Julie Piekarski when *The Facts of Life* changed from an ensemble cast to it's signature Blair-Jo-Natalie-Tootie alignment). Tori Spelling portrayed Screech's girlfriend Violet in a few episodes, Leah Remini served as Zack's girlfriend during the six episodes set at the Malibu beach resort, an unbilled Denise Richards appeared in the final episode of the Malibu run, and a now-buxom Punky Brewster played a snob for one show in the final season. Weirdly, a leather-clad girl named Tori (Leanna Creel) became the main character for half of the last season when Thiessen and Berkley left the show, but then they both reappeared at graduation and Creel was never seen again (I'll address the so-called "Tori Paradox" in a moment).

But—beyond that—the writers of *Saved by the Bell* always seemed to suggest that most adolescents are exactly the same and exist solely as props for the popular kids, which was probably true at most American high schools in the 1980s.[2] The only other important personality in the Bayside universe is Mr. Belding (Dennis Haskins), who is a principal of the John Hughes variety; there is no glass ceiling to his stupidity. However, Belding differs from the prototypical TV principal in that he tended to be completely transfixed by the school's most fashionable students; he really wanted Zack to like him, and Belding and Morris would often join forces on harebrained schemes.

On the surface, *Saved by the Bell* must undoubtedly seem like everything one would expect from a dreadful show directed at children, which is what it was. But that's not how it was consumed by its audience. There was a stunning recalibration of the classic "suspension of disbelief vs. aesthetic distance" relationship in *Saved by the Bell*, and it may have accidentally altered reality (at least for brief moments).

Here's what I mean: In 1993, *Saved by the Bell* was shown four times a day. If I recall correctly, two episodes were on the USA Network from 4:00 to 5:00 P.M. CST, and then two more were on TBS from 5:05 to 6:05. It's possible I have these backward, but the order doesn't matter; the bottom line is that I sometimes watched this show twenty times a week. So did my neighbor, a dude named (I think) Joel who (I think) was studying to become a pilot. Sometimes I would walk over to Joel's place and watch *Saved by the Bell* with him, and he was the type of affable stoic who never spoke. He was one of those quiet guys who would offer you a beer when you walked into his apartment, and then he'd

2. This is less true now, since unpopular kids are more willing to wear trench coats to school and kill everybody for no good reason.

silently drink by himself, regardless of whether you joined him or
not. Honestly, we never became friends. But we sort of had this
mute, parasitic relationship through *Saved by the Bell*, and I will
always remember the singular significant conversation we had:
We were watching an episode where Belding was blackmailing
Zack into dating his niece, and Joel suddenly got real incredulous
and asked, "Oh, come on. Who the fuck has that kind of relationship with their high school principal?"

Of all the things that could have caused Joel to bristle, I
remain fascinated by his oddly specific observation. I mean, Bayside High was a school where students made money by selling a
"Girls of Bayside" calendar, and it was a school where oil was discovered under the football team's goalposts. This is a show where
Zack had the ability to call time-out and *stop time* in order to nar-
rate what was happening with the plot. There is never a single
moment in the *Saved by the Bell* series that reflects any kind of
concrete authenticity. You'd think Zack's unconventional relationship with an authority figure would be the least of Joel's
concerns. However, this was the only complaint he ever lodged
against the *Saved by the Bell* aesthetic, and that's very telling.

Now, I realize there is some precedent for this kind of discon-
nect: Trekkies generally have no problem with the USS *Enterprise*
moving at seven times the speed of light, but they roll their eyes
in disgust if Spock acts a little too jovial. Within any drama, we
all concede certain unbelievable parameters, assuming specific
aspects of the story don't go outside the presupposed reality.
But I think Joel's take on *Saved by the Bell* is different than the
usual contradiction. What it made me realize is that people like
Joel (and like me, I suppose) were drawn to this unentertaining
show because we felt like we knew what was going to happen next.
Understanding *Saved by the Bell* meant you understood what was
supposed to define the ultrasimplistic, hyperstereotypical high
school experience—and understanding that formula meant you
realized what was (supposedly) important about growing up.
It's like I said before: Important things are inevitably cliché.

Zack's relationship with Belding—and his niece—was just too creative, and bad television is supposed to be reassuring. Nobody needs it to be interesting.

Take a show like *M*A*S*H*, for instance. *M*A*S*H* consciously aspired to be "good television." Its goal was to be intellectually provoking (particularly over its final four seasons), so almost every plot hinged on a twist: The North Korean POW was actually more ethical then the South Korean soldier, Colonel Potter's visiting war buddy was actually corrupt, a much-decorated sergeant was actually killing off his black platoon members on purpose, etc., etc., etc. The first ten minutes of every *M*A*S*H* episode set strict conditions; the next twenty minutes would illustrate how life is not always as it seems.[3] This—in theory—is clever, and it's supposed to teach us something we don't know. Meanwhile, *Saved by the Bell* did the opposite. The first ten minutes of every episode put a character (usually Zack) in a position where he or she was tempted to do something that was obviously wrong, and their friends would warn them that this was a mistake. Then they would do it anyway, learn a lesson, and admit that everyone was right all along. *Saved by the Bell* wasn't ironic in the contemporary sense (i.e., detached and sardonic), and it wasn't even ironic in the literal sense (the intentions and themes of the story never contradicted what they stated ostensibly). You never learned anything, and you weren't supposed to.

Take the episode from the gang's senior year, where they went to a toga party hosted by a bloated jock nicknamed Ox. They all

---

3. In fact, *M*A*S*H* followed this template so consistently that these twists ultimately became completely predictable; whenever I watch *M*A*S*H* reruns, I immediately assume every guest star is a flawed hypocrite who fails to understand the horror of televised war. It should also be noted that there is one *Saved by the Bell* script that borrows this formula: When beloved pop singer Jonny Dakota comes to Bayside High to film an antidrug video, we quickly learn that he is actually a drug addict, although that realization is foreshadowed by the fact that Jonny is vaguely rude.

get drunk, but Zack claims to be able to drive Lisa's car home.[4] Before they climb into the vehicle, they all note how this is dangerous, because Zack might wreck the car. And (of course) he does just that. Obviously, NBC would claim this was a "message" episode, and it was supposed to show teenagers that alcohol and the highway are a deadly combination. But there's really no way anyone would *learn* anything from Zack's booze cruising. There's no kid in America who doesn't know that drinking and driving is dangerous, and there's no way that you could argue *Saved by the Bell* made this sentiment any more "in your face" than when Stevie Wonder sang "Don't Drive Drunk." It served no educational purpose, and it served no artistic purpose. But what it did was reestablish everyone's moral reality. If *Saved by the Bell* was a clichéd, uncreative teen sitcom (and I think we would all agree that it was), it needed to deliver the clichéd, uncreative plot: If these kids drink and drive, they will have to have a bad accident—but no one will actually die, because we all deserve a second chance. As I watched that particular episode in college, I took satisfaction in knowing that American morality was still basically the same as it had been when I was thirteen years old. It proved I still understood how the mainstream, knee-jerk populace looked at life, even though my personal paradigm no longer fit those standards.

Saved by the Bell was well-suited for conventional moralizing, because none of the characters had multifaceted ethics (or even situational ethics). Every decision they made was generated by whatever the audience would expect them to do; it was almost like the people watching the show wrote the dialogue. This was damaging to the *Saved by the Bell* actors, all of whom went to ridiculous lengths to avoid being typecast as their TV identities

4. It's been several years since I've seen this episode, but what I particularly remember about it is that—while intoxicated—all the kids sing a song in the car . . . and in my memory, the song they sing is Sweet's "Fox on the Run." However, that just can't be. It was probably something like "Help Me Rhonda."

once the show ended. Berkley was the most adamant about her reinvention, taking the lead role in the soft-porn box-office failure *Showgirls*, which even her costars couldn't fathom. "I wouldn't see why you'd want to go so far afield to change your image that you'd take a role so demanding or drastic as that," said a remarkably candid Screech in an 2002 interview with *The Onion A.V. Club*. "It pretty much was just the exploitation of a Saturday-morning icon, I feel. I don't think that the movie had any more substance than, 'Hey, we should go check it out to see the girl from *Saved by the Bell* naked!' That's pretty much what everyone went to the theater to see."

Yet Berkley was not alone; she was merely the only one who exposed her nipples. Thiessen elected to become the new Shannen Doherty on *Beverly Hills, 90210* and smoked pot in her very first episode. Lopez portrayed a homosexual as the star of *Breaking the Surface: The Greg Louganis Story*. Diamond started a prog rock band (!) who call themselves Salty the Pocket Knife. Gosselaar may have actually made the most disturbing transition, as he dyed his hair black and joined the cast of *NYPD Blue*, one of the most serious police dramas on TV; he essentially became an altogether different person. Only Lark Voorhies moved in a "logical" direction, taking a role on the soap opera *The Bold and the Beautiful*.

I'm not sure what all that signifies, really. I suppose it just proves how trapped these people must have felt, although some of that is clearly their own fault; Zack, Slater, Screech, and Kelly all appeared in the lone season of *Saved by the Bell: The College Years*, and Screech played a faculty member for most of the seven-season run of *Saved by the Bell: The New Class*. Those latter two shows—neither of which I watched consistently—made for a comfortable transition of loss: I saw the *Saved by the Bell* characters constantly, then periodically, and then not at all. It was actually a lot like my relationship with the friends from college who used to watch the show with me; I once saw guys like Joel constantly, then periodically, and then never. Which brings me to the aforementioned "Tori Paradox," a desperate move by the *Saved by the Bell* producers that accidentally became the program's most realistic avenue (and probably the clearest example of how there's nothing more true than a cliché).

The Tori Paradox is a little like the season of *Dukes of Hazzard* when Bo and Luke were momentarily replaced by their cousins Coy and Vance, two guys who were exactly like them (so much so that the blond guy still preferred to drive). Here's the crux of the incongruity: For half of the "senior year" at Bayside, Jessie (Berkley) and Kelly (Thiessen) are completely part of the action, just as they'd been for the last three seasons. However, they're suddenly absent for twelve consecutive episodes, having been replaced by "Tori," an attractive, brassy brunette in a black leather jacket who displays elements of both their personalities. Within moments of her arrival, Tori is completely absorbed into the Bayside gang; she's romantically pursued by Zack and Slater and generally behaves as if she has always been one of their closest friends. This lasts until the graduation episode (aired in prime time), when Kelly and Jessie suddenly reappear as if nothing ever happened. Meanwhile, Tori does not appear at graduation and is not even mentioned.

The motivation for these moves were purely practical; Berkley and Thiessen wanted to leave the cast, but NBC wanted to squeeze out a dozen more episodes of a show that was now quite popular (and being rerun four times a day on other networks). NBC essentially shot the graduation special (and another prime-time movie, *Saved by the Bell Hawaiian Style*), embargoed them for later use, and queued up the Tori era. It was the easiest way to extend the series. However, this rudimentary solution created a seemingly unfathomable scenario: Since both the "Tori episodes" and the "Kelly/Jessie episodes" were shown concurrently—sometimes on the same day—we were evidently supposed to conclude that these adventures were happening at the same time. Whenever we were watching Zack's attempts to scam on Tori, we were asked to assume that Kelly and Jessie were in the lunch room or at the mall or sick, and it was just a coincidence that nobody ever mentioned them (or introduced them to Tori, or even recognized their existence).

On paper, this seems idiotic, borderline insulting, and—above all—*unreal*. But the more I think back on my life, the more I've come to realize that the Tori Paradox might be the only element of *Saved by the Bell* that actually happened to me. Whenever I try to remember friends from high school, friends from college, or even just friends from five years ago, my memory always creates the illusion that we were together constantly, just like those kids on *Saved by the Bell*. However, this was almost never the case. Whenever I seriously piece together my past, I inevitably uncover long stretches where somebody who (retrospectively) seemed among my closest companions simply wasn't around. I knew a girl in college who partied with me and my posse constantly, except for one semester in 1993—she had a waitressing job at Applebee's during that stretch and could never make it to any parties. And even though we all loved her, I can't recall anyone mentioning her absence until she came back. And sometimes *I* was the person cut out of life's script: That very same semester, all my coworkers at our college newspaper temporarily decided I was a jerk and briefly froze me out of their lives; we later reunited, but now— whenever they tell nostalgic stories from that period—I'm always confused about why I can't remember what they're talking about . . . until I remember that I wasn't included in those specific memories. A few years later I started hanging out with a girl who liked to do drugs, so the two of us spent a year smoking pot in my poorly lit apartment while everyone else we knew continued to go out in public; when I eventually rejoined all my old acquaintances at the local tavern, I could kind of relate to how Kelly Kapowski must have felt after Tori evaporated. Coming and going is more normal than it should be.

So what does that mean? Maybe nothing. But maybe this: Conscious attempts at reality don't work. The character of Angela on ABC's short-lived drama *My So-Called Life* was byzantine and unpredictable and emotionally complex, and all that well-crafted nuance made her seem like an individual. But Angela was so much an individual that she wasn't like anyone but herself; she didn't reflect any archetypes. She was real enough to be interesting, but too real to be important. Kelly Kapowski was never real, so she ended up being a little like everybody (or at least like someone everybody used to know). The Tori Paradox was a lazy way for NBC to avoid thinking, but nobody watching at home blinked; it was openly ridiculous, but latently plausible. That's why the Tori Paradox made sense, and why it illustrated a greater paradox that matters even more: *Saved by the Bell* wasn't real, but neither is most of reality.

Life is chock-full of lies, but the biggest lie is math. That's particularly clear in the discipline of probability, a field of study that's completely and wholly fake. When push comes to shove—when you truly get down to the core essence of existence—there is only one mathematical possibility: Everything is 50-50. Either something will happen, or something will not.

When you flip a coin, what are the odds of it coming up heads? 50-50. Either it will be heads, or it will not. When you roll a six-sided die, what are the odds that you'll roll a three? 50-50. You'll either get a three, or you won't. That's reality. Don't fall into the childish "it's one-in-six" logic trap. That is precisely what all your adolescent authority figures want you to believe. That's how they enslave you. That's how they stole your conviction, and that's why you will never be happy. Either you will roll a three, or you will not; there are no other alternatives. The future has no memory. Certain things can be impossible, and certain things can be guaranteed—but there is no sliding scale for *maybe*. Maybe something will happen, or maybe it won't. That's all there is. What are the chances that your sister will die from ovarian cancer next summer? 50-50 (either she'll die from ovarian cancer or she won't). What are the chances that your sister will become America's most respected underwater welding specialist? 50-50. It will happen, or it won't. There are two possibilities, and both are plausible and unknown. The odds are 2:1. These facts are irrefutable.

Quasi-intellectuals like to claim that math is spiritual. They are lying. Math is not religion. Math is the antireligion, because it splinters the gravity of life's only imperative equation: Either something is true, or it isn't. Do or do not; there is no try.

12   Sulking with Lisa Loeb
on the Ice Planet Hoth   1:41

It's become cool to like *Star Wars*, which actually means it's
totally uncool to like *Star Wars*. I think you know what I mean by
this: There was a time in our very recent history when it was
"interesting" to be a *Star Wars* fan. It was sort of like admitting
you masturbate twice a day, or that your favorite band was They
Might Be Giants. *Star Wars* was something everyone of a certain
age secretly loved but never openly recognized; I don't recall
anyone talking about *Star Wars* in 1990, except for that select
class of *über*geeks who consciously embraced their sublime nerdi-
ness four years before the advent of Weezer (you may recall that
these were also the first people who told you about the Internet).
But that era has passed; suddenly it seems like everyone born
between 1963 and 1975 will gleefully tell you how mind-blowingly
important the *Star Wars* trilogy was to their youth, and it's slowly
become acceptable to make Wookie jokes without the fear of
alienation. This is probably Kevin Smith's fault.

What's interesting about this evolution is that the value of a
movie like *Star Wars* was vastly underrated at the time of its
release and is now vastly overrated in retrospect. In 1977, few
people realized this film would completely change the culture of
filmmaking, inasmuch as this was the genesis of all those blockbuster movies that everyone gets tricked into seeing summer
after summer after summer. *Star Wars* changed the social perception of what a movie was supposed to be; George Lucas,
along with Steven Spielberg, managed to kill the best era of
American filmmaking in less than five years. Yet—over time—

Star Wars has become one of the most overrated films of all time, inasmuch as it's pretty fucking terrible when you actually try to watch it. *Star Wars*'s greatest asset is that it's inevitably compared to 1983's *Return of the Jedi*, quite possibly the least-watchable major film of the last twenty-five years. I once knew a girl who claimed to have a recurring dream about a polar bear that mauled Ewoks; it made me love her.

However, the middle film in the *Star Wars* trilogy, *The Empire Strikes Back*, remains a legitimately great picture—but not for any cinematic reason. It's great for thematic, social reasons. It's now completely obvious that *The Empire Strikes Back* was the seminal foundation for what became "Generation X."[1] In a roundabout way, Boba Fett created Pearl Jam. While movies like *Easy Rider* and *Saturday Night Fever* painted living portraits for generations they represented in the present tense, *The Empire Strikes Back* might be the only example of a movie that set the social aesthetic for a generation coming in the future. The narrative extension to *The Empire Strikes Back* was not the Endor-saturated stupidity of *Return of the Jedi*; it was *Reality Bites*.

I concede that part of my bias toward *Empire* probably comes from the fact that it was the first movie I ever saw in a theater. This is a seminal experience for anyone, and I suppose it unconsciously shapes the way a person looks at cinema (I initially assumed all theatrical releases were prefaced by an expository text block that was virtually incomprehensible). The film was set in three static locations: The ice planet Hoth (which looked like North Dakota), the jungle system Dagobah (which was sort of like the final twenty minutes of *Apocalypse Now*), and the mining

---

1. I know nobody uses the term *Generation X* anymore, and I know all the people it supposedly describes supposedly hate the supposed designation. But I like it. It's simply the easiest way to categorize a genre of people who were born between 1965 and 1977 and therefore share a similar cultural experience. It's not pejorative or complimentary; it's factual. I'm a "Gen Xer," okay? And I buy shit marketed to "Gen Xers." And I use air quotes when I talk, and I sigh a lot, and I own a Human League cassette. Get over it.

community of Cloud City (apparently a cross between Las Vegas and Birmingham, Alabama). It's often noted by critics that this is the only *Star Wars* film that ends on a stridently depressing note: Han Solo is frozen in carbonite and torn away from Princess Leia, Luke gets his paw hacked off, and Darth Vader has the universe by the jugular. *The Empire Strikes Back* is the only blockbuster of the modern era to celebrate the abysmal failure of its protagonists. This is important; this is why *The Empire Strikes Back* set the philosophical template for all the slackers who would come of age ten years later. George Lucas built the army of clones that would eventually be led by Richard Linklater.

Now, I realize *The Empire Strikes Back* was not the first movie all future Gen Xers saw. I was eight when I saw *Empire*, and I distinctly remember that a lot of my classmates had already seen *Star Wars* (or at least its first theatrical rerelease) and of course they all loved it, mostly because little kids are stupid. But *Empire* was the first movie that people born in the early seventies could understand in a way that went outside of its rudimentary plotline. And that's why a movie about the good guys losing—both politically and romantically—is so integral to how people my age look at life.

When sociologists and journalists started writing about the sensibilities that drove Gen Xers, they inevitably used words like *angst-ridden* and *disenfranchised* and *lost*. As of late, it's become popular to suggest that this was a flawed stereotype, perpetuated by an aging media who didn't understand the emerging underclass.

Actually, everyone was right the first time.

All those original pundits were dead-on; for once, the media managed to define an entire demographic of Americans with absolute accuracy. Everything said about Gen Xers—both positive and negative—was completely true. Twenty-somethings in the nineties rejected the traditional working-class American lifestyle because (a) they were smart enough to realize those values were unsatisfying, and (b) they were totally fucking lazy. Twenty-somethings in the nineties embraced a record like Nirvana's *Nevermind* because (a) it was a sociocultural affront to the vapidity of the Reagan-era paradigm, and (b) it fucking rocked. Twenty-somethings in the nineties were by and large depressed about the future, mostly because (a) they knew there was very little to look forward to, and (b) they were obsessed with staring into the eyes of their own self-absorbed sadness. There are no myths about Generation X. It's all true.

This being the case, it's clear that Luke Skywalker was the original Gen Xer. For one thing, he was incessantly whiny. For another, he was exhaustively educated—via Yoda—about things that had little practical value (i.e., how to stand on one's head while lifting a rock telekinetically). Essentially, Luke went to the University of Dagobah with a major in Buddhist philosophy and a minor in physical education. There's not a lot of career opportunities for that kind of schooling; that's probably why he dropped out in the middle of the semester. Meanwhile, Luke's only romantic aspirations are directed toward a woman who (literally) looks at him like a brother. His dad is on his case to join the family business. Most significantly, all the problems in his life can be directly blamed on the generation that came before him, and specifically on his father's views about what to believe (i.e., respect authority, dress conservatively, annihilate innocent planets, etc.).

Studied objectively, Luke Skywalker was not very cool. But for kids who saw *Empire*, Luke was The Man. He was the guy we wanted to be. Retrospectively, we'd like to claim Han Solo was the single-most desirable character—and he was, in theory. But Solo's brand of badass cool is something you can't understand until you're old enough to realize that being an arrogant jerk is an attractive male quality. Third-graders didn't want to be gritty and misunderstood; third-graders wanted to be Mark Hamill. And even though obsessive thirty-year-old fans of the trilogy hate to admit it, these were always kids' movies. Lucas is not a Coppola or a Scorsese or even a De Palma—he makes movies that a sleepy eight-year-old can appreciate.[2] That's his gift, and he completely admits it. "I wanted to make a kids' film that would . . . introduce a kind of basic morality," Lucas told author David Sheff. And because the *Star Wars* movies were children's movies, Hamill had to be the center of the story. Any normal child was going to be drawn to Skywalker more than Solo. That's the personality we swallowed. So when all the eight-year-olds from 1980 turned twenty-one in 1993, we couldn't evolve. We were just old enough to be warped by childhood and just young enough not to realize it. Suddenly, we all wanted to be Han Solo. But we were stuck with Skywalker problems.

There's a scene late in *The Empire Strikes Back* where Luke and Vader are having their epic light-saber duel, and one particular shot is filmed from behind Mark Hamill. Within the context of this shot, Darth Vader is roughly twice the physical size of Luke; obviously, the filmmakers are trying to illustrate a point about the massive size of the Empire and the relative impotence of the fledgling Jedi. Not surprisingly, they all go a bit overboard: Vader's head appears larger than Luke's entire torso, which sort of overextends any suspension of disbelief a rational adult might harbor. But to a wide-eyed youngster, that image looked completely reasonable: If Vader is Luke's father (as we would learn minutes later), then Vader should seem as big as your dad.

As the scene continues, Luke is driven out onto a catwalk, where he loses his right hand and is informed that he's the heir to the intergalactic Osama bin Laden. He more or less tries to commit suicide. Now, Luke is saved from this fate (of course), and since this *is* a movie, logic tells us that (of course) Vader will fall in the next installment of the series, even though it will take three

2. Case in point: When *Episode I—The Phantom Menace* came out in 1999, all the adults who waited in line for seventy-two hours to buy opening-night tickets were profoundly upset at the inclusion of Jar Jar Binks. "He's annoying," they said. Well, how annoying would R2D2 have seemed if you hadn't been in the third fucking grade? Viewed objectively, R2D2 is like a dwarf holding a Simon.

years to get there. This is all understood. But that understanding is an adult understanding. As an eight-year-old, the final message of *The Empire Strikes Back* felt remarkably hopeless: Luke's a good person, *but Luke still lost*. And it wasn't like the end of *Rocky*, where Apollo Creed wins the split decision but Rocky wins a larger victory for the human spirit; Darth Vader beats Luke the way Ike used to beat Tina. A psychologist once told me that—over the span of her entire career—she had never known a man who didn't have some kind of creepy, unresolved issue with his father. She told me that's just an inherent part of being male. And here we have a movie where the hero is fighting every ideology he hates, gets his ass kicked, and is then informed, "Oh, and by the way: I'm your dad. But you knew that all along."

In this same scene, Darth Vader tells Skywalker he has to make a decision: He can keep fighting a war he will probably lose, or he can compromise his ethics and succeed wildly. Many young adults face a similar decision after college, and those seen as "responsible" inevitably choose the latter path. However, an eight-year-old would never sell out. Little kids will always take the righteous option. And what's intriguing about Gen Xers is they never really wavered from that decision. Luke's quandary in *The Empire Strikes Back* is exactly like the situation facing Winona Ryder in 1994's *Reality Bites*: Should she stick with the nice, sensible guy who treats her well (Ben Stiller), or should she roll the dice with the frustrating boho bozo who treats her like crap (Ethan Hawke)? For a detached adult, that answer seems obvious; for people who were twenty-one when this move came out, the answer was just as obvious but completely different. As we all know, Winona went with Hawke. She had to. When Gene Siskel and Roger Ebert reviewed *Reality Bites*, I recall them complaining that Ryder picked the wrong guy; as far as I could tell, choosing the wrong guy was the whole point.

You don't often see *Reality Bites* mentioned as an important (or even as a particularly good) film, but it grows more seminal with every passing year. When it was originally released, all its

Gap jokes and AIDS fears and Lisa Loeb songs merely seemed like marketing strategies and ephemeral stabs at insight. However, it's amazing how one film so completely captured every hyper-conventional ideal of such a short-lived era; *Reality Bites* is a period piece in the best sense of the term. And in the same way I have a special place in my heart for the first film I saw inside a movie house, I reserve a special place in my consciousness for the first film so unabashedly directed toward the condition of my own life. I was graduating from college the spring *Reality Bites* was released, and—though it didn't necessarily seem like a movie *about* me—it was clearly a movie *for* me. Eighteen months earlier, everyone I knew had seen Cameron Crowe's *Singles*, which we initially viewed as a youth movie. When we went back and rented *Singles* in the summer of 1994, I was suddenly struck by how old its cast seemed. I mean, they had full-time jobs and wanted to get married and have babies. *Singles* was just a normal romantic comedy that happened to have Soundgarden on the soundtrack. *Reality Bites* was an equally mediocre movie, but it validated a lot of mediocre lives, most notably my own. As I stated earlier, all the clichés about Gen Xers were true—but the point everyone failed to make was that our whole demographic was comprised of cynical optimists. Whenever my circa-1993 friends and I would sit around and discuss the future, there was always the omnipresent sentiment that the world was on the decline, but *we* were somehow destined to succeed individually. Everyone felt they would somehow be the exception within an otherwise grim universe. This is why Ryder had to pick Hawke. Winona made the kind of romantic decision most people my age would have made in 1994: She pursued a path that was difficult and depressing, and she did so because it showed the slightest potential for transcendence. Not coincidentally, this is also the Jedi's path. Adventure? Excitement? The Jedi craves not these things. However, he does crave something greater than the bloodless existence of his father. Quite simply, Winona Ryder *is* Luke Skywalker, only with a better haircut and a killer rack.

Part of the reason so many critics think *The Empire Strikes Back* is the best *Star Wars* movie is just a product of how theater works: *Empire* is the second act of a three-act production, and the second act is usually the best part. The second act contains the conflict. And as someone born in the summer of 1972, I've sort of come to realize I'm part of a second-act generation. The most popular three-act play of the twentieth century is obvious: The Depression (Act I), World War II (Act II), and the sock-hop serenity of Richie Cunningham's 1950s (Act III). The narrative arc is clear. But the play containing my life is a little more amorphous and a little less exciting, and test audiences are mixed: The first act started in 1962 and has a lot of good music and weird costumes, but the second act was poorly choreographed. Half the cast ran in place while the other half just sat around in coffeehouses, and we all tried to figure out what we were supposed to do with a society that had more media than intellect (and more irony than personality). Maybe the curtain on Act II fell with the World Trade Center. And as I look back at the best years of my life, I find myself wondering if maybe I wasn't unconsciously conditioned to exist somewhere in the middle of two better stories, caught between the invention of the recent past and the valor of the coming future. Personally, I don't think I truly understand invention or valor; they seem like pursuits that would require a light saber.

Within the circuits of my mind, the moments in *The Empire Strikes Back* I most adore are whenever Yoda gives his little Vince Lombardi speeches, often explaining that—in life—there is no inherent value to effort. "Do, or do not," says the greenish Mugsy Bogues. "There is no *try*." And that's an inspiring sentiment. It's the kind of logic that drives the world. But in my heart of hearts, the part of the film I can't shake is when Luke Skywalker and Han Solo are riding around Hoth on tauntans, which are (for all practical purposes) bipedal space horses. When things get rough, Han Solo cuts open the belly of a tauntan and stuffs

Luke inside the carcass; he saves him from a raging blizzard by encasing him in a cocoon of guts. I assume we're supposed to find this clever and disgusting (or maybe even inventive and heroic). But I just know I'd rather be inside the belly of the beast.

So I'm eating supper in a Kentucky Fried Chicken, and this crazy old woman who looks like a disheveled version of Minnie Pearl taps me on the shoulder and asks, "Can you buy me some chicken?" I, of course, say, "What?" Because this does not seem like an appropriate question. She asks again, "Can you buy me some chicken?" This time I flatly say no. Then she changes her query and asks, "Can I have a dollar to buy me some chicken?" I again decline, and she skulks away, exiting the establishment and camping out in front of the KFC sign on the sidewalk.

Ten minutes later, I finish the last nibble of my buttermilk biscuit, all the while watching this old woman through the window. She continues to unsuccessfully panhandle. As I leave the restaurant and begin walking home, I pass this woman and she stops me again. "Can you buy me some chicken?" she asks. Again I say, "What?" She proceeds to repeat her question, and—upon my silence—asks if she can instead have a dollar to buy some chicken for herself.

To me, this just seems like a poor business philosophy. I realize street people don't really provide a "service," per se, but—if you had to quantify what they *do* contribute into some kind of discernible social role—the most flattering description might be that they make us feel like we're part of a civilization. They are part of the urban landscape, they are reminders of how life is wicked, and they are profiles in courage.

Or at least they *could* be profiles in courage, if they weren't so goddamn inconsiderate. How can you not remember talking to me, old woman? It's not like you're haunted by career responsibilities and bombarded by stimuli; in the past ten minutes, you've merely asked random strangers for free chicken. Is recalling that I've already declined to give you my charity too much to ask? Must you treat me like a complete stranger? As members of the same civilization, can I not expect the courtesy of a knowing glance when you beg for chicken a second time?

That's the problem with homeless people: To them, we're all just a number.

13   The Awe-Inspiring Beauty of Tom Cruise's Shattered, Troll-like Face   1:51

Last night I awoke at 3:30 A.M. with a piercing pain in my abdomen, certain I had been infected by some sort of Peruvian parasite that was gnawing away at my small intestine. It felt like the Neptunes had remixed my digestive tract, severely pumping up the bass. Now, the details of my illness will not be discussed here, as they are unappetizing. However, there was one upside to this tragedy: I was forced to spend several hours in my bathroom reading old issues of *Entertainment Weekly*, which inadvertently recalibrated my perception of existence.

As a rule, I do not read film reviews of movies I have not seen. Honestly, I've never quite understood why anyone would want to be informed about the supposed value of a film before they actually experience it. Somewhat paradoxically, I used to earn my living reviewing films, and it always made me angry when people at dinner parties would try to make conversation by asking if they should (or shouldn't) see a specific film; I never wanted to affect the choices those people made. When writing reviews, I actively avoided anything that could be perceived as an attempt at persuasion. Moreover, I never liked explaining the plot of a movie, nor did I think it was remotely interesting to comment on the quality of the acting or the innovation of the special effects.

Perhaps this is why many people did not appreciate my film reviews.

However, the one thing I *did* like discussing was the "idea" of a given film, assuming it actually had one. This is also why I prefer reading film reviews of movies I've already seen; I'm always more interested in seeing if what I philosophically absorbed from a motion picture was conventional or atypical, and that can usually be deduced from what details the critic focuses on in his or her piece. This was particularly true on the morning of my cataclysmic tummy ache, when I stumbled across *EW*'s January 4, 2002, review of *Vanilla Sky*.

I am keenly aware that I am the only person in America who thought *Vanilla Sky* was a decent movie. This was made utterly lucid just forty-five seconds after it ended: As I walked out of the theater during the closing credits, other members of the audience actually seemed angry at what they had just experienced (in the parking lot outside the theater, I overheard one guy tell his girlfriend he was going to *beat her* for making him watch this picture!). Over the next few days, everything I heard about *Vanilla Sky* was about how it was nothing but a vanity project for Tom Cruise and that the story didn't make any sense; the overwhelming consensus was that this was an overlong, underthought abomination. This being the case, I was not surprised to see *EW*'s Owen Gleiberman give *Vanilla Sky* a grade of D+. His take seemed in-step with most of North America. However, I found myself perturbed with one specific phrase in O.G.'s review:

> The way that the film has been edited, none of the fake-outs and reversals have any weight; the more that they pile up, the less we hold on to any of them. We're left with a cracked hall of mirrors taped together by a *What is reality?* cryogenics plot and scored to [director] Cameron Crowe's record collection.

The phrase I take issue with is the prototypically snarky "*What is reality?*" remark, which strikes me as a profoundly misguided criticism. That particular question is precisely why I think *Vanilla Sky* was one of the more worthwhile movies I've seen in the past ten years, along with *Memento, Mulholland Drive, Waking Life, Fight Club, Being John Malkovich, The Matrix, Donnie Darko, eXistenZ,* and a scant handful of other films, all of which tangentially ask the only relevant question available for contemporary filmmakers: "*What is reality?*" It's insane of Gleiberman to suggest that posing this query could somehow be a justification for hating *Vanilla Sky*. It might be the only valid reason for loving it.

By now, almost everyone seems to agree that the number of transcendent mass-consumer films shrinks almost every year, almost to the point of their nonexistence. In fact, I'm not sure I've heard anyone suggest otherwise. Granted, there remains a preponderance of low-budget, deeply interesting movies that never play outside of major U.S. cities; Todd Solondz's twisted troika of *Welcome to the Dollhouse, Happiness,* and *Storytelling* is an obvious example, as are mildly subversive minor films like *Pi* and *Ghost World*. P. T. Anderson and Wes Anderson make great films that get press and flirt with commerce. However, the idea of making a sophisticated movie that could be brilliant *and* commercially massive is almost unthinkable, and that schism is relatively new. In the early seventies, *The Godfather* films made tons of money, won bushels of Academy Awards, and—most notably—were anecdotally regarded as damn-near perfect by every non-Italian tier of society, both intellectually and emotionally. They succeed in every dimension. That could never happen today; interesting movies rarely earn money, and Oscar-winning movies are rarely better than good. *Titanic* was the highest-grossing film of all time and the 1998 winner for Best Picture, so you'd think that might be an exception—but I've never met an intelligent person who honestly loved it. *Titanic* might have been the least watchable movie of the 1990s, because it was so obviously designed for audiences who don't really like movies (in fact, that was the key to its success). At this point, winning an Oscar is almost like winning a Grammy.

I realize citing the first two *Godfather* films is something of a cheap argument, since those two pictures are the pinnacle of the cinematic art form. But even if we discount Francis Ford Coppola's entire body of work, it's impossible to deny that the chances of seeing an *über*-fantastic film in a conventional movie house are growing maddeningly rare, which wasn't always the case. It wasn't long ago that movies like *Cool Hand Luke* or *The Last Picture Show* or *Nashville* would show up everywhere, and everyone would see them collectively, and everybody would have their consciousness shaken at the same time and in the same way. That never happens anymore (*Pulp Fiction* was arguably the last instance). This is mostly due to the structure of the Hollywood system; especially in the early 1970s, everybody was consumed with the auteur concept, which gave directors the ability to completely (and autonomously) construct a movie's vision; for roughly a decade, film was a director's medium. Today, film is a producer's medium (the only director with complete control over his product is George Lucas, and he elects to make kids' movies). Producers want to develop movies they can refer to as "high concept," which—somewhat ironically—is industry slang for "no concept": It describes a movie where the human element is secondary to an episodic collection of action sequences. It's "conceptual" because there is no emphasis on details. Capitalistically, those projects work very well; they can be constructed as "vehicles" for particular celebrities, which is the only thing most audiences care about, anyway. In a weird way, film studios are almost *requiring* movies to be bad, because they tend to be more efficient.

However, there's also a second reason we see fewer important adult films in the twenty-first century, and this one is nobody's fault. Culturally, there's an important cinematic difference between 1973 and 2003—and it has to do with the purpose movies serve. In the past, film validated social evolution. Look at Jack Nicholson: From 1969 to 1975, Nicholson portrayed an amazing array of characters—this was the stretch where he made *Easy Rider, Five Easy Pieces, Carnal Knowledge, The Last Detail,*

The King of Marvin Gardens, Chinatown, and *One Flew Over the Cuckoo's Nest.* It might be the strongest half decade any actor ever had (or at least the strongest five-year jag since the fall of the studio system). And what's most compelling is that all the people he played during that run were vaguely unified by a singular quality. For a long time, I could never put my finger on what that was. I finally figured it out when I came across a late-eighties profile on Nicholson in *The New York Times Magazine:* "I like to play people who haven't existed yet," Jack said. "A future something."

Nicholson was particularly adroit at embodying those future somethings, but he was not alone. This was what good movies did during that period—they were visions of a present tense that was just around the corner. When people talk about the seventies as a Golden Era, they tend to talk about cinematic techniques and artistic risks. What they should be discussing is sociology. The filmmaking process is slow and expensive, so movies are always the last idiom to respond to social evolution; the finest films from the seventies were really just the manifestation of how art and life had changed in the sixties. After a generation of being entertained by an illusion of simplicity and the clarity of good vs. evil, a film like *Five Easy Pieces* offered the kind of psychological complexity people were suddenly relating to in a very personal way. What people like Nicholson were doing was *introducing* audiences to the new American reality: counterculture as the dominant culture.

Unfortunately, that kind of introduction can't happen in 2003. It can't happen because reality is more transient and less concrete. It's more difficult for a film to define and validate the current of popular culture, because that once linear current has been splintered; it's become a cracked Volvo windshield, spider-webbing itself in a manner that's generally predictable but specifically chaotic (in other words, we all *sort of* know where the national ethos is going, but never *exactly* how or *exactly* why or *exactly* when). Cinematically, this creates a problem. Traditional character models like "The Everyman" and "The Antihero" and

"The Wrongly Accused" are no longer useful, because nobody can agree on what those designations are supposed to mean anymore (in Christopher Nolan's *Memento,* all three of those labels could simultaneously be applied to the same person). Modern movies can no longer introduce impending realities; they can't even explain the ones we currently have. Consequently, there's only one important question a culturally significant film can still ask: What *is* reality?

I'll concede that *Vanilla Sky* poses that question a little too literally at times, inasmuch as I vaguely recall one scene where Tom Cruise is riding in an elevator and someone looks at him and literally asks, "What is reality?" The cryogenics subplot is also a tad silly, since it sometimes seems like an infomercial for Scientology and/or an homage to Arnold Schwarzenegger's *Total Recall.* But fuck it—I'm not going to overcompensate and list a bunch of criticisms about a movie I honestly liked, and I *did* like *Vanilla Sky.* And what I liked was the way it presented the idea of objectivity vs. perception, which is ultimately what the "What is reality" quandary comes down to. In *Vanilla Sky,* Cruise plays a dashing magazine publisher. He likes to casually bang Cameron Diaz, but he falls in love with the less attainable Penelope Cruz (it is a credit to Cruz that she makes this situation seem plausible; Penelope is so cute in this film that I found myself siding with Cruise and thinking, "Why the hell would anyone want to have sex with a repulsive hosebag like Cameron Diaz?"). When Diaz figures out that Cruise has been unfaithful, she goes bonkers and tries to kill them both by driving a car off a bridge. She dies, but Cruise escapes—with a horribly disfigured face. Despite his grotesque appearance, he still pursues a satisfying relationship with Cruz and intends to repair his mangled grill through a series of plastic surgeries. Against all odds, his life (and his face) improves. But then it turns out that the diabolical Diaz is still alive . . . or maybe not . . . maybe she and Cruz are actually the same person . . . or maybe neither exists, because this is all a fantasy. Frankly, whatever answer Crowe wanted us to deduce is irrelevant. What matters is that Cruise ultimately has to decide between a fake world that feels real and a real world that feels like torture.

Cruise chooses the latter, although I'm not sure why. Keanu Reeves makes the same choice in *The Matrix*, electing to live in a realm that is dismal but genuine. Like *Vanilla Sky*, the plot of *The Matrix* hinges on the premise that everything we think we're experiencing is a computer-generated illusion: In a postapocalyptic world, a band of kung fu terrorists wage war against a society of self-actualized machines who derive their power from human batteries, all of whom unknowingly exist in a virtual universe referred to as "the matrix." *The Matrix* would suggest that everything you're feeling and experiencing is just a collective dream the whole world is sharing; nobody is actually living, but nobody's aware that they aren't.

For Reeves's character, Neo, choosing to live in the colorless light of hard reality is an easy decision, mostly because *The Matrix* makes the distinction between those two options very clear: reality may be a difficult brand of freedom, but unreality is nothing more than comfortable slavery. Cruise's decision in *Vanilla Sky* is similar, although less sweeping; his choice has more to do with the "credibility" of his happiness (his fake life would be good, but not *satisfying*). Both men prefer unconditional reality. This is possibly due to the fact that both films are really just sci-fi stories, and science fiction tends to be philosophy for stupid people.[1] Every protagonist in a sci-fi story is ultimately a moral creature who does the right thing, often resulting in his own valiant destruction (think Spock in *The Wrath of Khan*). But what's intriguing about Keanu and Cruise is that I'm not sure I agree that choosing hard reality *is* the "right thing." *The Matrix* and *Vanilla Sky* both pose that question—which I appreciate—but their conclusions don't necessarily make logical (or emotional) sense. And that doesn't mean these are bad movies; it just

---

1. As opposed to this essay, which tends to be philosophy for shallow people.

forces us to see a different reflection than the director may have intended. It probably makes them *more* intriguing.

The reason I think Cruise and Reeves make flawed decisions is because they are not dealing with specific, case-by-case situations. They are dealing with the entire scope of their being, which changes the rules. I would never support the suggestion that ignorance is bliss, but that cliché takes on a totally different meaning when the definition of "ignorance" becomes the same as the definition for "existence."

Look at it this way: Let's assume you're a married woman, and your husband is having an affair. If this is the only lie in your life, it's something you need to know. As a singular deceit, it's a problem, because it invalidates every other truth of your relationship. However, let's say *everyone* is lying to you *all the time*— your husband, your family, your coworkers, total strangers, etc. Let's assume that no one has ever been honest with you since the day you started kindergarten, and you've never suspected a thing. In this scenario, there is absolutely no value to learning the truth about anything; if everyone expresses the same construction of lies, those lies *are* the truth, or at least a kind of truth. But the operative word in this scenario is *everyone*. Objective reality is not situational; it doesn't evolve along with you. If you were raised as a strict Mormon and converted into an acid-eating Wiccan during college, it would seem like your reality had completely evolved—but the only thing that would be different is your perception of a world that's still exactly the same. That's not the situation Cruise and Reeves face in these movies. They are not looking for the true answer to one important question; they are choosing between two unilateral truths that apply to absolutely everything. And all the things we want out of life—pleasure, love, enlightenment, self-actualization, whatever—can be attained *within either realm*. They both choose the "harder" reality, but only because the men who made *The Matrix* and *Vanilla Sky* assume that option is more optimistic. In truth, both options are exactly the same. Living as an immaterial cog in the matrix would be no better or worse than living as a fully-aware human; existing in a cryogenic dreamworld would be no less credible than existing in corporeal Manhattan.

The dreamworld in Richard Linklater's staggering *Waking Life* illustrates this point beautifully, perhaps because that idea is central to its whole intention. *Waking Life* is an animated film about a guy (voiced by Wiley Wiggins) who finds himself inside a dream he cannot wake from. As the disjointed story progresses, both the character and the audience conclude that Wiggins is actually dead. And what's cool about *Waking Life* is that this realization is not the least bit disturbing. Wiggins's response is a virtual nonreaction, and that's because he knows he is not merely in a weird situation; he is walking through an alternative reality. Instead of freaking out, he tries to understand how his new surroundings compare to his old ones.

There are lots of mind-expanding moments in *Waking Life*, and it's able to get away with a lot of shit that would normally seem pretentious (it's completely plotless, its characters lecture about oblique philosophical concepts at length, and much of the action is based on people and situations from Linklater's 1991 debut film, *Slacker*). There are on-screen conversations in *Waking Life* that would be difficult to watch in a live-action picture. But *Waking Life* doesn't feel self-indulgent or affected, and that's because it's a cartoon: Since we're not seeing real people, we can handle the static image of an old man discussing the flaws of predestination. Moreover, we can accept the film's most challenging dialogue exchange, which involves the reality of our own interiority.

The scene I'm referring to is where Wiggins's character meets a girl and goes back to her apartment, and the girl begins explaining her idea for a surrealistic sitcom. She asks if Wiggins would like to be involved. He says he would, but then asks a much harder question in return: "What does it feel like to be a character in someone else's dream?" Because that's who Wiggins realizes this person is; he is having a lucid dream, and this woman is his own subconscious construction. But the paradox is that this woman is able to express thoughts and ideas that Wiggins himself could never create. Wiggins mentions that her idea for the TV show is great, and it's the kind of thing he could never have come up with—but since this is *his* dream, he must have done exactly that. And this forces the question that lies behind "What is reality?": *"How do we know what we know?"*

This second query in what brings us to *Memento,* probably the most practical reality study I've ever seen on film. The reason I say "practical" is because it poses these same abstract questions as the other films I've already mentioned, but it does so without relying on an imaginary universe. Usually, playing with the question of reality requires some kind of *Through the Looking Glass* trope: In *Waking Life,* Wiggins's confusion derives from his sudden placement into a dream. Both *The Matrix* and *Vanilla Sky* take place in nonexistent realms. *Being John Malkovich* is founded on the ability to crawl into someone's brain through a portal in an office building; *Fight Club* is ultimately about a man who isn't real; *eXistenZ* is set inside a video game that could never actually exist. However, *Memento* takes place in a tangible place and merely requires an implausible—but still entirely *possible*—medical ailment.

Memento is about a fellow named Leonard (Guy Pearce) who suffers a whack to the head and can no longer create new memories; he still has the long-term memories from before his accident, but absolutely no short-term recall. He forgets everything that happens to him three minutes after the specific event occurs.[2] This makes life wildly complicated, especially since his singular goal is to hunt down the men who bonked him on the skull before proceeding to rape and murder his wife.

2. Unfortunately, this does create the one gaping plot hole the filmmakers chose to ignore entirely, probably out of necessity: If Leonard can't form new memories, there is no way he could comprehend that he even has this specific kind of amnesia, since the specifics of the problem obviously wouldn't have been explained to him until after he already acquired the condition.

Since the theme of *Memento* is revenge and the narrative construction is so wonderfully unconventional (the scenes are shown in reverse order, so the audience—like Leonard—never knows what just happened), it would be easy to find a lot of things in this movie that might appear to define it. However, the concept that's most vital is the way it presents memory as its own kind of reality. When *Memento* asks the *"What is reality?"* question, it actually provides an answer: Reality is a paradigm that always seems different and personal and unique, yet never really is. Its reality is autonomous.

There's a crucial moment in *Memento* where Leonard describes his eternal quest to kill his wife's murderers, and the person sitting across from him makes an astute observation: This will be the least satisfying revenge anyone will ever inflict. Even if Leonard kills his enemies, he'll never remember doing so. His victory won't just be hollow; it will be instantaneously erased. But Leonard disagrees. "The world doesn't disappear when you close your eyes, does it?" he snaps. "My actions still have meaning, even if I can't remember them."

What's ironic about Leonard's point is that it's completely true—yet even Leonard refuses to accept what that sentiment means in its totality. Almost no one ever does.

I'm not sure if anyone who's not a soap opera character truly gets amnesia; it might be one of those fictional TV diseases, like environmental illness or gum disease. However, we all experience intermittent amnesia, sometimes from drinking Ketel One vodka[3] but usually from the rudimentary passage of time. We refer to this phenomenon as "forgetting stuff." (*Reader's note: I realize I'm not exactly introducing ground-breaking medical data right now, but bear with me.*) Most people consider forgetting stuff to be a normal part of living. However, I see it as a huge problem; in a way, there's nothing I fear more. The strength of your memory dictates the size of your reality. And since objective reality is fixed, all we

3. Holland's #1 memory-destroying vodka!

can do is try to experience—to *consume*—as much of that fixed reality as possible. This can only be done by living in the moment (which I never do) or by exhaustively filing away former moments for later recall (which I do all the time).

Taoists constantly tell me to embrace the present, but I only live in the past and the future; my existence is solely devoted to (a) thinking about what will happen next and (b) thinking back to what's happened before. The present seems useless, because it has no extension beyond my senses. To me, living a carpe diem philosophy would make me like Leonard. His reality is based almost entirely on faith: Leonard believes his actions have meaning, but he can't experience those meanings (or even recall the actions that caused them). He knows hard reality is vast, but his soft reality is minuscule. And in the film's final sequence, we realize that he understands that all too well; ultimately, he lies to himself to expand it. In a sense, he was right all along; his actions do have meaning, even if he doesn't remember them. But that meaning only applies to an objective reality he's not part of, and that's the only game in town.

It's significant that the character of Rita in David Lynch's *Mulholland Drive* is a woman with total amnesia, and that we're eventually forced to conclude that she might be nothing but a figment of another character's imagination.[4] It's almost like Lynch is saying that someone who can't remember who they are really doesn't exist. Once your reality closes down to zero, you're no longer part of it. So maybe that's the bottom line with all of these films. Maybe the answer to *"What is reality?"* is this: Reality is both reflexive and inflexible. It's not that we all create our own reality, because we don't; it's not that there is no hard reality, because there is. We can't alter reality—but reality can't exist unless we know it's there. It depends on us as much as we depend on it.

---

4. For those of you who've seen *Mulholland Drive* and never came to that conclusion, the key to this realization is when the blonde girl (Naomi Watts) masturbates.

We're all in this together, people.

Semidepressing side note: Eight months after reading Owen Gleiberman's review in *EW*, I woke up with another tummy ache in the middle of the night (this time at a Days Inn in Chicago). The only thing I had to read was the July 15 issue of *Time* magazine that came with the hotel room, so I started looking at the "letters" page. All the letters were about Tom Cruise (*Time* had just done a cover story on Cruise after the release of Steven Spielberg's film version of Philip K. Dick's *Minority Report*). These are two of them:

> I was glad to see Tom Cruise, the most respected person in show biz, on the cover of *Time*. In general, Hollywood actors contribute little to society, other than mere amusement. Cruise, however, is different. He isn't simply another mindless entertainer. He is a role model who overcame his childhood problems by being confident and motivated.
>
> —Daniel Liao, Calgary

> Was this article intended to help Tom Cruise regain his clean-cut image? He lost so much of it when he left his wife and children. Most alpha males need to control the women in their lives, and since Nicole Kidman has come into her own, it appears that Cruise moved on to a woman he had more control over. Are you going to be doing a cover on Kidman? She is the one who has had to go through the humiliation of being dumped by a famous husband and deal with being a single mom. She is a much more interesting person.
>
> —Susan Trinidad, Spanaway (Wash.)

My first reaction to these letters was guttural: "Since when does *Time* publish letters that are written by rival publicists?" However, as I sat there in pain, feeling as though my stomach was being vacuumed through the lower half of my torso and into the bowels of this Illinois hotel, I was struck by the more frightening realization: *These are* not *publicists!* They are just everyday people, and they are some of the people I am trying to understand reality alongside. Somehow, there are literate men in Canada who believe Tom Cruise is a respected role model and "different" from all the other actors who contribute nothing but "mere amusement." Somehow, there are women in the Pacific Northwest who think Nicole Kidman is interesting and wonderful and an icon of single motherhood, and that little five-foot-seven Cruise is an "alpha male" (even though everyone I know halfway assumes he's gay). These are the things they feel strongly about, because these are things they know to be true.

We don't have a fucking chance.

I hate punk rock.

Actually, that's not true; I kind of like punk rock, sometimes. What I hate are people who *love* punk rock. There has never been a genre of anything that has made more people confused about what art is capable of doing, and they all refuse to shut up about it.

A few years ago, one of my favorite humans of all time died from bone cancer. A few hours after the funeral, I found myself in a conversation with someone who was as depressed as I was and almost as drunk. But—in order to avoid talking about our friend, probably— we started talking about pop music, and this guy kept saying, "Punk rock saved my life." He said it like four times in ten minutes. "When I was in high school," he insisted, "punk totally saved my life. If not for that music, I wouldn't be here today. Punk rock saved my life, man."

I have heard those exact words said thousands of times by hundreds of people, and none of them are ever joking. They exist in a culture of certainty. They want to believe what they are saying *so much*. They want to believe that this sentiment is literally true. And all I could do while I listened to this dude tell me how punk rock saved his life was think, Wow. Why did my friend waste all that time going to chemotherapy? I guess we should have just played him a bunch of shitty Black Flag records.

14   Toby over Moby   1:66

In November of 2000 I reviewed a concert by the Dixie Chicks in downtown Cleveland. A sold-out show. A big deal, sort of. And at the time, I didn't know a goddamn thing about the Dixie Chicks, beyond what information could be gleaned from their name (which—in my defense—is probably more expository than just about any other pop moniker I can think of, except for maybe the Stooges).

I can't recall if I liked this concert, but I suspect I probably enjoyed half of it. I mostly vaguely recall that Nathan from MTV's *The Real World 7: Seattle* was somehow involved with the event's promotion, and I clearly remember getting several angry phone calls from readers who read my review the next morning and thought I was cruel for suggesting that Chicks singer Natalie Maines had an "oddly shaped body, fleshy cheekbones, and weird fashion sense." It turns out Natalie Maines was pregnant. I am nothing if not underinformed.

But ANYWAY, Natalie's uterus is not the issue here. What struck me about this show was the audience, which appeared to be a cross-section of forty-one-year-old gay males outfitted from Old Navy and fifteen-year-old teenage girls with above-average teeth. I had never before seen so many teenage girls at a concert with *real* musicians, which is what the Dixie Chicks are. Obviously, we're all used to seeing thousand of adolescent females at Britney Spears and 'NSYNC concerts, but those shows have nothing to do with music; those are just virgin-filled Pepsi commercials. It's a teenage girl's *job* to like that shit. But the Dixie Chicks aren't part of that marketing scheme; there was one stunning moment in the middle of the evening's festivities where

Martie Seidel shredded on her fiddle like she was trying to start a California brushfire, and the foggy arena air tasted exactly like the omnipresent ozone from every pre-grunge, big-hair heavy metal show I attended in the late eighties. I looked around the building and I saw all my old friends from high school, only now they had breasts and were named Phoebe. And that's when I realized that teenage girls are the new teenage boys, which is why the Dixie Chicks are the new Van Halen, which is why country music is awesome.

Contrary to what you may have heard from Henry Rollins or/and Ian MacKaye and/or anyone else who joined a band after working in an ice cream shop, you can't really learn much about a person based on what kind of music they happen to like. As a personality test, it doesn't work even half the time. However, there is at least *one* thing you *can* learn: The most wretched people in the world are those who tell you they like every kind of music "except country." People who say that are boorish and pretentious at the same time. All it means is that they've managed to figure out the most rudimentary rule of pop sociology; they know that hipsters gauge the coolness of others by their espoused taste in sound, and they know that hipsters hate modern country music. And they hate it because it speaks to normal people in a tangible, rational manner. Hipsters hate it because they hate Midwesterners, and they hate Southerners, and they hate people with real jobs.

Now, obviously, this hipster distaste doesn't apply to *old* country music, because everybody who's cool *loves* that stuff (or at least claims to). Nobody questions the value of George fucking Jones. It's completely acceptable for coolies to adore the idea of haggard nineteen-year-old men riding in cabooses and having their hearts shattered, which is why alternative country is the most popular musical genre of the last twenty-five years that's managed to remain completely unpopular (if you follow my meaning). I once asked Uncle Tupelo founder Jay Farrar about how his audiences changed as alt country became a phenomenon.

"What audiences are you talking about?" he asked me back. "Do you mean the two hundred rock critics who actually care?" Farrar was sort of joking when he said that, but he wasn't laughing. And he was probably more right than wrong. Columbia decided to rerelease all of Farrar's early Uncle Tupelo albums on the imprint label Legacy, but it seems like the only people buying them are simply buying them *again*. On the surface, that's a bit sad, because it seems like Uncle Tupelo wrote great songs that deserve to be significant. However, the operative word in that sentence is "seems." What they really wrote were great songs that had no genuine significance whatsoever. I think the person who explained this most clearly was indie rocker/average poet David Berman of the Silver Jews, speaking to the *Nashville Scene* right after he moved to Tennessee. One gets the impression the reporter must have made reference to the "authenticity" of modern country music when she asked Berman a question:

"One thing that cracks me up in the Nashville local music scene," Berman said in response, "is this verbal battle between Music Row and alt-country. Alternative country, to me, is just as ridiculously empty in a different way—it's just that they're not in power. All these people singing about a life they never knew—it's really a fetishization of Depression-era country life. If authenticity is the issue, then there's something more authentic to me about Wal-Mart country, which speaks to the real needs of the people who listen to it, more than talking about grain whiskey stills."

Granted, the best alt country songs *feel* authentic, and that should be enough (and in the idiom of pop music, it usually is). The problem is that guys like Farrar embrace a reality that's archaic and undesirable; the only listeners who appreciate what they're expressing are affluent intellectuals who've glamorized the alien concept of poverty. The lyrics on a track like "Screen Door" off *No Depression* have the texture of something old and profound, but they're not; technically, those lyrics are more modern than everything off Nine Inch Nails' *Pretty Hate Machine*. And more important, they're only viewed to be profound by people who've never had the experience described in the lyrics.[1] Truly depressed people don't need depressing music. I don't think I would have had any interest in hearing lines like, *"Down here, where we're at / Everybody is equally poor"* when I was sixteen, sitting in my parents' basement in rural North Dakota, only vaguely aware that I (and everyone I knew) had no fucking money. I probably would have thought Jeff Tweedy was whining. Oddly (or maybe predictably), I love that song today. But that's because the lyrics no longer apply to the actual condition of my life. I would guess the prototypical Uncle Tupelo fan earns around $52,000 a year and has two VCRs. I would also guess they don't shop at Berman's aforementioned Wal-Mart, which is where mainstream country music sells like Pokémon.

"I definitely don't feel a part of what I call the straighter country music industry of Nashville," said critical alt country darling Lucinda Williams in a 2001 *Billboard* interview. "I'm definitely not connected with that world. Nashville is so straight. I guess I'm sort of considered an outlaw here with Steve Earle. They used to write grittier stuff. It's gotten so puritanical . . . I don't want to be identified with the stuff that's on country radio now. Country music to me is Hank Williams and Loretta Lynn."

Well, good for you, Lucinda. It's nice to see you've jammed the pretension of Kill Rock Stars into country music. Granted, there is some truth to what Williams says; she's certainly doing what she can to keep her own music "grittier," inasmuch as she likes to make albums about gravel roads. But this quote is really just an example of why Lucinda Williams's music won't matter in twenty years. Oh, she'll be *remembered historically*, because the brainiacs who write pop reference books will always include her name under W. She'll be a nifty signpost for music geeks. But her songs will die like softcover books filled with postmodern poetry,

---

1. This is similar to the way rich white kids in places like suburban Connecticut fell in love with N.W.A. records in the early nineties.

endorsed by Robert Pinsky and empty to everyone else. Lucinda Williams does not matter.

The Dixie Chicks, however, do matter. They matter in the way *big things* matter . . . which is to say they matter without duplicity, which is to say they matter the way Van Halen did in 1981.[2] What you have with the Dixie Chicks is real bluegrass music that doesn't sound like traditional roots music, just as Eddie Van Halen played blues-based guitar licks that didn't sound anything like John Lee Hooker. Like Van Halen, the Dixie Chicks added a blond singer to make the band an arena-ready megaforce, and—like Van Halen—the Dixie Chicks kicked a singer out of the band when she seemed like dead weight. The Dixie Chicks' best song is "There's Your Trouble," which is about the pain of seeing your man with the wrong woman, and Maines ain't talkin' 'bout love, because love is rotten to the core. But all those coincidences are really just peripheral. The single-biggest proof that the Dixie Chicks are Van Halen is their audience; they are singing to the same teenage boys, except those boys are now teenage girls.

Here's what I mean: For the past twenty-five years, culture has been obsessed with making males and females more alike, and that's fine. Maybe it's even enlightened. But what I've noticed—at least among young people—is that this convergence has mostly just prompted females to adopt the worst qualities of men. It's like girls are trying to attain equality by becoming equally shallow and selfish. Whenever I see TV shows like Fox's defunct *Ally McBeal* or HBO's *Sex and the City,* I find myself perplexed as to how this is sometimes viewed as an "advancement" for feminism; it seems to imply that it's empowering for women to think like all of the stupidest men I know (myself included). We've all heard the argument that there is an eternal double standard about promiscuity: The cliché is that girls who sleep around are inevitably labeled "sluts" while guys who make the rounds are

2. Although it should be noted that David Lee Roth seemed to have no problem with Ronald Reagan hailing from California.

dubbed "studs" (in fact, I hear people making *this particular point* far more often than I hear anyone literally calling women "sluts" or men "studs"). What's interesting about that argument is the way it's been absorbed by my generation and all the generations that have followed: The consensus is that this double standard is wrong, so—therefore—we should *all* have sex with as many peo-ple as possible, regardless of our gender. Somehow, this became logical. And that's why modern fifteen-year-old girls are like fif-teen-year-old boys from 1981: They're saturated not only with internal sexual intensity, but also with the social belief that they *should* be having sex. And this manifests itself in strange ways. In the 1960s, the Rolling Stones realized that if you could make an audience unconsciously think about fucking, you could control the way they respond to music. Mick and Keith manufactured sexual aggression. Van Halen didn't have to manufacture that sen-timent, because their audience was already an ocean of lust, desperately wanting The Big Loud Show. In 1981, that ocean was adolescent boys. But Sarah Jessica Parker and Calista Flockhart have turned adolescent girls into adolescent boys, and those girls want their own Van Halen. And their version of Van Halen is Martie Seidel playing "Eruption" on a fiddle.

This is one example of why Wal-Mart country will never become unpopular, even though nobody I know seems to openly embrace it: It's flexible, and it's reflexive. It's flexible because nobody in the media (outside of Tennessee) seems to care how it operates, so it can quietly make adjustments and corrections to fit its zeitgeist; country music evolves a little like the stock mar-ket. It's reflexive because it doesn't place an artistic premium on creating new ideas; nobody expects Clint Black to be the *first* guy to come up with *anything*. Nobody even expects him to write his own songs. As a consequence, the organic themes in Wal-Mart country filter *up* from its audience. They actually come from the people shopping in Wal-Mart. And when those Wal-Mart shop-pers eventually hear their own ideas on the radio, it somehow seems fresh. While rock and hip-hop constantly try to break

171

through to a future consciousness—and while alt country tries to replicate a lost consciousness from the 1930s—modern country artists validate the experience of living right here, right now.

This started to become clear as glass in the early 1990s. At the time, the presumption in the media was that grungy Sasquatch rockers were emerging as a more "realistic" reflection of public sentiment, apparently because the musicians dressed like laid-off factory employees and down-tuned their guitars. This was not without justification; I will concede that this posit seemed completely sensible at the time. But—with the exception of the second Nirvana album, the first three Pearl Jam records, and maybe four or five Soundgarden songs—that music has not sustained a significant life outside its brief window of import. Most of that music already comes across as dated as disco. But what *has* continued to matter are crappy country songs like Trisha Yearwood's 1991 single "She's in Love with the Boy," which probably means it isn't entirely crappy.

"She's in Love with the Boy" is almost like something the Ronettes could have done: A sweet girl named Katie is dating a local bonehead named Tommy, and everyone in town—particularly Katie's father—thinks she can do better. However, their love is ultimately vindicated by Katie's mother, who explains that she was once dating a local bonehead whom everyone hated, and that man became Katie's father. Certainly, this is not an innovative narrative (in fact, I think it was actually an episode from the 1991 season of *The Wonder Years*, costarring David Schwimmer as "the bonehead"). However, there are two elements to this song that make it amazingly evocative to a certain kind of listener. The irony is that they're the same elements that make intellectuals despise modern country music.

The first is that the lyrics to this song are highly specific, but secretly universal. I'm referring particularly to lines like *"But later on, outside the Tastee Freeze / Tommy slips something on her hand / He says, "My high school ring will have to do / Till I can buy a wedding band."* Proposing marriage at a Tastee Freeze is not exactly romantic, but it *is* important, just as it was when scruffy little Johnny Cougar mentioned eating chili dogs "outside the Tastee Freeze" in the song "Jack and Diane." Tastee Freezes are iconic structures in the rural Midwest, because they say something about your hometown; they irrefutably prove your community does not have enough of a population to sustain a Dairy Queen. In fact, you don't even have enough of a population to sustain an ice cream facility *with indoor seating* (you might notice that both Yearwood and Cougar describe encounters that take place *outside* the Tastee Freeze, presumably in the parking lot). Tastee Freezes are the places that remind you how isolated you are; a Tastee Freeze is like an oasis. And even though they're everywhere, you don't realize that until you move away. It's a circular reality: Tastee Freezes exist where people are disconnected from the rest of the world—and that very disconnection makes them all seem autonomous. So when Yearwood mentions this kind of coquettish proposal between two overtly archetypical teenagers, it cuts an amazingly wide swath. It's what David Berman means when he says that Wal-Mart country reflects the lives of its audience. There are thousands of people in this country who still can't believe Trish Yearwood perfectly described the teenage experience of someone they know in real life. And the amazing thing is that they're all correct.

However, there's another reason why a song like "She's in Love with the Boy" is so successful, and it's even less complicated. "She's in Love with the Boy" is easy to understand—and I don't mean intellectually. I mean *literally*. A huge part of why somebody like Yearwood connects so deeply with so many people (she has career sales approaching 11 million) is because her words can be easily heard and immediately contextualized, even when a person casually hears them one time. I'm sure that sounds like a moronically obvious argument for what makes a piece of music good, but I've come to realize it's one of those painfully obvious things that everyone who's allegedly enlightened seems to deny.

Whenever you talk to collegiate musicologists about music,

they will often complain that rock writers place entirely too much emphasis on the content of song lyrics. Academics tend to argue that lyrics have only nominal importance; they will say that pop critics tend to see pop songs as having two parts—words and music—and that this is an example of ignorance. They think the words to a song like the Beatles' "Helter Skelter" are only a fraction of the total creation; the lyrics have no more individual importance than the guitar chords, or Ringo's drum fills, or George Martin's production, or any other component. Moreover, they'll tell you that song lyrics are not really poetry, because they only matter when they're married to a specific piece of music and are often used as filler; lyrics usually say very little about the songwriter and are more important for how practical they are (i.e., "Can I match a melody to this?") than for how deep they are (i.e., "What does this mean?"). What's funny is that rock writers sort of validate those suggestions, but only because they take the appreciation of lyrical content too far. They're exclusively focused on how *clever* lyrics are, even if that cleverness is only appreciated by their peers (for example, rock critics love David Berman's buddy Stephen Malkmus, and he is indeed very talented—although I sometimes wonder how funny jokes about Geddy Lee's voice are to people who have never listened to a Rush album).[3]

The net result of all this is that discernible lyrics are—by and large—dismissed. The elitist belief is that hearing what an artist is saying is either (a) totally irrelevant, or (b) only relevant when difficult. And what these elitists forget is that normal people never think like that. Normal people want to hear what artists are saying, and normal people tend to perceive the vox as the sole identity of the artistic product. This is completely clear to anyone who steps back and just looks at what material works outside of New York and L.A. I find it amusing that so many pundits have tried to create explanations for why Eminem is so polarizing (people say

3. And don't even get me *started* on the line "You're my fact-checking cuz"!

that it's just because he's white, or that it's all because of Dr. Dre, or that it's just because he's controversial, etc.). To me, the biggest reason is obvious: He enunciates better than any rapper who ever lived. *He's literally good at talking.* The first time you hear an Eminem song, you can decide whether or not you find him entertaining. That seems to be a central quality for anyone who deeply resonates with blue-collar Americans. I once did a feature for *SPIN* magazine that tried to explain why Morrissey has become a cult figure with Latino teenagers in California, and I suggested a variety of explanations for why a forgotten, asexual Oscar Wilde fanatic would resonate with Hispanic kids in East L.A. What I came to realize is that relating to Morrissey is easy for anyone who puts forth the effort to try; Moz sings about universal problems (loneliness, alienation, emotional fraud), and he sings about those problems in a way that's oddly literal. His voice is clear, the meanings can be appreciated on two (and sometimes three) different levels, and you can always hear every thought. He lets you get close to him. I'm more surprised that Latinos are the *only* kids who still love him.

What I'm saying is that lyrics do matter, and people who say they're overemphasized by critics are wrong. The significance of lyrics in pop music is not overrated; in fact, it's probably underrated. And this is what people overlook about modern country music. They fail to see that it's a word-based idiom, and words are far more effective than pianos or guitars. The manipulation of sonics makes someone like Moby a genius, but he'll never have the middle-class importance of someone like Toby Keith.

Now, I know what you're thinking: You're thinking that this is a profoundly depressing argument, because it implies that the only things that can be culturally important are things that appeal to the lowest common denominator. But that's not what I'm suggesting. I realize that Toby Keith seems like a troglodyte, especially when he appears in those long-distance commercials with Terry Bradshaw and ALF—but it's not his simplicity that makes him vital. It's his clarity. Keith writes songs like 1993's

"Should've Been a Cowboy," and what's compelling is that you can't deconstruct its message. "Should've Been a Cowboy" is not like Bon Jovi's "Wanted Dead or Alive," where Jon Bon Jovi claimed to live *like* a cowboy; Toby Keith wants to be a cowboy *for real.* "I should have been a cowboy," he sings. "I should have learned to rope and ride." Somewhat amusingly, the cowboys Toby references in his songs are all fake cowboys (*Gunsmoke*'s Marshal Dillon, cinematic crooners Gene Autry and Roy Rogers), but fake cowboys are the only kind that Keith—and most of America—ever wanted to embody. When I was fourteen, I liked Bon Jovi, and part of the reason why was because I liked the idea of riding a steel horse and using whiskey bottles as wall calendars. I aspired to turn my life into that of a modern-day cowboy,[4] and that always seemed vaguely possible. But whenever I go back to my hometown and see the people I grew up with—many of whom are still living the same life we all had twelve years ago as high school seniors—I realize that I was very much the exception. Lots of people (in fact, most people) do not dream about morphing their current life into something dramatic and cool and metaphoric. Most people see their life as a job that they have to finish; if anything, they want their life to be *less* complicated than it already is. They want their life to only have one meaning. So when they imagine a better existence, it's either completely imaginary (i.e., Toby's nineteenth-century Lone Ranger fantasy) or staunchly practical (i.e., Yearwood's description of the girl who just wants to get married without catching static from her old man). The reason Garth Brooks and Shania Twain have sold roughly 120 million more albums than Bob Dylan and Liz Phair is not because record buyers are all a bunch of blithering idiots; it's because Garth and Shania are simply better at expressing the human condition. They're less talented, but they understand more people.

The paradox, of course, is that I'm writing this essay while

4. Like Tesla!

staring at my CD rack, which currently holds seventeen Dylan and Phair records and exactly three country records released after 1974. And in a weird way, that makes me happy. I have at least one thing in common with Bob Dylan: Neither one of us understands how the world works. When push comes to shove, we're both Reba's bitch.

Here is the easiest way to explain the genius of Johnny Cash: Singing from the perspective of a convicted murderer in the song "Folsom Prison Blues," Cash is struck by pangs of regret when he sits in his cell and hears a distant train whistle. This is because people on that train are "probably drinkin' coffee." And this is also why Cash seems completely credible as a felon: He doesn't want freedom or friendship or Jesus or a new lawyer. He wants coffee.

Within the mind of a killer, complex feelings are eerily simple.

This is why killers can shoot men in Reno just to watch them die, and the rest of us usually can't.

15   This Is Zodiac Speaking   1:79

The killing machine wore a cowboy hat, and he was a real sweet-heart.

Let me drag you back to the summer of 2001. I was in a karaoke bar in a Washington town called Lacey, a little place out-side Olympia, which is a little place outside Seattle. That's when my friend Sarah appears to have danced with a serial killer. Sarah spent ten minutes twirling and whirling to Brooks & Dunn with an (allegedly) fucked-up weirdo who may have killed at least five women throughout the Pacific Northwest. I suppose this fella did seem a tad creepy (at least to me), but not in a "I'm gonna drag you home to rape you and kill you and defile your corpse" sort of way. That would be an exaggeration on the behalf of my memory. He just seemed like the kind of person who aspired to buy a used Trans Am and possibly wore Brut cologne.

The bar was a joint strangely called Mehfil, and—for some odd reason—it's attached to an Indian restaurant; you could kind of smell curry fused with warm Budweiser, assuming that's possible (perhaps it was just the scent of lumberjack sweat). The reason we were in Mehfil was because certain friends of mine think karaoke is "fabulously ironic," apparently because stupid, white-trash divorcées often sing Linda Ronstadt's "It's So Easy" in public. What honestly seemed more ironic was that the vast majority of people in this particular bar were semi-intellectual twenty-two-year-old hippies from the nearby fake college of Evergreen, all of whom were trying to feel superior by mocking the (maybe) eight or nine buck-toothed regulars who earnestly sing at Mehfil as an extension of their actual life. In places like Olympia, coolness and condescension are pretty much the same thing.

179

However, one of those sincere regulars at Mehfil was a man named Michael Braae, and he was getting the last laugh, mostly by (allegedly) killing local girls at random. But we didn't know that at the time, of course; we were just getting hammered on Maker's Mark and Pepsi when Braae sauntered up to my friend Sarah and politely asked her to dance.

Now, Sarah is not exactly Giselle; I can recall that there was at least one other woman at the bar that night who was more striking than she. But Sarah is definitely attractive, and she's a good drinker, and she has luxurious red hair that smells like papayas. Moreover, Sarah just looks *nice*; she is the kind of person who makes you want to tell your secrets. Her eyes are guileless and enthusiastic at the same time. And part of me suspects that's why Michael Braae thought she'd be a perfect girl to dance with, and—at least in theory—shoot in the skull, which is what some investigators believe he did to a girl named Marchelle Morgan a month before he was arrested.

Fortunately, Sarah's brush with Braae did not end with any skull shooting. "Cowboy Mike" (that's what everyone called him at the bar) merely danced with her twice (and he was a pretty nifty dancer). We all watched them from across the room. When they finished, Sarah sheepishly ditched him and returned to our table of well-acquainted drunks; later that night, we teased her about having a new boyfriend while picking up some relatively terrible food at a Jack in the Box restaurant. And we never thought about Cowboy Mike again . . . until the Olympia cops apprehended him four weeks later. Sarah got to see his charming face on the front page of her newspaper. It seems he had jumped off a bridge into Evel Knievel's Snake River, fleeing from local authorities who didn't want him to kill any more of his guileless, enthusiastic, red-haired dance partners.

Somehow, I seem to have acquired three friends who have known serial killers. I find Sarah's encounter especially intriguing, mostly because I happened to witness it firsthand; by total coincidence,

I was visiting the very night Braae tried to flirt with her. However, the reason I find that encounter so interesting is not because I sat five feet from an alleged monster, nor is it because I've casually looked into the eyes of evil, nor is it that I feel like I've vicariously brushed against some twisted version of celebrity. It's mostly because something now seems different about Sarah, even though she's exactly the same. There's a sexy residue to the whole Serial Killer Experience; somehow, it morphs the way I look at all the people who simply happened to collide with them (either by choice or by accident). There's something amazingly *modern* about meeting a man who kills innocent strangers arbitrarily. It has a way of making someone's personality abstractly sophisticated.

This is probably because serial killing is the most modern of high crimes, even though it's not new in any official sense (Jack the Ripper's 1888 London spree is the most obvious proof of this, but there are certainly others). The metaphoric newness of serial killing has nothing to do with chronology; it has to do with its meaning. At least culturally, there is something accelerated about the notion of killing strangers for no valid reason. It's one of those nightmare situations we collectively try to rationalize into nonexistence, almost as if it's entirely fictional. And most of the time, that rationalization makes sense: If a man is trying to kill you, his reasons—though flawed—are still *usually* within the scope of explanation; perhaps he wants to shoot you because you're sleeping with his wife (or perhaps he just thinks you are, which is just as bad). If someone is trying to break into your house after midnight, he probably has a clear motive; he probably needs money to buy crack or crystal meth or Wonder Bread. Most American crime is no random accident. I suppose nobody deserves to die, but it certainly seems like most people in America who get murdered have put themselves in a position where getting shot or stabbed is not an unthinkable consequence; their lifestyle dictates a certain degree of risk. However, that's not the case with serial killer victims. I realize serial killers tend to ice prostitutes more often than anyone else, but they're not killing them *because* they're prostitutes; it's not like serial killers are sexual moralists.[1] Hookers are simply easier to kill (no one notices when they disappear). If given the choice, the typical serial killer would just as soon shoot a dental assistant. In fact, he'd just as soon shoot someone like *you*, and maybe someday he will. This is why serial killing strikes me as such a modern act: It validates the seemingly irrational fear that someone you've never met before will just decide to capriciously end your life. It's not *figuratively* senseless (like a gangland killing, which is stupid but still explicable), it's *literally* senseless (inasmuch as there's no connection between the two involved parties and no benefit to the assailant, beyond giving him the opportunity to masturbate on—or into—a corpse).

My obsession with serial killers began when I was ten years old. My fourth-grade teacher told our class that we should never hitchhike, because the only people who picked up hitchhikers were perverted serial killers. This advice was complicated by what my fifth-grade teacher told us the following year; she said that we would all have driver's licenses in a few years, and the one rule we always needed to remember was never to pick up hitchhikers. This was because all hitchhikers were serial killers. According to what I learned in public school, every person on every freeway was trolling for destruction. I used to imagine nomadic, sadistic drifters thumbing rides with bloodthirsty Volkswagen owners, both desperately waiting for the first opportunity to kill each other. Hitchhiking seemed like an ultraviolent race against time.

Keeping this threat in mind, I began casually studying serial killers in my spare time, mostly through TV documentaries on

---

1. It should be noted that certain experts disagree with me on this point; some are prone to classify one genre of serial killers as "mission-oriented," which means they aspire to kill specific people (such as hookers) in order to improve society. Other classifications include "visionary motive" types (who imagine voices inside their head), "thrill-oriented" killers (who find the process of murder exciting), and "lust killers" (who actively get a sexual thrill from torture and execution).

PBS and British books with comical names like *The Mammoth Book of Murder* and *The Mammoth Book of Killer Women*. Due to my age (and my interest in the band W.A.S.P.), I suspect part of me was intrigued by the necrophilia gruesomeness of the police reports. However, what I found more fascinating were the skewed details about the killers' lives, all of which seemed more original and more clichéd than anything I experienced through literature or film. It didn't "almost" seem funny; it seemed *completely* funny, pretty much all the time. I will never forget the 1985 arrest of Richard Ramirez, the infamous California "Night Stalker." At one point in his court hearing, Ramirez held up his hand with a pentagram scrawled on the palm and hissed the word *"Evil!"* My cousin Greg and I were twelve when this happened, and we saw this particular image on television while attending a weeklong Catholic retreat that was hosted by local nuns. For the whole week, we drew pentagrams on our paws with ballpoint pens and constantly said *"Evil!"* in the hope of amusing the girls at this event, most of whom loved Culture Club and wore Esprit T-shirts. This was the same week we learned how to be altar boys.

However, my interest in guys like Ramirez went a little further than Greg's, since he *only* saw all this as comical. At a very early age, an understanding of serial killers seemed important to me. The fact that Ramirez and I had the same favorite AC/DC song ("Night Prowler") didn't freak me out, but it certainly made me wonder if I was somehow predisposed to freakish impulses. My all-time favorite serial killer was the never-captured Zodiac, the San Francisco–based mastermind who bragged to newspapers about his murders through a byzantine code and may have actually killed people because of his interest in math.[2] Somehow, that sounded like something I would come up with. I didn't

2. One of the Zodiac's many coded missives included a reference to the semi-esoteric mathematical concept of "radians," which are 57.3-degree arcs used to calculate circles ($2 \times$ pi radians $= 360$ degrees). Amazingly, it turns out Zodiac's victims were always found at perfect radian intervals in relation to the summit of nearby Mount Diablo. It does not appear that this could be a coincidence,

relate to these guys, per se, but I always wondered if I was a "serial person"—a Midwestern Zodiac who simply had no desire to kill.

This is why I can't resist badgering my acquaintances who have encountered genuine madmen; perhaps my obsession with serial killers has less to do with what makes them different from everyone else and more to do with what makes them similar to those of us who don't feel compelled to kill hookers. As I said, I have three such chums: Beyond serving as a firsthand witness to Sarah's dance-a-thon with the second-rate death machine Cowboy Mike, I also know a guy who became friends with John Wayne Gacy (the much publicized "Clown Killer") and another who attended high school with Jeffrey Dahmer (the most stridently prototypical serial killer in pop history). Much to their unilateral annoyance, I continually find myself compelled to ask them different versions of the same question: *What does it mean to know a serial killer?* And it seems like the answer is the same every single time.

It was on the last day of 2001 that I discovered I knew a man who knew John Wayne Gacy (or maybe it was on the first day of 2002, depending on how you quantify time). Near the conclusion of a rather dull New Year's Eve party, I found myself chatting with a dude named Eric Nuzum, who works as the programming director for the National Public Radio station in Kent, Ohio. I was mostly arguing with his clever Asian girlfriend about the value of Bjork (she seemed to think Bjork was the cat's pajamas), but the conversation somehow touched tangentially on the fact that Nuzum has one of John Wayne Gacy's paintings hanging in his living room. I was immediately curious about this, but I found that Nuzum was reticent to talk about the subject (beyond casu-

---

especially since one of Zodiac's victims was a cabdriver who was instructed to drive to a specific location before being shot. This kind of "evil mathematical genius" behavior is part of the reason some people erroneously suspected that Unabomber Ted Kaczynski had been the Zodiac Killer as a younger man.

ally admitting that he did, in fact, have one of Gacy's paintings and that he did, in fact, carry on a friendship with the sociopath for roughly three years while the ex-clown sat on death row). I managed to pry a few more details about this relationship from him at the party, but I could tell he wasn't exactly stoked about being hammered with questions about Gacy in the context of a New Year's Eve fiesta. However, I asked him if I could interview him at length about Gacy at a later date, and he said, "Oh, probably." When I e-mailed him about that possibility a month later, he was clearly more enthusiastic about having such a conversation. And by the time I finally showed up at his house, he seemed downright *excited* to be talking about John Wayne Gacy, at times behaving like I was a psychiatrist and he was a patient reminiscing about formative experiences from his childhood. It almost felt like the old *Bob Newhart Show*.

What happened, I think, was that my journalistic interest in Nuzum's relationship with Gacy—as opposed to my prurient interest in Gacy himself—sort of jarred Eric into realizing that there was something noteworthy about having made small talk with someone who was about as nocuous as any twentieth-century American. This is especially true when one considers that Nuzum was not some kind of obsessive death groupie; his involvement with Gacy stemmed from involvement with an anticensorship group called Refuse and Resist (Nuzum is something of a First Amendment fanatic, having written a book titled *Parental Advisory: Music Censorship in America*). It seems Nuzum had discovered that Gacy was the only inmate in the entire Illinois penal system who wasn't allowed to sell his paintings commercially, and—being the spunky twenty-four-year-old idealist that he was—Nuzum decided to remedy this injustice. His first step was contacting Gacy by mail (he had to make sure Gacy *wanted* to be liberated), and things just kind of took off from there.

Like most incarcerated humans, Gacy loved mail; unlike most incarcerated humans, Gacy was picky about his friends. When anyone wrote to him, he returned a typed, two-page survey that

asked fifty-two questions about artistic affinities, political ide-
ologies, and personal values. Nuzum still has that form. The
most ironic section of the questionnaire asks the applicant to
describe what kind of advice he or she would offer to children;
one assumes Gacy's honest advisement would have been, "Don't
struggle while I sodomize you." But the bottom line is that
Nuzum responded to the fifty-two questions and slowly found
himself a new pen pal. After a year of writing, Gacy began calling
him on the telephone (collect, of course).

"He had HBO in his cell, so we talked about what was on HBO
a lot," Nuzum recalls. "He liked classic movies, but he really
seemed more interested in mainstream crap like *Footloose*. His
tastes weren't very sophisticated. But sometimes I suspect that he
liked big, bang-up Hollywood movies like *Patriot Games* because
he knew they were culturally popular with people on the outside,
and that made him feel more normal."

While Nuzum was telling me about Gacy's appreciation for
the early work of Kevin Bacon, I found my eyes drifting over to
the rudimentary portrait of Elvis Presley on his wall. This was the
painting he had mentioned at the party. The image was of a relatively young Elvis, sadly staring at the ground against a sky-blue
background. In the lower right corner, I could see the signature of
"J.W. Gacy." It's not a stellar painting; I doubt Nuzum would
hang it in his living room if it didn't come from someone who
snuffed the life out of thirty-three Chicagoans and stuffed them
into the crawl space beneath his home.

Now, I realize there are people who would find Nuzum's dec-
orating decision pretty fucked-up. They wouldn't hang one of
Gacy's paintings in their house if he had twice the talent of
Picasso, and some might even suggest that Nuzum inadvertently perpetuates the gothic glamour of mass murder; by hanging a mediocre painting in this living room, it proves that (a)
Gacy is a celebrity, and (b) killing people warrants celebrity
stature. I don't think it's a coincidence that America is the most
celebrity-driven culture on earth *and* the homeland for more

serial killers than virtually every other country combined. Serial killing is glam killing (or at least it seems that way after a culprit gets caught).

But here's where things get complex: Nuzum is barely interested in Gacy's murders. It's really the one aspect of history's most sinister clown[3] he doesn't enjoy discussing. However, I don't think it's because he's in any sort of denial; Nuzum is certain that Gacy did terrible, terrible things. It's just that Eric happens to be one of those hyperkinetic NPR liberals who spends his free time rescuing kittens from the pound. The deeper reality, I suspect, is that he feels *sorry* for John Wayne Gacy, and that—somehow—he was part of a society that makes people like Gacy exist.

"I guess I always had this image of a brilliant, maniacal genius who constructed these complicated plans to satisfy his sexual urges and kill, kill, kill," Nuzum tells with his fingers interlocked behind his head and his pupils fixed on the ceiling. "But the fact of the matter is that he really wasn't that smart. There's such a vast difference between trying to understand this kind of crime and trying to understand anything else. With someone like O. J. Simpson, you could argue that he killed two people and he knew exactly what he was doing. With someone like Timothy McVeigh, one assumes he was able to rationalize the 168 people he killed as causalities of war. But this is different. You know, Gacy always insisted to me that he never killed animals when he was younger, which is usually common with serial killers. For him, it was all sexually based. That was his motivation for everything. But what does that mean? I still don't understand it."

It sort of dawned on me that—the more I talked to Nuzum

3. In fact, Eric gets kind of annoyed when people dwell on the fact that Gacy sometimes dressed as "Pogo the Clown" and performed at children's birthday parties. "I think the clown stuff is really overdone," he says. "He was just doing that as part of a civic group—it was really just an outreach of his political involvement." Weirdly, this is true: Gacy was a political junkie who was once photographed with then–First Lady Rosalynn Carter. You'd think the GOP could do something with this.

about this—the further our conversation devolved from the original *"What does it mean to know a serial killer"* question, which indicated to me that I probably wasn't going to find the answer from him. All I really learned was that I am less compassionate than just about everyone I know. If I had known John Wayne Gacy, I suspect I would have been fascinated by his impending execution; I would have constantly asked him about his thoughts on death and his expectations for the afterlife, and how the experience of living changes once your life suddenly has an exact expiration date. To me, his lethal injection would have been the summit of our rapport. But Nuzum didn't see it like that at all.

"I was very upset when he was put to death," Eric told me. "In fact, when it became obvious that it was just a matter of time, that's when our relationship ended. I stopped accepting his collect calls. I would like to say that I cut things off because his phone calls got weird—and they certainly did near the end, because he'd ramble for twenty minutes and I wouldn't even say a sentence—but the truth is that it just got hard to think about what it was going to be like when he was dead.

"If I learned anything from the time I knew him, though, it's that I think I now have a wider view of heinous crimes than most people. Once you get to know a murderer as a person, you actually start to rationalize things less, and you start to see things more clearly. For example, one time we were talking on the phone very casually about television, and one of the guards happened to walk by Gacy while we were talking. Gacy immediately freaked out and started raving about how this person had woken him up the night before by shining a flashlight on him. Judging from Gacy's reaction, you would have sworn this guard raped his mother. He lost control and just went ballistic. But thirty seconds later, he was completely fine. And I remember thinking, 'I can totally see how this person could kill children.' He was just a guy with a huge problem."

Jeffrey Dahmer had a problem, too. In fact, he had a bunch of them, and they kept getting worse. He was an alcoholic (not good). He was a self-loathing homosexual (even worse). He was a murderer (which downplays the sexual struggle), he was a cannibal (maybe the only habit that makes murdering people seem borderline normal), and he longed to surround himself with corpses in the hope that they would become surrogates for the human relationships he could not sustain in day-to-day life ('nuff said). There isn't a dimension of serial killer lore that Dahmer didn't embody, including the obligatory tortured adolescence. When he was a high school student in Ohio, Dahmer life's was profoundly sad and predictably disturbing. I know this because that's when Derf used to hang out with him.

"Derf" is John Backderf, a comic book artist I worked with at a newspaper in Akron, Ohio. Dahmer is a huge deal in Akron, because that's his hometown. Technically, he graduated from a joint educational facility called Revere High School, which was comprised of kids from two small towns: Bath (a relatively affluent suburb) and Richfield (a town best known for hosting the now-destroyed Richfield Coliseum, the former home for countless hair metal concerts and the Cleveland Cavaliers). But for all practical purposes, those communities are just extensions of suburban Akron. And what's interesting about Akron is that—due to a variety of socioeconomic reasons—the community tends to spawn things that could not have come from anywhere else in America. The band Devo is one example. Jeffrey Dahmer is another.

I had been working at the *Akron Beacon Journal* for less than a month when someone told me that Derf grew up with Dahmer, which was weird for two reasons. The first is obvious—it's always surprising to meet someone who used to have gym class with a cannibal. However, what was even stranger is that I had never even met this Derf character; some coworker just felt compelled to tell me there was a person on staff who went to high school with J. Dahmer. This same person also told me that the legal name of Derf's little son Max was supposedly "Maximum Volume

Backderf," which seemed only slightly less unreasonable than eating from the corpse of a Milwaukee homosexual.

When I eventually met Derf that summer, he turned out to be very cool; he was sort of this *über*-sarcastic, unrepentant, aging punk rocker who always wore a Greek fishing hat and would stroll by my desk twice a week to tell me that every band I liked was terrible. And when I finally asked him if he really knew Dahmer, his reaction was to say, "Well, of course I did," as if I had just asked him if he hated Pink Floyd's *The Wall*. He proceeded to give me a comic he published titled *My Friend Dahmer*, an illustrated twenty-six-page narrative of his youthful memories of a demented scamp known simply as "Jeff."

Without being the least bit exploitive, *My Friend Dahmer* paints an eerily vivid portrait of the young Akronian weirdo and suggests that all the signs of his future monstrosities would have been clearly visible to anyone who had cared enough to pay attention. The title is technically misleading, as Dahmer appears to have had no real friends whatsoever in high school—but Derf and his geeky cronies were probably the closest approximation. They would pay him $35 to go to the local mall and perform his "Dahmer shtick," which amounted to him pretending to have cerebral palsy (it seems his mother's interior decorator suffered from the condition, prompting Dahmer to mimic the spastic, seizurelike movements). Dahmer's preperformance ritual was to shotgun six beers in the backseat of a car, which was the same thing he did every single day before school. Beyond the summer after tenth grade, Derf can't recall ever seeing Dahmer when he wasn't either "in character" or completely and utterly intoxicated.

People picked on Dahmer, but he didn't respond; he mostly existed as a zombie who occasionally blurted out the indecipherable phrase "Baaaa!" at inappropriate times. He was a victim waiting to become a victimizer. And he finally made that transition one month after he, Derf, and two hundred other kids graduated from Revere. It was the summer of 1978, and Jeffrey destroyed his first human.

"Believe it not, I consider Dahmer something of a tragic figure," Derf once told me while munching on a bowl of Honey Nut Cheerios. "My relationship with him ended just before he killed that first guy, but I honestly believe he could have been stopped. Some adult could have stepped in when he was younger, I think, and changed the path he was on. But the moment he actually killed someone, any sympathy I might have had for him disappeared. When he crossed over to the other side, he became a monster to me, and he deserved a bullet in the back of the head."

Certainly, there is something paradoxical about Derf's assessment of Dahmer. His portrait of J.D. in *My Friend Dahmer* aggressively humanizes the killer, often to the point where he becomes almost likable. However, the moment Dahmer took someone's life, Derf says his perception suddenly mirrored that of the rest of America. And as our conversation continued, I started to suspect Derf's relationship with this guy was a little more complicated than even Derf was aware of. This was particularly clear when I asked him if he was *glad* that Dahmer went to Revere High. My specific question was this: If we concede that Dahmer was destined to commit these crimes regardless of where he grew up, would Derf have preferred that Jeffrey been raised in someplace like Cincinnati or Dayton, thereby making him someone he never knew? Or is he happy that—if *someone* had to go to the mall with the young Dahmer—it was him?

"Well, since I've led an exceedingly dull life in all other regards, having known Dahmer has certainly been periodically interesting and sporadically surreal," he answered. "For example, last night I was watching one of those *Saturday Night Live* reruns on Comedy Central. It was an episode from one of the really bad years. But there was this skit where a guy is singing some stupid song, and he mentions Jeffrey Dahmer. And it suddenly hits me that he's talking about a guy I used to pass in the halls every day. That never stops being strange, I guess. But is it really *interesting*? I don't know. I mean, how interesting would it have been to have known Michael J. Fox in high school? It's kind of the same thing."

191

It's noteworthy that Derf mentions Michael J. Fox as a metaphor for knowing Dahmer; Nuzum made a similar comparison when discussing John Wayne Gacy, but his metaphor was Cameron Diaz. I suspect this kind of celebrity analogy is common. However, part of me deeply disagrees with the accuracy of those comparisons, and here's why: The fame a serial killer achieves is a sicker—but more authentic—brand of fame. There are thousands of thin young women in Hollywood who wanted to be Cameron Diaz, and hundreds of them could have done exactly that. There are five hundred girls who could have had her career. There is nothing inherently special about Cameron Diaz; until she made a movie, she was just an attractive person. At some point, she *became* Cameron Diaz. But Jeffrey Dahmer didn't *become* Jeffrey Dahmer the first time he killed somebody. That's always who he was. Derf claims he "turned into a monster" the day he killed his first victim, but I think that's mostly just what he'd like to believe; more than almost anyone, Derf knows that Dahmer was always just a guy who couldn't (or at least *didn't*) relate to the normal boundaries of right and wrong. To know that kind of person is to know the darkest kind of power. To me, that has to mean something. But Derf will always disagree with me.

"What kind of meaning would you expect this to have? The guy was a parasite," Derf tells me, his mouth still half-filled with Cheerios. "He gave nothing to society, and his effect on me is pretty negligible. What is there to learn? These questions seem like bullshit to me."

Which brings us back to little red-haired Sarah . . .

"I really must say that I feel sort of ambivalent about the whole Cowboy Mike situation," Sarah tells me over the phone. She has just finished her second beer of the night, but she does not seem drunk; her boyfriend is trying to fall asleep in the other room. "In a way, I think you care about this more than I do.

Because honestly, I would say my knowledge of serial killers is slightly below average."

This is funny for two reasons. It's mainly funny because Sarah has inexplicably concluded that there is (a) a universally accepted level for serial murder knowledge, and that (b) she somehow falls just below the national median. But it's also funny because it's true; if I didn't keep bringing it up, I sometimes think Sarah would completely forget she danced with a man who might have killed her if given the opportunity.

"That night was actually something I tried not to think about for several months, and I guess I succeeded," she said. "It initially seemed strange in the sense that I suppose I could have ended up like one of those women on those Lifetime movies who are always getting beaten. Had I been single, something terrible could have happened that night. I certainly can't imagine that I would ever have gone home with that person, but I can imagine maybe having a cigarette with the guy. He was really a gentleman. And he didn't so much seem *creepy* as much as he just seemed unusually skinny."

Well, great. Serial killers aren't necessarily spooky; they simply have high metabolisms. And they like to watch *Footloose*. And to know them means nothing, even if it does. Apparently, there is no one on earth who needs to meet a serial killer more than me; only then will I realize these people are meaningless. Get ready, all ye lonely hitchhikers. My car awaits your empty eyes, your random perversity, and your hand of perpetual doom. One way or the other, I need the truth. The next dance is mine, Cowboy.

Timothy McVeigh was executed on June 11 of 2001. Around the time of his execution, the *Chicago Tribune* ran a breakdown of all 168 people killed in the Oklahoma City bombing. Here are some examples of how the victims were mentioned:

- **Donald Earl Burns Sr., 63,** taught woodworking for many years.
- **John Van Ess, 67,** played national championship basketball as a student at Oklahoma A&M.
- **Karen Gist Carr, 32,** was a member of Toastmasters International.

There's nothing intrinsically wrong with any of those details. However, as I read and reread every little bio on the list, I found myself deflated by the realization that virtually everyone's life is only remembered for one thing. J. D. Salinger wrote *Catcher in the Rye*; for all practical purposes, that's it. He may as well have done nothing else, ever. As time passes, that book becomes his singular legacy. He's certainly famous, but 98 percent of the world doesn't know about anything else he's ever done. Eli Whitney invented the cotton gin; every other element of his existence is totally irrelevant. Bill Buckner let a ground ball go through his legs in the World Series and cost the Red Sox a championship; in fifty years, everything else about his career will be a footnote.

This doesn't just apply to second-rate celebrities, either. It's equally true for normal citizens (case in point: Oklahoma City bombing victim Oleta Christine Biddy was undoubtedly a complex human, but the readers of the *Chicago Tribune* only know that she "always had a smile on her face"). Beyond your closest friends, you can probably describe everyone you know with one sentence.

I think this is what motivates people to have children. Everyone agrees that creating life is important, so having a child guarantees you've done at least one act of consequence. Moreover, it extends the window for greatness; if your kid becomes president, your biography becomes "the parent of a president." The import of your existence can be validated by whoever you bring into the world. But this doesn't always work. In fact, sometimes it makes things worse. Which is why the most depressing thing about the Oklahoma City bombing is that there's now an innocent woman whose one-sentence newspaper bio will forever be, "She was Timothy McVeigh's mother."

16 All I Know Is What I Read in the Papers 1:95

As of the writing of this particular book, I have 43 "close friends,"[1] 196 "good friends,"[2] and 2,200 "affable acquaintances."[3] Due to the circumstances of my chosen existence, almost half of these people—somewhere in the neighborhood of 40 percent—currently work (or once worked) in some sort of media capacity. This means that the other 60 percent do not (or have not). This being the mathematical case, I feel as though I have a pretty solid grasp on the communication industry, as I have ties to both (a) the people presenting the news and (b) the people consuming it. And it has been my experience that they all pretty much hate it.

I would never try to convince someone not to hate the media. As far as I can tell, it's a completely reasonable thing to hate. Whenever I meet someone who feels a sense of hatred for a large, amorphous body—the media, the government, Ticketmaster, the Illuminati, Anna Nicole Smith, whatever—I fully support their distaste. It's always better to be mad at something vast and unspecific and theoretical, as these entities cannot sue you for defamation. But here's my one problem with media bashers, both inside and outside the journalistic profession: They inevitably hate the wrong things. Just about everyone I know who

1. These are people I would phone immediately if I was diagnosed with lung cancer.
2. These are people whose death from lung cancer would make me profoundly sad.
3. These are people I would generally hope could recover from lung cancer.

has problems with newspapers (or magazines, or CNN, or Ted Koppel, et al.) is completely misdirecting their anger.

You say you want to hate the media? Fine. I happen to love the media, and I think it's just about the only organism in America that works more often than it doesn't. But if you're truly serious about finding things to hate about your local newspaper, and you want to write letters to the editor that will actually make valid criticisms, I will help you.

DON'T WORRY ABOUT AGENDAS.
WORRY ABOUT RANDOM CIRCUMSTANCE.

This is—indisputably and inarguably—the biggest misconception people make about the media. Everybody seems to be concerned that journalists are constantly trying to slip their own political and philosophical beliefs into what they cover. This virtually never happens. And I am not being naive when I say this; it really doesn't happen.[4] There are thousands of things that affect the accuracy of news stories, but the feelings of the actual reporter is almost never one of them. The single most important impact of any story is far less sinister: Mostly, it all comes down to (a) who the journalist has called, and (b) which of those people happens to call back first.

Are media outlets controlled by massive, conservative corporations? Well, of course they are. Massive conservative corporations own everything. Are most individual members of the media politically liberal? Absolutely. If talented writers honestly thought the world didn't need to be changed, they'd take jobs in advertising that are half as difficult and three times as lucrative. So—in theory—all the long-standing conspiracies about media motives are true. But—in practice—they're basically irrelevant, at

4. Obviously, I'm not counting the *New York Post* or *The National Enquirer* or anything else that defines itself as a tabloid, as those publications have no relationship to journalism.

least in the newspaper industry. There is no way the espoused Aryan masterminds who run the world can affect the content of any daily story; they usually have no idea what the hell is going on with anything in the world, and certainly not with what anyone's writing about. I worked in the Knight Ridder chain for four years, and I never got the impression that the CEO read anything, except maybe *Golf Digest*.

The media machine is too bloated to "manufacture consent." What filters down from the queen bee is nominal; there is no successful macro agenda. Meanwhile, individual reporters—the drones who do all the heavy lifting—tend to be insane. Being a news reporter forces you to adopt a peculiar personality: You spend every moment of your life trying to eradicate emotion. Reporters overcompensate for every nonobjective feeling they've ever experienced; I once got into a serious discussion over whether or not the theft of a live fetus from the womb of a kidnapped pregnant woman could be publicly classified as a "tragedy." What civilians in the conventional world need to realize is that *journalists are not like you.* They have higher ethics and less common sense. For example: Let's say somebody was trying to pass a resolution that created stricter pedophilia laws. Most normal people would think to themselves, "Well, I'm against kids being molested and so is everybody I've ever met, so—obviously—if I was asked to write a story about this resolution, I'd make sure people understood it was a positive thing." Reporters never think like this. A reporter would spend the next three hours trying to find an activist who'd give them a quote implying it was unconstitutional to stop people from performing oral sex on five-year-old boys. Journalists aren't trying to tell you their version of what's right and what's wrong, because anyone who's been a reporter for five years forgets how to tell the difference.

That's why the biggest influence on the content of most news stories is simply who calls back *first*. Most of the time, that's the catalyst for everything else that evolves into a news story. Since breaking the news is a competition-based industry, almost everything is done on deadline—and since journalism is founded on the premise that reality can only be shown through other people's statements, reporters are constantly placing phone calls to multiple sources with the hope that all of them (or at least *one* of them) will give the obligatory quotes the writer can turn into a narrative. That's why the first person who happens to return a reporter's phone message dictates whatever becomes the "final truth" of any story. Very often, the twenty-four-second-shot clock simply runs out before anyone else can be reached; consequently, that one returned phone call is all the information the journalist can use. And even when everyone else *does* calls back before deadline, the template has already been set by whoever got there first; from now on, every question the reporter asks will be colored by whatever was learned from the initial source. Is this bad? Yes. Does it sometimes lead to a twisted version of what really happened? Yes. But it's not an agenda. It's timing.

Don't obsess over the notion of insidious politics creeping into your newspaper. Leftist crackpots and faceless corporate hacks rarely affect the news. High school volleyball games affect the news—or at least they do if a reporter's kid happens to be one of the players. You see, high school volleyball games often start at 6:30 P.M., so that reporter is not going to wait at his desk past six o'clock to see if his phone rings. His wife will kill him if he does. Or maybe he *does* wait for that call; maybe he skips his daughter's game because he really needs the mayor to return his phone call in order to technically say "no comment" about an issue that the reporter already *knows* the mayor won't comment upon. Maybe our steadfast reporter waits and waits and waits, and at 7:20 he decides to get a Dr Pepper. This requires him to walk across the newsroom to wherever they keep the vending machines, and—while he pops his quarters into the pop machine—his phone rings. It's the mayor. But maybe the mayor hates using voice mail, and maybe the mayor inexplicably assumes this reporter is actually a bleeding-heart socialist, so he hangs up without leaving a message. Two hours later, our metro reporter still doesn't have his obligatory "no comment," so the newspaper's metro editor tells him that the story needs to be held for at least one day so that they can get a response from the mayor. But twenty-four hours later, a hospital catches on fire, and that fire becomes the day's major news event. Meanwhile, the story about the mayor is suddenly old news, and—because of the fire—it's no longer on the front page; now it's buried on page B3. Most readers won't even notice it. But a handful of people who hate the mayor *will* notice it, and they'll assume the newspaper buried this story on purpose, either because (a) the reader is liberal, so he or she thinks the paper's aging Caucasian owner is in cahoots with the mayor, or because (b) the reader is conservative, so he or she thinks the liberal media is trying to raise taxes and mandate abortions and keep the tax-happy, baby-killing mayor in power. And all of this has nothing to do with politics, and it has nothing to do with agendas. It has to do with some guy wanting Dr Pepper. And shit like this happens *all the time.*

DISTRUST THE PROPER PEOPLE.

Über-idiotic people tend to think of the entire newspaper as one organism; they think that stories, columns, editorials, and advertisements are all exactly the same. Mildly intelligent people understand that there's a difference between what's on the front page and what's on the OpEd page. However, only a select few are aware that most of what's in a newspaper is either fact-plus-fiction or truth-minus-fact, which evens out to be just about the same thing.

Here's what I mean: People get nervous when they read stories in newspapers, because they always think they're being lied to or manipulated (this goes back to the aforementioned "agenda" presumption). They always think they're not getting the whole story. Actually, they're getting more than the whole story; they're getting the whole story, plus a bunch of stuff that has nothing to do with anything.

Remember our thirsty reporter who was waiting for the mayor to call him back? Well, let's say he finally leaves the office and swings by Stop-N-Go (maybe he wants another Dr Pepper). While walking toward the counter with his beverage in hand, a crazed loner walks into the store and shoots the convenience store employee in the face, killing him instantly. The reporter watches this shooting happen. The crazed loner then begins screaming like a maniac, and two cops rush in and apprehend him. Now, remember—the reporter sees all of this firsthand. And as a consequence, he calls up his editor on a cell phone and volunteers to write a story about the event. And he probably writes something like this . . .

> RANDOM CITY, USA—The owner of a local Stop-N-Go was killed tonight in a brutal act of seemingly random violence. The alleged perpetrator was immediately taken into custody but firmly denies his involvement in the crime. "I never shot nobody," said the alleged gunmen, who is also wanted for murder in seventeen other states.

Actually, I'm sort of exaggerating: I'm sure a copy editor would undoubtedly feel obligated to remove the word *brutal*. But by and large, this would be seen as a reasonable accounting of the events. This is why all reporters eventually go insane: Even if you see a guy shoot someone—in fact, even if a guy shoots *you* in the face, and you watch the bullet come out of the chamber of the .38 he's holding—the event needs to be described as an "alleged" crime, and that alleged criminal needs to allege that he had no part in anything that allegedly happened.

Now, I realize this is essential to journalism, and I certainly don't disagree with the principle behind that journalistic tradition. But these "essential" rules do create one rather embarrassing contradiction: Most serious news stories are peppered with information that is laughably false, and reporters are always fully aware of how false that information is. Newspapers are constantly quoting people who are openly lying, and almost every sound bite you hear in the broadcast media is partially false. And there's nothing anyone can do about it. It's not that the truth is being ignored; it's just that the truth is inevitably combined with a bunch of crap that's supposed to make news stories unbiased and credible, but really just makes them longer and less clear. The motivation for doing this is to foster objectivity, but it actually does the complete opposite. It makes finding an objective reality impossible, because you're always getting facts *plus* requisite grains of "equalizing" fiction.

In his book *Explaining Hitler*, author Ron Rosenbaum applauds a group he calls the "First Explainers," a collection of 1920s journalists who worked at publications like the *Munich Post* and risked their lives in order to illustrate the impending danger of the coming führer. He paints these guys as heroes. However, I'm not sure if modern reporters would even be allowed to perform that kind of watchdog function if a new Hitler-esque character emerged in the twenty-first century; he would probably just be referred to as a "charismatic, neoconservative upstart."

As a result of this ham-fisted faux objectivity, skeptical news consumers often find themselves suspecting that a deeper truth can be found on the newspaper opinion pages, or through talk radio, or via egocentric iconoclasts like Bill O'Reilly or Michael Moore. The assumption is that—since these pundits openly admit their biases—you can trust their insights more. They display less guile, and you know where they're coming from. But this is not true. You may find these people interesting and you may find them entertaining, but they offer nothing for anyone who doesn't already agree with their espoused stance. George Will and Maureen Dowd are both more effective writers than I could ever hope to become, but all their political insights are unabashed propaganda, even when they happen to be right: They sometimes tell the truth, but they're always subtracting facts. That's what they get paid to do. They are paid to manipulate and simplify issues that are too complex for casual observers to understand independently. What makes them good columnists is their ability to present a version of the truth that somehow seems self-evident; they are urbane cult leaders. I will never understand people who complain that the media can't be trusted, yet still inexplicably think they can learn something of value from Molly Ivins or Cal Thomas. Most of the time, political columnists and political commentators are trying to persuade you not to think critically about anything.

SPORTS REPORTERS HATE SPORTS.

Nobody realizes how much the people who write about sports despise the subject they write about. There is nothing they hate more. I know that seems paradoxical, and most of them would never admit it in public. But give them four drinks in a deserted tavern, and you will hear the truth: The people paid to inform you about the world of professional, collegiate, and high school athletics would love to see all sports—except for maybe the NCAA basketball tournament—eradicated from the planet.

What's depressing is that this was not always the case for these people. Back when today's sportswriters were still enthusiastic young fellows playing outside at recess, they loved sports. It was the only thing they loved, usually. They were the kind of kids who would watch a baseball game on TV and keep the official book, and they worshiped Brent Musburger and they memorized statistics from the *World Almanac* and they cried when Dwight Clark caught a pass in the back of the end zone to beat the Dallas Cowboys in 1981. Very often, the only important connection they had with their fathers was watching *Monday Night Football*. All their adolescence, these guys dreamed of a life where they could think about sports for a living. So they all went to college and got journalism degrees, and they all got jobs as sportswriters. And five years later, they all find themselves watching games from the press box and secretly wishing they were holding sniper's rifles.

If you want to become jaded and bitter in the shortest period possible, become a sportswriter. You will spend your Friday nights trying to talk to high school kids who have nothing to say, and you will have to ask them questions until they give you a quote that proves it. You will spend your Saturday afternoons talking to college players who will earnestly discuss the importance of academics and school spirit two hours before they rape the first girl unluckiest enough to chug a GHB kamikaze. And if you become *really* good at your job, you will eventually get to live in hotels for weeks at a time, alongside millionaire pro athletes who—if not for their ability to perform one socially irrelevant act—would quite possibly kill you and steal your car. And you will still remember statistics from the *World Almanac,* but now those memories will make you mad.

However, athletes aren't the worst part about being a sportswriter; after a few months, the players merely become literary devices. The worst part about being a sportswriter is that no one will ever have a normal conversation with you for the rest of your life. Everyone you meet will either (a) want to talk about sports, or (b) assume *you* want to talk about sports. Strangers will feel qualified to walk up to you in a café and complain about Rasheed Wallace; upon your introduction, your girlfriend's father will immediately ask you oddly specific questions about the New York Rangers. You may have insightful thoughts on the Middle East, but no one will care; they will be interested in your thoughts on middle relieving.

Over time, you will see your life disappear into sweat and contract negotiations and descriptions of the wishbone offense. And you will hate it. And normal sports fans deserve to know this. They deserve to know that the people telling them about the Utah Jazz enjoy pro basketball about as much as Catholic priests enjoy watching *The Thorn Birds*. I honestly feel the best sports journalism of the last ten years has been Jim Rome's work on his radio program *The Jungle,* since Rome seems to be the only man who aggressively accepts one very important truth: The single-best part about loving sports is *hating* sports.

CELEBRITY JOURNALISM IS A NEW KIND
OF MEANINGLESSNESS.

During the summer of 2001, you may recall a temporary hubbub about Tom Junod, a writer for *Esquire* magazine who did a profile on Michael Stipe of R.E.M. The controversy was that Junod admitted to fabricating much of the story, particularly details that made Stipe appear as an iconoclastic weirdo who stuck pennies on his eyes and consumed packets of sugar for no apparent reason.

My initial reaction to Junod's piece was that it was the wrong thing to do, and I still feel that way. Considering that almost nobody believes the media as it is, I can't see how lying on purpose can possibly be to anyone's benefit. But Junod claims he did this in order to make people reevaluate how the press covers celebrity, and that's valid. It's valid because conventional celebrity journalism is inevitably hounded by two problems: Either the subject is lying, or the writer is guessing. Junod just happened to embrace both of those obstacles simultaneously.

The problem with interviewing famous people is that—much of the time—they don't know anything. And I don't mean they don't know about religion or world affairs or physics; I mean they don't know anything about what they're supposedly being interviewed about. Quite often, you will see an actor discussing the character he's playing in a certain film, and he'll be explaining what kind of person this character is and what that character represents in a metaphoric sense (this happens all the time on Bravo's *Inside the Actors Studio*, America's single most embarrassing TV program). This is crazy. The actor didn't create that character; a screenwriter did. The actor didn't decide what the character represents outside the narrative; that's what the director tries to do. In a big-budget Hollywood movie, the actor has one responsibility: He needs to look visually compelling and recite the lines somebody else wrote for him. That's the whole gig. But in order to promote movies, actors and actresses need to give interviews at press junkets, because nobody wants to read an interview with some nebbish screenwriter. As a consequence, celebrity journalism is usually just attractive people trying to make up answers to questions they barely understand.

But those fabrications are only half the dilemma; part of the blame must fall on the reporter. It's almost impossible for journalists to cover celebrities without collapsing into conjecture. Unless they work for a major magazine or a mammoth newspaper, reporters rarely spend much time with the celebrities they cover; very often, an artist will do eight twenty-minute phone interviews with eight different writers in the span of a single morning, and that's all each writer has to work with. And since this artist probably said the exact same things in all eight interviews, all the writer can do is look at his ten rudimentary quotes and try to figure out how they can be used to prove that this person is somehow interesting.

Great example: In 1998, I interviewed Dave Pirner of the band Soul Asylum. Relative to most alt rockers, he was a pretty good talker; we discussed his liberal political views and the state of the music industry and—very briefly—his defunct relationship with Winona Ryder. All in all, we were on the phone for maybe thirty-five minutes. I started writing my Pirner profile as soon as the call ended, and I found myself using his casual insights to paint an incredibly vivid portrait of both his personal life and the cultural significance of his band. I saw tragic parallels between his ill-fated romance with Ryder and the unavoidable illusion of a meteoric rise to fame, and the whole story turned out to be an amazingly well-constructed psychological profile of a rock star who needed to pass the apex of his fame before he could take the time to appreciate what he had lost. It was a very good story. But then something dawned on me: *What the fuck do I know about David Pirner?* I talked to this dude for thirty-five minutes, and we spent the first ten discussing the coolest bars in uptown Minneapolis. How could I possibly think I gained any meaningful understanding of this man's existence through one completely innocuous phone conversation? I could have written the whole story without even talking to him, and it wouldn't have been any more (or less) accurate.

But you know what? My deadline for that Soul Asylum piece was 6:00 P.M. that same day, and I came to this realization at around 5:45. I could not change my life (or his) in fifteen minutes. I ran a spell check on the article and sent it to my editor, and then I went home. And everybody read my story, and everybody fucking loved it.

That's celebrity journalism.

IT IS ASSUMED YOU CAN'T READ.

If I have learned anything from working in journalism, it's that people who read newspapers apparently can't read newspapers. That's all I've ever been told. Every discussion I've ever had with an editor has stressed that people despise the process of reading. What people want, I am told, are shorter stories that never jump to a different page (stories that jump to different pages are apparently too confusing for people to follow, although it certainly seems like people manage to comprehend books, which tend to be spread over many, many many pages). People also like graphics, especially pie graphs. Photographs are also profoundly important, even if it's just a photograph of someone standing in front of the T.G.I. Friday's they happen to manage. And don't forget about sky boxes! People desperately need "sky boxes," which are eye-catching charts that tell them about news stories hidden inside the same paper everyone assumes they don't want to read. HOWEVER, the one thing *nobody* wants is sentences, and they certainly don't want paragraphs. People *despise* paragraphs. Focus groups have proven this.

Let me briefly describe what happened: At some unspecific point in history (during the height of the Vietnam War, probably), the television industry started kicking the newspaper industry's ass, mostly because TV was able to deliver the bare bones of information at a much faster speed. It was like newspapers were a horse and buggy, and TV was a train. So how did newspaper magnates combat this dilemma? By trying to design a really, really fast horse.

What newspapers tried to do was make reading feel like watching TV. Logically, they should have tried to do the opposite; they should have started writing longer, more complex stories, and they should have tried to deliver all the things the broadcast medium does not have the capacity to offer. But newspapers did the opposite. They tried to compete with the broadcast media by being flashier and less intellectual, which is why the newspaper industry is now controlled by page designers.

Truthfully, I'm not even sure the average consumer knows that people called "page designers" even exist, but these individuals dictate everything you read (and—more to the point—everything you don't). Intellectually, the newspaper industry is now controlled by guys like Mario Garcia, the consultant who redesigned *The Wall Street Journal* when it went to full color in April of 2002. In all likelihood, you have never heard the name Mario Garcia before today—yet he is the kind of man constructing your consciousness.

Here's how the newspaper process operates: Reporters write stories. Those stories are read by midlevel editors who tend to make minor content changes. The stories are then pushed to the "copy desk," where copy editors check for grammar mishaps and factual errors (copy editors also write the headlines). Eventually the stories get to the "design desk," where a page designer decides how to place this information on the tangible paper page—they decide how to incorporate the news alongside the photographs, graphics, sky boxes, and everything else that really doesn't matter. Their goal is to make the page look pretty; they are akin to architects. Quite simply, they are trying to create a newspaper than can be appreciated by the illiterate.

If you subscribe to a daily newspaper, you will notice that—once or twice a year—the paper will run a short story that mentions all the journalism awards that particular newspaper has won in some kind of quasi-notable journalism contest. Editors run these self-congratulatory stories because they think it makes the publication seem credible. However, winning awards in journalism is like winning awards at the Special Olympics; everyone is a winner. Every single person I have ever worked with could technically be classified as "an award-winning journalist," because everyone who enters journalism contests eventually wins *something*. However, these competitions are especially important to page designers. Since the only people who care about newspaper design are other newspaper designers, they are constantly giving awards to each other. And those meaningless plaques and certificates have become the driving force behind how the world consumes information. When you pick up the front page of any news publication, you are looking at someone's attempt to win a design contest; everything that comprises that page—the words, the images, and even the white spaces between those words and images—are nothing more than props. In the eyes of the modern newspaper designer, all of those elements have equal value. This is not an exaggeration; stroll past any newspaper design desk and you will hear people talking about the "creative use of white space." This means people are discussing ways to better utilize the parts of the paper that are blank (this includes the gaps between columns and the borders at the top and bottom of a page). Just think about that for a moment: *People are literally discussing the creative significance of nothingness.*[5]

Now, page designers will insist that all they want to do is help writers and that their only true goal is to direct the eyes of readers to the stories they need to see the most. Sometimes I believe them; one of my best friends designs news pages for a living, and he might be the best journalist I've ever met. But good intentions can't compete with bad policy, and that's what the emphasis on newspaper design is. It's now a journalistic philosophy, and it's becoming the dominant one. What's most troubling about the

5. Then again, maybe these people are just way Zen.

growing influence of newspaper designers is that it becomes a self-fulfilling prophecy: As newspapers and magazines become more obsessed with shorter, breezier stories and visual gimmickry, readers adopt that sensibility as normalcy. We are losing the ability to understand anything that's even vaguely complex.

At the moment, the leaders of Knight Ridder and Gannett and Thompson and all the other media chains are wrong; people who buy newspapers can still read them. But give them time. They'll be right soon enough.

Today I got a phone call from Minnesota, and the person asked me how this book was going. I said it was going fine. Then he asked if I had any hopes for its success.

"Well, here is my hope," I said. "I hope the book is published and distributed at least six weeks before a rogue terrorist manages to build and unleash a one-kiloton nuclear warhead in the vicinity of Times Square, since I am told that the blast would instantly incinerate at least twenty thousand people, including me and everyone in my office. It is my understanding that—even if I wasn't killed by the initial blast—it's almost certain that I would be dead within twenty-four hours of the explosion, probably via intense radiation poisoning but possibly from third-degree burns and blindness, both of which would make evacuation from the urban chaos virtually impossible. And to a lesser extent, I hope that this book is available on amazon.com before the discharge of a cobalt-60 "dirty bomb" that would turn Manhattan into a cauldron of walking death that—if I'm really, really lucky—will only give me a hyper-accelerated case of skin cancer. And of course I'd love to see this book in paperback before somebody detonates a uranium-rich suitcase bomb, stolen from Belarus or Ukraine."

"That's interesting," the caller said in response. "I suppose this technically makes you an optimist."

17 I, Rock Chump 2:11

I used to think there was nothing worse than being trapped in a conversation with someone who knows absolutely nothing about anything. However, an acquaintance taught me this wasn't true. "There's one thing worse than talking to a person who knows about nothing," he said, "and that's talking to someone who knows about nothing *except* music."

You know the kind of person to which my friend refers. You've met him at underattended rock concerts and in empty downtown taverns, and he inevitably adores the Moody Blues. But try to imagine if one of those people was so adroit at being singularly obsessive that he actually got paid for it. Imagine if the weirdo who seems to live in your nearest locally owned record store suddenly had a 152 IQ and a degree from Tufts. And now imagine a hundred of those people coming together for four rainy days in Seattle, all of them totally fucking stoked for the opportunity to compare *The Kinks Are the Village Green Preservation Society* with Danish physicist Niels Bohr's field theory on radioactive decay.

Prepare to rock and/or roll.

What I have just described was a glimpse of life inside the palatial walls of the Experience Music Project, home for the first annual Pop Music Studies Conference (a summit boldly titled "Crafting Sounds, Creating Meaning: Making Popular Music in the U.S.") Held in April 2002, the conference brought together a wide array of respected academics and snarky rock critics who were asked to "think about pop music in the abstract." What this really meant is that one hundred people who like Sigur Rós way too much came together to read self-penned manuscripts that were either too goofy to be classified as scholarship or too pedantic to be seen as commercially viable.

I was one of these people.

Now, let me be completely clear about something: I had a wonderful time at EMP. I'm precisely the kind of supergeek who enjoys forty-minute conversations about side three of Lou Reed's *Metal Machine Music* album. The pencil-necked eggheads at "Crafting Sounds, Creating Meaning" are—sadly—my people. If I was Jewish, EMP would have been my Israel. Yet even I cannot deny that this conference was probably the *least* rock 'n' roll experience I've ever had.

Thursday, April 11, 5:20 P.M.: I have just arrived outside the EMP building, a monstrosity of postmodern architecture nestled in the shadow of the Space Needle. Frankly, EMP looks ridiculous from the outside (it's bulbous, multicolored, and possibly made out of aluminum). However, the inside is gorgeous. I can't believe how clean these bathrooms are, particularly the porcelain urinals. This being a "rock conference," I wonder if we will later snort cocaine off these fixtures.

It takes me about ten minutes to realize this is not going to happen; most of the people at this conference barely even drink. We're all mingling upstairs in the EMP bar (I think it's referred to as the "Liquid Lounge"), and I'm introduced to Douglas Wolk, a writer for the *Village Voice* and *SPIN* and the bass player for a metacommunicative band called The Media. I can immediately tell that Wolk is interesting, but we're both struggling with casual conversation, so I offer to buy him a drink. He wants an orange juice. This is fine (I have nothing *against* orange juice, per se), but it quickly dawns on me that this sensibility will pretty much be the norm for the weekend. At least in the conventional, stereotypical, Nikki Sixxian definition of the term *debauchery*, EMP is a "no rocking" zone.

I wander about the mixer, trying to mix. A few people are discussing how the Avalanches are overhyped, an odd argument to

212

make about a band that 98 percent of America has never even heard of. There is lots of handshaking, and everyone seems to be saying "I love your work" or "I love your book" to whomever they happen to be standing alongside. Some people are upset that EMP has only provided free cookies for the mixer (there had been a rumor about chicken wings), but the cookies are crisp. A graduate student from Bowling Green University and I talk about the Wu-Tang Clan's obsession with kung-fu movies; when I tell this guy he looks like the lead singer of Nickelback, he threatens to punch me.

There aren't many women at this conference. I see one tall female with pigtails who looks mildly attractive, so I saunter up and try to make conversation. It turns out she's a twenty-four-year-old freelance writer from San Francisco, and she's not even actively involved with the conference; she just wanted to hang out with rock journalists (!) and meet Simon Reynolds, the British author of a drug-friendly rave book called *Generation Ecstasy*. I try to talk shop with this woman, but her shop appears to exist in Narnia; she tells me her ultimate goal is to publish a fictional biography about Alex Chilton built on the premise that Chilton was actually sired by a sexual tryst between a woman and an alligator. "The research is totally kicking my ass right now," she tells me. "Basically, I need to learn more about alligators. And about the Delta blues."

Tonight, Solomon Burke is speaking in a room the EMP staff refers to as their "sky church," but I elect to go to some dive bar four blocks away from the museum. I meet an amazing blond girl from a local Seattle alternative paper, and we do not drink orange juice; we end up having somewhere between eight and four thousand cocktails, and we play Lynyrd Skynyrd's "Tuesday's Gone" on the jukebox in order to slow dance without leaving the comfort of our booth. I go to bed around 3:30 A.M., confident that I have rocked more than enough for my juice-drinking brethren.

Friday, April 12, 9:40 A.M.: I just woke up. The conference apparently started at 8:30 A.M. What kind of self-respecting rocker gets up for *anything* at 8:30? Doesn't anyone here own *Appetite for Destruction*? Do these people not realize that even if you wake up around seven, you're not supposed get out of bed until nine? I wander down to the lobby of the Courtyard Marriott at 10:05, assuming there will be several other panelists feeling exactly like me, which is to say "below average." But there's only one guy, and he's reading the newspaper. It appears that everyone else made it to the 8:30 A.M. welcoming remarks. There's an upside to being juice drinkers, I guess.

The first three-person panel I sit through is titled "Self-Image." The initial presenter is *New York Times* writer Kelefa Sanneh, and his paper is sort of funny. Of course, what's even funnier is watching the audience when he plays snippets of N.W.A. to illustrate his points; suddenly, the room is filled with old white people bobbing their heads along with Ice Cube, desperately trying to show everyone just how much they love hip-hop. That's one of the unspoken prerequisites at this conference: You must overtly love whatever music seems the most detached from your own personal experience. Apparently, this proves you're a genius. As a consequence, all the white people talk about how much they love rap, all the young females insist they love misogynistic cock rock, and all the aging academics praise Pink and the Backstreet Boys. Other sentiments that are essential to publicly express at a rock conference are as follows: All unpopular music should be more popular; all popular music should be less popular (unless it's aggressively vapid, which thereby makes it transcendent); authenticity is essential; authenticity is ridiculous; music is the soundscape through which we experience reality; there will never be another *Trout Mask Replica*. It's also essential to have a "mentor," or at least to claim that you do. Former *SPIN* writer and current EMP program manager Eric Weisbard tells me he's an "unapologetic Robert Christgau protégé." I meet at least two people who openly describe themselves as Chuck Eddy rip-off artists. A writer from Austin tells me his mentor during college was Rob Sheffield. All the academics give props to older academics no one else has ever heard of. And most peculiarly, an unnamed woman with a tragic hairdo asks me if I'm from "the Greil Marcus school of criticism or the Lester Bangs school of thought." I say the latter, but only because I like cough syrup.

DePaul sociologist Deena Weinstein follows Sanneh, and she compares the social contract within a working rock band to the fictionalized existence of the jackalope. I must concede that this is a clear example of "thinking about music in the abstract." Later that morning, I attend a presentation titled "Duran Duran: Video Band?" It turns out the answer to that particular query is, "yes." This strikes me as significantly less abstract.

Jon Pareles of the *New York Times* is the "star" of an afternoon symposium mysteriously dubbed "Dos and Don'ts," and he makes references to the Heisenberg Principle and the formation of Zaire. Pareles follows an affable presentation from University of Iowa's Thomas Swiss (he discusses Jewel's poetry) and precedes a boring British academic who drones on about reggae before advocating the death of capitalism ("I am a socialist," he said during the Q & A portion of the symposium, "and I think we need to change society"). I'm not exactly sure what any of this has to do with pop music, but I do learn that Jewel moved 432,000 hardcover copies of *A Night Without Armor*, thereby making her the best-selling American poet of the past fifty years. At least *she's* not a socialist.

I eat lunch at Turntable, the Experience Music Project restaurant. Now—if someone wanted to be critical of EMP as an inadvertently "antirock" entity—this meal would have been a perfect metaphor, as it was the epitome of ruining something visceral. I ordered "old fashioned" chicken and dumplings, but I ended up getting the horrific modern incarnation of what some booksmart Seattle hippie imagines the Deep South should taste like. I almost felt like I was being *punished* for ordering something simple. And I suspect that's how anti-intellectuals feel about things like the EMP Pop Conference. They would prefer consuming the philosophical equivalent of McDonald's, which would be asking a fifteen-year-old kid why Hoobastank kicks ass. And it turns out I could have literally done both of these things; EMP is two blocks from a McDonald's, and Hoobastank was playing with Incubus that very night at Key Arena.

However, I ultimately do neither. I just eat my dreadful dumplings and wait around to hear Robert "The Dean of Rock Critics" Christgau discuss whether or not American pop music is still exceptional, although the only part of his speech I remember is when he says, "I don't see any new Nirvanas lurking around, and I don't plan to." I guess he doesn't like Hoobastank, either.

Saturday, April 12, 11:00 A.M.: Right now I'm listening to Sarah Dougher, and she seems deeply offended by something (and possibly by everything). Dougher is a musician and a teacher at Evergreen State College in Olympia, and she's taking issue with the fact that her symposium, titled "Personal Stories," is the only panel at the conference composed exclusively of women. It appears she also has problems with the way her panel is named: "I make music in a sexist world that views the male experience as *general* and the female experience as *personal*," she says. To me, the latter designation actually seems preferable to the former, but what do I know? Dougher later mentions that academia and music are "two of the most sexist professions that exist," further solidifying my suspicion that people attend Evergreen in order to avoid attending life.

This sense of utter unreality is a problem with several of the academic papers at this event; they're often written from completely detached perspectives. Yesterday, some dude from Middle Tennessee State gave a speech about how the threat of terrorism is not worth the chilling effect the recently legislated "Patriot Act" could have on political artists like Sting. This might be true . . . although I'm guessing it's considerably easier to downplay the threat of terrorism when you work at Middle Tennessee State. I don't see a lot of jets crashing into downtown Murfreesboro.

Still, it would be disingenuous if I didn't mention how innovative (and how clever) some of these presentations truly were. Craig Seymour of the *Atlanta Journal-Constitution* talked about "boy band slash fiction," outlining how certain fans of 'NSYNC like to imagine Justin Timberlake getting fisted by Lance Bass. Glenn Dixon surmised that much of the Contemporary Christian genre is driven by artists who literally want to fuck Jesus Christ. And the aforementioned Wolk's juice-fueled explanation of how CDs are inappropriately remastered for pop radio was fascinating and insightful. These are all examples of people who truly *did* think about music in new, unconventional ways.

But here's the depressing rub: You know who's *not* thinking about music in new, innovative ways? Musicians. At least not the musicians who came to this conference.

You see, Saturday night was supposed to be the big collision of sound and fury; this was when local "rock stars" were going to take part in a high-profile EMP symposium, simulcast on public radio. The four participants were Mark Arm of Mudhoney, Carrie Brownstein of Sleater-Kinney, Sam Coomes of Quasi, and all-around indie rock impresario Calvin Johnson.

And they all had nothing to say.

For two hours, I watched four people stare at the audience, all trying to prove they were cool enough not to care about the attention. None of them had any prepared statements (well, Brownstein *claimed* she did, but then she elected not to read it). None of them wanted to answer any of the moderator's inquiries, and they made fun of half the audience members who dared to ask them questions. Coomes spent all 120 minutes trying to act confused; Arm preferred to play surly; Brownstein opted for a nervously bookish vibe; Johnson just tried to seem weird. At one point, Calvin bemoaned the fact that—since the end of the World War II era—Americans won't even sing "Happy Birthday" at parties, apparently because our willingness to sing in public has become "atrophied." Clearly, Calvin Johnson has never been to an Olive Garden.

"I try not to analyze the process of listening to music," Brown-

217

stein begrudgingly said. "The less I think about my art, the better," reiterated Arm. If you take these artists at their word, there
is no intellectual element whatsoever to rock music; all you do is
walk out on stage and emote. According to them, there's never
anything to think (or write) about; in fact, attempts to do so sully
the entire creative process.

Luckily, hardly any of the visiting critics or academics attended
the musicians' panel, as it happened to be scheduled during
suppertime. And honestly, I'm glad they didn't go. Who needs to
hear that your life's work is irrelevant? I prefer to imagine all of
America's rock geeks breaking bread together, talking about Silk-
worm songs and Clinic b-sides and forgotten Guided by Voices
shows and—maybe for the first time in their lives—feeling completely and utterly normal. I'm sure their orange juice never
tasted so sweet.

Whenever I can't sleep, I like to lie in the darkness and pretend I've been assassinated. I've found this is the best way to get comfortable. I imagine I'm in the coffin at my funeral, and people from my past are walking by my corpse and making comments about my demise. It's quite reassuring: At least at my imaginary funerals, it's amazing how many of my female friends were secretly in love with me.

Some people think this habit makes me a freak, but I disagree. I'm always shocked when friends tell me they don't like to think about death; I think about dying constantly, and I think everybody else should, too.

I recall once sitting around a bonfire and asking all the folks staring into the flames what they fantasize about more: dying or having sex. I thought I knew what was going to happen: I thought everybody would immediately answer "sex," but—as we talked about the question in detail and slowly lowered our shields of enforced normalcy—the honest people would admit that they actually thought about dying a lot more than they thought about fucking. Much to my surprise, everyone insisted that they fantasize about sex constantly and *never* dream about

being killed, which seems insane to me. Relatively speaking, having sex is so easy. People do it all the time. It's so pedestrian; fantasies about making love are rarely necessary and usually contrived. However, dying is always original. It's always a onetime limited engagement, and (depending on your theology) it's either the defining moment of existence or the final corporeal sensation in the universe's most remarkable coincidence. How can anyone not be consumed by that? I'm constantly thinking about how bullets would burn into my lungs, or if my eyes would remain open if my skull shattered a windshield, or if cancer cells itch, or how it will sound if and when I drown. I cannot shake the notion of my head being swatted off by a grizzly bear, or of my rib cage being pulverized by a madman with a ballpeen hammer, or of being buried alive. There has never been a day in my life when I didn't daydream about having both my collarbones crushed into powder. And these are not things I necessarily *want* to happen; these are just things that warrant consideration (certainly more consideration than how I'd most prefer to orgasm).

In all likelihood, you don't think about dying enough.

18   How to Disappear Completely and Never Be Found   2:20

I'm having a crisis of confidence, and I blame Jesus.

Actually, my crisis is not so much about Jesus as it is about the impending rapture, which I don't necessarily believe will happen. But I don't believe the rapture *won't* happen, either; I really don't see any evidence for (or against) either scenario. It all seems unlikely, but still plausible. Interestingly enough, I don't think there is a word for my particular worldview: "Nihilism" means you don't believe in anything, but I can't find a word that describes partial belief in *everything*. "Paganism" is probably the closest candidate, but that seems too Druidesque for the style of philosophy I'm referring to. Some would claim that this is kind of like "agnosticism," but true agnostics always seem too willing to side with the negative; they claim there are no answers, so they live as if those answers don't exist. They're really just nihilists without panache.

Not me, though. I'm prone to believe that just about any religious ideology is potentially accurate, regardless of how ridiculous it might seem (or be). Which is really making it hard for me to comment on *Left Behind*.

According to the blurb on its jacket, the *Left Behind* book series has more than 40 million copies in print, which would normally prompt me to assume that most of America is vaguely familiar with what these books are about. However, that is not the case. By and large, stuff like *Left Behind* exists only with that bizarre subculture of "good people," most of whom I've never met and never will. These are the kind of people who are fanatically good—the kind of people who'll tell you that goodness isn't even that much of an accomplishment.

Left Behind is the first of eleven books about the end of the world. It was conceptualized by Dr. Tim LaHaye, a self-described "prophecy scholar," and written by Jerry B. Jenkins, a dude who has written over a hundred other books (mostly biographies about moral celebrities like Billy Graham and Walter Payton). The novel's premise is that the day of reckoning finally arrives and millions of people just disappear into thin air, leaving behind all their clothes and eyeglasses and Nikes and dental work. All the humans who don't evaporate are forced to come to grips with why this event happened (and specifically why God did not select them). The answer is that they did not "accept Christ as their personal savior," and now they have seven years to embrace God and battle the rising Antichrist, a charismatic Romanian named Nicolae Carpathia, who is described by the author as resembling "a young Robert Redford."

Everything that happens in *Left Behind* is built around interpretations of Paul's letters and the Book of Revelation, unquestionably the most fucked-up part of the Bible (except maybe for the Book of Job). It's the epitome of a cautionary tale; every twist of its plot mechanics scream at the reader to realize that the clock is ticking, but it's not too late—there is still time to accept Jesus and exist forever in the kingdom of heaven. And what's especially fascinating about this book is that it's a best-selling piece of entertainment, even though it doesn't offer intellectual flexibility; it's pop art, but it has an amazingly strict perspective on what is right and what is wrong. In *Left Behind*, the only people who are accepted by God are those who would be classified as fundamentalist wacko Jesus freaks with no intellectual credibility in modern society. Many of the *Left Behind* characters who aren't taken to heaven—in fact, almost all of them—seem like solid citizens (or—at worst—"normal" Americans). And that creates a weird sensation for the *Left Behind* reader, because the post-Rapture earth initially seems like a better place to live. Everybody boring would be gone. One could assume that all the infidels who weren't teleported into God's kingdom must be pretty cool: All the guys would be drinkers and all the women would be easy, and you could make jokes about homeless people and teen suicide and crack babies without offending anyone. Quite frankly, my response to the opening pages of *Left Behind* was "Sounds good to me."

Things in *Left Behind* get disconcerting pretty rapidly, however, and part of what I found disconcerting was that its main character is a reporter named Buck Williams, which was also the name of a retired NBA power forward regularly described as the league's hardest worker. As a result, I kept imagining this bearded six-foot-nine black guy as the vortex of the story, which really wouldn't have been that much of a stretch, especially since the real Buck Williams was involved with the "Jammin' Against the Darkness" basketball ministry. If the Rapture came down tonight, I'm guessing Buck would be boxing out J.C. by breakfast.

A mind-numbing percentage of pro athletes are obsessed with God. According to an episode of Bryant Gumbel's *Real Sports* on HBO, some studies suggest that as many as 40 percent of NFL players consider themselves "born again." This trend continues to baffle me, especially since it seems like an equal number of pro football players spend the entire off-season snorting coke off the thighs of Cuban prostitutes and murdering their ex-girlfriends.

That notwithstanding, you can't ignore the relationship between pro sports and end-of-days theology, and its acceleration as an all-or-nothing way of life. In the 1970s, the template for a religious athlete was a player like Roger Staubach of the Dallas Cowboys, someone who was seen as religious simply because everybody knew he was Catholic. The contemporary roster for God's Squad is far more competitive; if you're the kind of fellow who'd be "left behind," you don't qualify. These are guys like Kurt

Warner of the St. Louis Rams, a person who would consider being called a zealot complimentary.

Warner is an especially interesting case, because his decision to become "born again" appears to have helped his career as a football player. Here was a guy who couldn't make an NFL roster, was working in a grocery store, and was married to a dying woman. And then—inexplicably—his life completely turns around and he becomes the best quarterback in the NFL (and his wife lives!). Warner gives all the credit for this turnaround to his "almighty savior Jesus Christ," and that explanation seems no less plausible than any other explanation. In fact, I find that I sort of want to believe him. In the fourth quarter of Super Bowl XXXVI, Warner made a break for the end zone against the New England Patriots; at the time, the Rams were down 17–3, and it was fourth and goal. Warner was hit at the one-yard line and fumbled, and a Patriot returned the ball ninety-nine yards for what seemed to be a game-clinching touchdown. However, this play was erased—quite possibly wiped clean by the hand of God. For no valid reason, Patriots linebacker Willie McGinest blatantly tackled Ram running back Marshall Faulk on the weak side of the play, forcing the referee to call defensive holding. I remember thinking to myself, "Holy shit. That made no sense whatsoever. I guess God really does care about football." St. Louis retained possession and Warner scored two plays later, eventually tying the game with a touchdown pass to Ricky Proel with under two minutes remaining.

I'm not sure why God would care about a football game, but he certainly seemed interested in this one. It looked like Warner's faith was tangibly affecting the outcome, which is a wonderful notion. However, New England ultimately won Super Bowl XXXVI on the final play—a forty-eight-yard field goal, kicked by a guy who grew up in South Dakota and is related to Evel Knievel. You can't question God, though: The following Monday, I happened to catch a few minutes of *The 700 Club*, and a Patriot wide receiver was talking about how God is awesome. With competitive spirituality, it's always a push.

• • •

Part of the never-ending weirdness surrounding *Left Behind* was the 2000 movie version that starred Kirk Cameron, still best known as Mike Seaver from the ABC sitcom *Growing Pains*. Cameron portrays the aforementioned Buck Williams, a famous broadcast journalist (this is a slight alteration from the book, where Williams is a famous magazine writer). If one views the literary version of *Left Behind* to be mechanical and didactic, the film version would have to be classified as boring and pedantic. But—once again—there's something oddly compelling about watching this narrative unfold, and it's mostly because of Kirk's mind-bending presence.

It's always peculiar when someone famous becomes ultra-religious (Prince being the most obvious example), but it's especially strange when he or she actively tries to *advocate* their religiosity. Cameron says he became a "believer" when he was seventeen or eighteen, but nobody really cared until he got involved with *Left Behind* and suddenly became the biggest Christian movie star in America (which—truth be told—is kind of like being the most successful heroin dealer on the campus of Brigham Young University). His wife is also in *Left Behind*, and she portrays a (relatively) immoral flight attendant named Hattie Durham.

When interviewed about *Left Behind* when it was first released, Cameron usually played things pretty close to the vest and always stressed that he wanted the film to deliver a point of view about the Bible, but also to work as a commercially competitive secular thriller. However, I did find this mildly controversial exchange from an interview Cameron did with some guy named Robin Parrish on a Christian music site operated by about.com:

> How accurate do you think *Left Behind* is? I mean obviously, there won't be a real-life Buck or Hattie or whoever. But the events that transpire in the story, how accurate do you think they are? The movie or the book?

Both.
I think one of the most appealing aspects of the *Left Behind* story is that these are events that could be happening today or tomorrow. It's very realistic. The events that happen in the story parallel, I think very realistically, the events depicted in the Bible. And whether you're a pre-Trib Rapture believer, or a mid-Trib, or a post-Trib . . .

Yeah, is there anything that people who *don't* believe in a pre-Tribulation Rapture can take away from this movie?
I'd encourage those people to take a look at the *Left Behind* film project Web site, which has answers to those kinds of questions. You know . . . I'm not a pre-Trib or post-Trib expert at defending this kind of stuff, but personally I think the movie is very accurate and in line with the Bible. There are some things in prophecy that we're just going to have to wait and see how they happen, that we're not going to really know until they do. The Bible says that Jesus is coming soon though, so I think more important than the pre-Trib or post-Trib debate is all of us being ready before either one happens.

Now, I have no real understanding of what a "pre-Tribulation Rapture" is supposed to signify symbolically; it refers to a Rapture that happens before the technical apocalypse, but I'm not exactly sure how that would be better or worse than a "mid-Tribulation" or "post-Tribulation" Rapture. Honestly, I don't think it's important. However, this point *is* important: Kirk Cameron thinks the idea of 100 million Christians suddenly disappearing is "very realistic." And I don't mention this to mock him; I mention this because it's the kind of realization that significantly changes the experience of watching this movie. In the film, Buck Williams goes from being a normal, successful person to someone who ardently wants the world to realize that there is no future for the unholy and that we must prepare for the political incarnation of Satan; apparently, the exact same thing happened to Cameron *in*

225

real life. In his mind, he has made a docudrama about a historical event that merely hasn't happened yet. This is not a former teen actor forced to star in an amateurish production because he needs the money; this is a former teen actor who consciously pursued an amateurish production with the hope of saving mankind. Relatively speaking, all those years he spent with Alan Thicke and Tracey Gold must seem like total shit.

There is something undeniably attractive about becoming a born-again Christian. I hear atheists say that all the time, although they inevitably make that suggestion in the most insulting way possible: Nothing offends me more than those who claim they wish they could become blindly religious because it would "make everything so simple." People who make that argument are trying to convince the world that they're somehow doomed by their own intelligence, and that they'd love to be as stupid as all the thoughtless automatons they condescendingly despise. That is not what I find appealing about the Born-Again Lifestyle. Personally, I think becoming a born-again Christian would be really cool, at least for a while. It would sort of be like joining the Crips or the Mossad or Fugazi.

Every rational person will tell you that all the world's problems ultimately derive from disputes that are perceived by the warring parties as "Us vs. Them." That seems sensible, but I don't know if it's necessarily true; all my problems come from the opposite scenario. I was far more interesting—and probably smarter, in a way—when I refused to recognize the existence of the color gray in my black-and-white universe. When I was twenty-one, I was adamantly anti-abortion and anti–death penalty; these were very clear ideas to me. However, things have since happened in my life, and now I have no feelings about either issue. And I'm sincere about that; I really have no opinion about abortion or the death penalty. Somehow, they don't even seem important. But that's what happens whenever you start to understand that most things cannot be emotively understood: You're able to make better conversation over snifters of brandy, but you become an unfeeling idiot. You go from *believing* in objective reality to *suspecting* an objective reality exists; eventually, you start trying to make objectivity mesh with situational ethics, since every situation now seems unique. And then someone tells you that situational ethics is actually an oxymoron, since the idea of ethics is that these are things you do *all the time*, regardless of the situation. And pretty soon you find yourself in a circumstance where someone asks you if you believe that life begins at conception, and you find yourself changing the subject to NASCAR racing.

This is not a problem for the born again. There are no other subjects, really; nothing else—besides being born again—is even marginally important. Every moment of your life is a search-and-rescue mission: Everyone you meet needs to be converted and anyone you don't convert is going to hell, and you will be partially at fault for their scorched corpse. Life would become unspeakably important, and every conversation you'd have for the rest of your life (or until the Rapture—whichever comes first) would really, really, *really* matter. If you ask me, that's pretty glamorous. And *Left Behind* pushes that paradigm relentlessly. Another one of its primary characters—airline pilot Rayford Steele—becomes born again after he loses his wife and twelve-year-old son. However, his skeptical college-aged daughter Chloe doesn't make God's cut, so much of the text revolves around his attempts to convert Chloe to "The Way." And the main psychological hurdle Steele must overcome is the fact that he's not an obtrusive jackass, which *Left Behind* says we all need to become. *"Here I am, worried about offending people,"* Rayford thinks to himself at the beginning of chapter 19. *"I'm liable to 'not offend' my own daughter right into hell."* The stakes are too high to concern oneself with manners.

This is ultimately what I like about the Born-Again Lifestyle: Even though I see fundamentalist Christians as wild-eyed maniacs, I respect their verve. They are probably the only people openly fighting against America's insipid Oprah Culture—the pervasive belief system that insists everyone's perspective is valid and that no one can be judged. As far as I can tell, most people I know are like me; most of the people I know are bad people (or they're good people, but they consciously choose to do bad things). We *deserve* to be judged.

I realize that liberals and libertarians and Michael Stipe are always quick to quote the Bible when you say something like that, and they'll tell you, "Judge not, lest ye be judged." And that's a solid retort for just about anything, really. But the thing with born agains is that they *want* to be judged. They can't fucking wait. That's why they're cool.

As I just mentioned, Rayford Steele loses his young son in *Left Behind*'s Rapture. As it turns out, every young child in this book vanishes, including infants in the process of being born. This is to indicate that they are "innocents" and have done no wrong. And oddly, this was the aspect of *Left Behind* I found most distasteful.

First of all, it kind of contradicts the book's premise, since we are constantly told that the ONLY way to get into heaven is to accept Christ, which no four-year-old (much less a four-*month*-old) could possibly comprehend. Granted, this is mostly a technicality, and I'm sure it's intentional (for most exclusivist born-again groups, the technicalities are everything; the technicalities are what save you). But my larger issue is philosophical: Why do we assume all children are inherently innocent? Innocent of what? I mean, any grammar school teacher will tell you that "kids can be cruel" on the playground; the average third-grader will gleefully walk up to a six-year-old with hydrocephalus and ask, "What's wrong with you, Big Head?" And that third-grader knows what he's doing is evil. He knows it's hurtful. Little boys torture cats and cute little girls humiliate fat little girls, and they know it's wrong. They do it *because* it's wrong. Sometimes I think children are the worst people alive. And even if they're not—even if some smiling toddler is as pure as Evian—it's only a matter of time. He'll eventually become the fifty-year-old car salesman who we'll all assume is morally bankrupt until he proves otherwise.

As far as I can tell, the nicest thing you can say about children is that they haven't done anything terrible *yet*.

So let's get to the core question in *Left Behind*: If the Rapture happened tonight, who gets called up to the Big Show? Judging from the text, the answer is "No one I know, and probably no one who would read this essay." *Left Behind* is pretty clear about this, and the authors go to great lengths to illustrate how many of the people passed over by God are fair, moral, and—for the most part—more heroic than prototypical humans. This is a direct reflection of the primary audience for hard-core Christian litera ture; one assumes those readers would typically possess those same characteristics and simply need a little literary push to become "higher" Christians.

The best example in *Left Behind* is Rayford Steele, the person with whom we're evidently supposed to "relate." Buck Williams is the star and the catalyst (especially in the film version), but his main purpose is to move the plot along and provide the conflict. It's through Rayford that we are supposed to understand the novel's theme and experience. The theme is that you're good, but being good is not enough; the experience is that you cannot be saved until you allow yourself to surrender to faith, even though that's not really how it works for Rayford.

On the very first page of *Left Behind*, we learn that Rayford has a bad marriage, and it's because his wife had developed an "obsession" with religion. We also learn that—twelve years prior—Rayford drunkenly kissed another woman at the company Christmas party and has never really forgiven himself. However, that guilt does not stop him from secretly lusting after the aforementioned Hattie Durham, even though he never actually touches her (interestingly enough, Rayford and Hattie do have a physical relationship in the film version of *Left Behind*, presumably because director Victor Sarin didn't think moviegoers would buy the whole Jimmy Carter "I've lusted in my heart" sentiment).

Suffice it to say that Rayford would generally be described as a very decent person in the secular universe, which is how most *Left Behind* readers would likely view themselves. However, he can't see the espoused "larger truth," which is that there is only a future for those who take the Kierkegaardian leap and believe everything the Bible states (and as literally as possible).

Rayford can't do this until his life is destroyed, so his conversion isn't all that remarkable (it actually seems like the most reasonable decision, considering the circumstances). In many ways, this is the book's most glaring flaw: It demands blind faith from the reader, but it illustrates faith as a response to terror. And since *Left Behind* isn't a metaphor—it presents itself as a fictionalized account of what *will* happen, according to the Book of Revelation—the justification for embracing Jesus mostly seems like a scare tactic. It's not a sophisticated reason for believing in God.

Of course, that's also the point: There is no sophisticated reason for believing in anything supernatural, so it really comes down to believing you're right. This is another example of how born agains are cool—you'd think they'd be humble, but they've got to be amazingly cocksure. And once you've crossed over, you don't even have to try to be nice; according to the born-again exemplar, your goodness will be a natural extension of your salvation. Caring about orphans and helping the homeless will come as naturally as having sex with coworkers and stealing office supplies. If you consciously do good works out of obligation, you'll never get into heaven; however, if you make God your proverbial copilot, doing good works will just become an unconscious part of your life.

I guess that's probably the moment where I just stop accepting all this born-again bullshit, no matter how hard I try to remain open-minded. Though I obviously have no proof of this, the one aspect of life that seems clear to me is that good people do whatever they believe is the right thing to do. Being virtuous is hard, not easy. The idea of doing good things simply because you're good seems like a zero-sum game; I'm not even sure if those actions would still qualify as "good," since they'd merely be a function of normal behavior. Regardless of what kind of god you believe in—a loving god, a vengeful god, a capricious god, a snooty beret-wearing French god, whatever—one has to assume that you can't be penalized for doing the things you believe to be truly righteous and just. Certainly, this creates some pretty glaring problems: Hitler may have thought he was serving God. Stalin may have thought he was serving God (or something vaguely similar). I'm certain Osama bin Laden was *positive* he was serving God. It's not hard to fathom that all of those maniacs were certain that what they were doing was right. Meanwhile, I *constantly* do things that I *know* are wrong; they're not on the same scale as incinerating Jews or blowing up skyscrapers, but my motivations might be worse. I have looked directly into the eyes of a woman I loved and told her lies for no reason, except that those lies would allow me to continue having sex with another woman I cared about less. This act did not kill 20 million Russian peasants, but it might be more "diabolical" in a literal sense. If I died and found out I was going to hell and Stalin was in heaven, I would note the irony, but I really couldn't complain. I don't make the fucking rules.

Just to cover all my doomed bases, I watched a few other apocalyptic movies after *Left Behind*: I rented *The Omega Code* and revisited *The Rapture*. The latter film—a 1991 movie starring Mimi Rogers—was a polarizing attempt to make the end of the world into a conventionally entertaining film, and I still think it's among the decade's more interesting movies (at least for its first seventy-five minutes). *The Rapture* opens with Rogers as a bored sex addict, and it ends with her dragging her child into the desert to wait for God's wrath. Part of the reason so many critics like this film is because writer/director Michael Tolkin "goes all the way" and resists the temptation to end the film with an unclear conclusion. That's commendable, but I wonder what the response would have been if Rogers didn't question God at the very end; her character essentially wants to know why God plays with people like pawns and created a totally fucked world when making a utopia would have been just as easy (and though I realize these are not exactly the most profound of existential questions, it's hard to deny that they're not the most important ones, either).

Within the scope of mainstream filmmaking—it was released on the same day as the Joe Pesci vehicle *The Super*—*The Rapture* clearly seems like a religious movie. But it's really not, because it doesn't have a religious point of view. When push comes to shove, Tolkin's script adopts a staunchly humanistic take: The Mimi Rogers character asks God why his universe doesn't make sense. Like most people, she thinks life should be a democracy and that God should behave like an altruistic politician who acts in our best interests. You hear this all the time; critics of organized religion constantly say things like, "There is no way a just God would send a man like Gandhi to hell simply because he's not a Christian." Well, why not? I'm certainly pulling for Gandhi's eternal salvation, but there's no reason to believe there's a logic to the afterlife selection process. It *might* be logical, and it *might* be arbitrary; in a way, it would be more logical if it was *totally* arbitrary. But the idea of questioning God's motives will always be a fiercely American thing to do; it's almost patriotic to get in God's face. I'm pretty sure a lot of my friends would love the opportunity to vote against God in a run-off election. Even I'd be curious to see who the other candidate might be (probably Harry Browne).

In contrast, 1999's *The Omega Code* is much like *Left Behind* in that it doesn't really offer any options besides buying into the whole born-again credit union. Since both stories are so dogged about the Book of Revelation, they share lots of plot points (i.e., two Israeli prophets screaming about the Second Coming, the construction of a church on The Dome of the Rock in Jerusalem, a miracle agricultural product that will end world hunger, etc.). The main difference is that *The Omega Code* has ties with Michael Drosnin's *The Bible Code*, arguably the goofiest book I've ever purchased in a lesbian bookstore. Drosnin's book claims the Torah is actually a three-dimensional crossword puzzle that predicted (among other things) the assassination of Yitzhak Rabin; more importantly, it allows computer specialists to learn just about anything—the date of the coming nuclear war (2006), the coming California earthquake (2010), and the best Rush album (*2112*). I have no idea why I bought this book (or why it was assumed to be of specific interest to lesbians), but it forms the narrative thread for *The Omega Code*, a movie that was actually less watchable than *Left Behind*. Surprisingly, *The Omega Code* earned about three times as much as *Left Behind* ($12.6 million to $4.2 million), even though it was made with a much smaller budget ($8 million and $17.4 million, respectively).

I'm not sure why *The Omega Code* made more at the box office than *Left Behind*; it's kind of like trying to deduce why *Armageddon* grossed more than *Deep Impact*. But the most plausible explanation is that *Left Behind* tried a marketing gamble that failed: It was released on video before it was released in theaters. At the end of the VHS version of *Left Behind*, there is a "special message" from Kirk Cameron. Kirk appears to be standing in the Amazon rain forest while explaining why the movie went to Blockbuster before it went to theaters. "You are part of a very select group," Cameron tells us, "and that group makes up less than one percent of the country . . . [but] what about the other 99 percent of the country?" The scheme by *Left Behind*'s production company (an organization that calls itself Cloud 10) was to have every core reader of *Left Behind* see the film in their living room in the winter of 1999 and then instruct each person to demand it be played theatrically in every city in America when it was officially released on February 2, 2000. "We need you to literally tell everyone you know," Kirk stressed in his video message.

I was working as the film critic for the *Akron Beacon Journal* in early 2000, and—all during January—I kept getting phone calls from strangers, telling me I needed to write a story about some upcoming movie that I had never heard of; I've now come to realize that these were *Left Behind* people. I can't recall if the film ever opened in Akron or not. Regardless, there is a part of me that would like to see this as an example of how *Left Behind* is different from other kinds of entertainment. Its audience truly felt it had a social and spiritual import that far exceeded everything else that opened that same weekend (such as Freddie Prinze Jr.'s *Head Over Heels*). And I'm sure that some of the people who called me that January truly did believe that a Kirk Cameron flick could save the world, and that it was their vocation to make sure all the sinners in suburban Ohio became aware of its existence.

However, I can't ignore my sinking suspicion that the makers of this movie merely assumed their best hope for commercial success was to manipulate the very people who never needed a movie or a book to learn how to love Jesus. They took people who wanted to rescue my soul and turned them into publicists. Which makes me think the people at Cloud 10 are probably a few tiers below Stalin, too.

There are eleven books in the *Left Behind* series, and many have excellent subtitles like *The Destroyer Is Unleashed* and *The Beast Takes Possession*, both of which may have been Ronnie James Dio records. I am not going to read any more of them, mostly because I know how they're going to end. I mean, doesn't everybody? I went back and read the Book of Revelations, which doesn't make much sense except for the conclusion—that's where it implicitly states that Jesus is "coming soon." Of course, Jesus operates within the idiom of infinity, so "soon" might be 30 billion years. Sometimes I find myself wishing that the world would end in my lifetime, since that would be oddly flattering; we'd all be part of humanity's apex. That's about as great an accomplishment as I can hope for, since I just don't see how I will possibly get into heaven, Rapture or otherwise.

When I was a little boy, I used to be very thankful that I was born Catholic. At the time, my Catholicism seemed like an outrageous bit of good fortune, since I considered every other religion to be fake (I considered Lutherans and Methodists akin to USFL franchises). Over time, my opinions on such things have evolved. But quite suddenly, I once again find myself thankful for Catholicism, or at least thankful for its more dogmatic principles. I'm hoping all those nuns were right: I'm angling for purgatory, and I'm angling hard.

Acknowledgments

Due to the schizophrenic nature of this collection, it would be impossible for me to thank everyone who—at one point or another—intangibly contributed to this manuscript. Consequently, I'm not going to try. However, I must express an avalanche of kudos to my editor at Scribner, Brant Rumble. Beyond being a brilliant editor, Brant might be the last sincere human in all of New York.

Additionally, there are a few random cats whose editorial insight directly influenced certain passages, and they are as follows:

Kate Condon
Bob Ethington
David Giffels
Scott Lowe
Jennifer Piro
Mark J. Price
Hillery Stone
Paul Tough
Michael Weinreb

I must likewise thank my supercagey agent, Daniel Greenberg, and my superfoxy lawyer, Amy Everhart. I'd also like to unleash my profound gratitude to everyone at *SPIN* whom I ever had lunch with (and especially to those whom I *always* have lunch with) and to everyone at *SPIN* I occasionally have drinks with (and especially to those who I *always* have drinks with).

Finally, I want to publicly apologize to anyone who ended up getting mentioned in this book simply because they had the misfortune of knowing me (either in the present or in the past). I'm not sure what compels me to ruin all our lives; I guess that's just the way I am. Sorry.

Index

INDEX

INDEX